About the Author

Noel Harvey lectures in management studies in the Regional Technical College Galway. He received his Ph.D. from the University of Wisconsin, Madison, and has carried out extensive research on the metalworking industry in America and Germany dealing with the effects of group work on employees. He is the co-author of *Sexual Harassment in the Workplace* and has written numerous articles for international business journals. An earlier version of this book, *Effective Supervisory Management in Ireland*, was published by NCIR Press in 1994.

The Challenge of Supervisory Management

Noel Harvey

Oak Tree Press
Dublin

Oak Tree Press
Merrion Building
Lower Merrion Street
Dublin 2, Ireland

A catalogue record of this book is
available from the British Library.

ISBN 1 86076 077 5

Printed in the Republic of Ireland by Colour Books Ltd.

CONTENTS

PREFACE

An earlier edition of this book was published by the NCIR Press and, not surprisingly, was centred around the Diploma in First Line Management (Supervision) course offered by the National College of Industrial Relations. In fact, many of the chapters of the book related very closely to modules of the diploma course.

With Oak Tree Press, this second edition presented an opportunity to break with the past and introduce new material, new concepts and new ideas. There are, to begin with, some new chapters and the old chapters have been revised and updated considerably. The second edition also has an up-to-date bibliography on supervisory management, and an index, indispensable features of any text which were missing from the first edition. Finally, and perhaps most importantly, this edition is driven by research. Using a detailed questionnaire I interviewed a large number of working people, mainly human resources managers, about their views and concerns on supervisory management. A survey was also administered to practising supervisors. It is this research which drives this edition.

Despite such changes, the second edition remains faithful to the first in general layout as well as content. In a sense this is testimony to the strength of the Diploma in First Line Management (Supervision) course. Another feature remains the same: the overriding concern of this book is to provide Irish working men and women, in supervisory management or other positions, a detailed, accurate and up-to-date account of the changing nature of supervisory management. Indeed, the job of the supervisor continues to change, demanding skill and dedication in equal amount. This book remains, as far as I am aware, the only book on supervisory management in Ireland.

I am grateful to many people, friends, colleagues and students, past and present, who provided insights and support in the writing of this and the previous edition. Pride of place goes to Adrian Twomey who provided, yet again, an insightful and knowledgeable chapter on employment law. The law is one area that supervisors in particular have to be aware of. Similarly, I extend my gratitude to Paddy Gunnigle for writing the foreword.

I would like to acknowledge the contribution of the following: Jim Walsh (Eastern Health Board); Thomas Cummins (IBM, Ireland); Dan Fitzpatrick and Bertie Collins (Dublin Fire Brigade); Colette Cregan, Riona Sheehan and Tony O'Flanagan (Aer Lingus); Christy Killeen, Charles Byrne and Ria Farron (RTE); Patrick Cregg (Garda Síochána); Lt. Col. Martin Egan (Air Corps); Martin Fitzpatrick (Avonmore); Lt. Col. Fitzgerald, Lt. Michael O'Brien and Lt. John Wynne (Army); Norman Croke (SIPTU); Brenda O'Sullivan (Central Bank); Matt Commiskey, Mike King and Paul Fox (Guinness); Eugene Hardiman (AGF-Irish Life Holdings); Commander Jim Robinson and Captain Liam Donnelly (Navy); Frank Smyth (Carlow); T. J. McIntyre (NCIR) and students of the "model office" in Galway RTC.

The following provided helpful and insightful comments on earlier drafts of individual chapters: Paddy Gunnigle and Joe Wallace (University of Limerick); Martin Naughton and Norman Croke (SIPTU); Les Richards (Organon); Sean O'Dwyer (Health and Safety Authority); Mick Creedon (Jesuit Centre for the Unemployed); Fergus Whelan and Tom Wall (ICTU); Bryan Howard Jones and Mick Loftus (NIMT); Bernard O'Hara and John Hynes (Galway RTC); Joe Peppard (TCD); Kevin O'Kelly (European Foundation for the Improvement of Living and Working Conditions); Kieran O'Dwyer (Garda Síochána); Irvine Ferris (Air Corps); Frances McDonnell (Dublin); Sam Malone (Dublin).

Last but not least, David Givens proved once again the talented and hard-working editor that he is and, I suspect, will continue to be, in spending countless hours working through the manuscript to get it into the shape you now have.

As with the first edition, the book is dedicated to Sandra and Peadar for making life very much worthwhile.

Noel Harvey
Galway, September 1997

FOREWORD

This book represents a significant contribution to the literature on Irish management. Despite a proliferation in the titles applied to the supervisory role, the position of first-line manager is ever more important in today's organisation. The move towards "leaner" organisation structures means that line managers undertake responsibility for a broad range of managerial tasks. An ever more competitive business environment presents increased challenges for first-line managers in areas such as managing people, dealing with changes in technology and addressing pressures for enhanced quality and productivity.

The text addresses these issues using a sound Irish research base. Dr. Harvey's extensive research on the role of first-line supervisors facilitates a greater understanding of supervisory management in Irish organisations. It also allows readers to consider the complexities of supervisory management practice and, particularly, the changing nature of supervisory work through extensive insights into management practice in Irish organisations.

The text draws on the extensive academic debate on supervisory management by addressing recent Irish and international work in the area. Of particular note are those chapters which address current developments in management practice such as teamworking, "world class manufacturing", and technological change. The text also examines recent changes in legislation which impact on first-line supervisors, particularly those in the area of labour law and health and safety.

Despite its strong academic emphasis, the book is written in a direct style which should be accessible to students and managers alike. In so doing, the text should help provide both theory and practical knowledge to enhance supervisory practice in organisations.

I enthusiastically welcome this book as an important addition to the emergent literature on Irish business and management and congratulate Noel Harvey on his work. I would also like to acknowledge the contribution of Oak Tree Press and their hard-working editor, David Givens, in facilitating the publication of research-based analyses of issues of contemporary interest in Irish business and economic life.

Paddy Gunnigle
Professor of Business Studies
Employment Relations Research Unit
Department of Personnel and Employment Relations
University of Limerick

Part One

THE FUNDAMENTALS OF SUPERVISORY MANAGEMENT

Chapter 1

UNDERSTANDING SUPERVISORY MANAGEMENT

THE OBJECTIVE OF THIS CHAPTER

The chapter provides a general overview of supervisory management. Issues covered include the definition of a supervisor, levels of management and the role of the supervisor in a business organisation.

After reading and studying this chapter, the reader should have the following:

- A broad understanding of what supervisors do
- An understanding of how a supervisor's position fits into the organisational structure
- A knowledge of the many responsibilities of supervisors.

A further examination of the managerial role of supervisory management and more specifically the functions of management is contained in the next chapter.

A DEFINITION OF A SUPERVISOR

The Oxford Dictionary defines a supervisor as "one who inspects or directs a body of employees". This is derived from the literal meaning of the term "super-visor" as one who looks from above, or an "overseer". Thus a supervisor is a person who directs, controls, and motivates, in short, supervises others.

There is no legal definition in Ireland of what constitutes a supervisor. This is not the case in America. There, a supervisor is defined in law (Section 2(11), National Labor-Management Relations Act of 1947) as follows:

> The term "supervisor" means any individual having authority, in the interest of the employer, to hire, transfer, suspend, lay off, recall, promote, discharge, assign, reward, or discipline other employees, or responsibility to direct them, or to adjust their grievances, or effectively to recommend such action, if in connection with the foregoing the exercise of such authority is not of a merely routine or clerical nature, but requires the use of independent judgement (Keys and Henshall, 1990).

This is a cumbersome definition and not entirely suitable to Ireland because supervisors in America, as can be seen from the above definition, often have wide power including the authority to hire and fire, which is generally not the case in Ireland.

Definitions used in Britain have more application to the Irish case. For example, Adair (1988, p. 1), borrowing from the Industrial Relations Code of Practice, defines a supervisor as a "member of the first-line of management responsible for a work group to a higher level of management". Similarly, Betts (1983, p. 5), in an earlier publication, defines a supervisor as "a person who is given authority and responsibility for planning and controlling work of a group by close contact". Finally, Bolton (1986, p. 27), another Briton who has written extensively in the area of supervisory management, states clearly: "The term supervisor is generally used to describe the first line of authority that spends the majority of his or her time on supervisory duties".

These definitions convey a number of points. Firstly, a supervisor is a person with responsibility or authority for others. Secondly, this responsibility is to higher level management for the performance of a work group under the supervisor's control.[1] Finally, the supervisor, as traditionally defined, is a manager who, typically, spends much of their time working with people.

This book will define a supervisor as:

---

[1] Adair (1988, p. 3) suggests that the supervisor should be in charge of a group that numbers "no more than 15". Six to eight people would seem the ideal group to manage. Group dynamics is discussed in Chapter 12.

> Anyone at the first level of management who has responsibility for the work of others.

This broad, if brief, definition serves many functions. In the first instance, by stressing the term "responsibility for", rather than, say, "authority over", we are recognising that the supervisory function is changing. In point of fact, a recurring theme of this book is that the role of the supervisor is changing from a disciplinary or authoritative role to one in which leadership and motivation are central. Secondly, the definition recognises that, even within organisations, there are many different types of supervisors and that their work will differ according to, among other things, the type of business the organisation or department performs, the number and type of staff being supervised and the variety and complexity of task(s) needed to be completed. Finally, the individual supervisor may bring to a position certain traits or qualities that in time define or modify a job.

THE IMPORTANCE OF SUPERVISORY MANAGEMENT

Supervision is both an important and common activity in business. Despite this, not everyone who is in charge of people, or indeed who are in supervisory positions, are called supervisors. An individual may thus perform the supervisory function, but not be called a supervisor. Executive officers in the civil service, a matron in a hospital, a Garda or an Army sergeant (or petty officer in the Navy) all fall into this category. Others may find themselves in charge of people without a corresponding change in their job titles. Terminology also favoured include chargehand, foreman (or forewoman), senior operative, assistant, line or junior manager, and plant or chief superintendent.

Disputes about terminology are to a large extent redundant. People who are in supervisory positions, regardless whether they are called supervisors or not, perform what is termed the supervisory function. If you are in charge of people, and have contact with them, then in all probability you are a supervisor regardless of what you are called. In this book, the term "supervisory management" (rather than first-line or front-line management) will be used, though it should be clear that the term refers to employees who perform supervisory roles whatever their specific job title.

SUPERVISORS AS FIRST-LINE MANAGERS

Supervisors are, first and foremost, managers, belonging to the level of management known as first-line (or front-line) management. As managers, they have responsibility for ensuring that the work is done. The work is generally carried out by employees under the direction or leadership of the supervisor. In some cases (and increasingly), the supervisor participates in the work; in other cases, particularly in the traditional firm, the supervisor does not participate but directs work. Either way, the supervisor is responsible and accountable for the work performed. Supervisory management therefore is the process of getting things accomplished with and through people by guiding and motivating their efforts toward common objectives.

This relationship between management, supervisors and employees is depicted in Figure 1.1.

FIGURE 1.1: SENIOR, MIDDLE AND FIRST-LINE MANAGEMENT

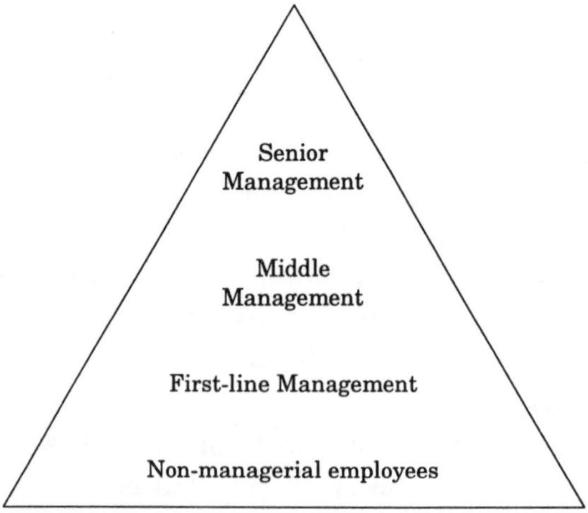

LEVELS OF MANAGEMENT

As Figure 1.1 demonstrates, there are three levels of management, commonly referred to as senior, middle and first-line management. As levels differ, so too do responsibilities. Senior management is concerned with the overall direction and competitiveness of the firm. It makes the plans that deal with the strategic or long-term future of the company. Middle management, by contrast, has as its responsibility the short-term functioning of the firm. It also co-ordinates the activities of the firm. First-line management makes sure the job gets done. This is the level of supervisory management, also referred to as front-line management.

The term "first-line management" is used because of the close contact supervisors have with employees. Higher level management deals with employees from a distance, typically controlling through indirect means. Supervisors, on the other hand, normally have daily contact with the employees they supervise, and deal with issues as they arise. Another way of putting this is that higher level management makes policy which is often framed in broad terms. Supervisors put such plans into operation. In order to do so, supervisors must understand what is expected of them, and be able to convey this to management, fellow supervisors, and to employees. Betts (1983) make this point very clear:

> Supervision implies operating at close range by actually overseeing or controlling, dealing with situations on the spot as they arise, whereas management implies controlling remotely by using other administrative means.

SUPERVISORY LEVELS

There are distinct levels within the ranks of supervisory management. A manufacturing plant, for example, may have many different types of supervisors, including a plant superintendent, general or departmental supervisors, and works supervisors. With different levels comes different responsibilities. Works supervisors will have direct responsibility for the performance of a work group, while superintendents have much broader responsibilities and answer directly to management. Hence, as an individual moves up to either the supervisory or management levels, they assume much broader managerial responsibilities and deal less, on a day-to-day basis, with people.

In the services sector, there are, equally, various levels of supervisory management. For example, in nursing the following jobs have supervisory authority: ward sister, charge nurse, deputy and chief nursing officer and director of nursing. Similarly, the Dublin Fire Brigade, as another example, has three levels of first-line manager: district officer, station officer, and sub-officer. A sub-officer is directly responsible for a working group of about 9 to 13 fire-fighters; above him (and increasingly her) is a station officer who is responsible for the day-to-day running of a fire station; finally, district officers manage a number of stations. Beyond the first level of management are third officers, and assistant and chief fire officers. Entry to such levels is typically restricted to graduates. In other organisations there are two broad levels of supervisory management; in the military, senior and junior NCOs (non-commissioned officers), and in private organisations, supervisors who are in charge of workers and supervisors who are in charge of other supervisors.

It should be noted that there is a movement in business to remove layers. Firms, in both the private and public sector, are getting smaller (downsizing is one term for this, rightsizing another). In some cases, this downsizing is taking the form of wholesale removal of layers of management, especially middle and first-line management. For example, organisations in both the US and Ireland, as they move into teams, often remove supervisors and re-employ them as either team leaders or facilitators. Similarly, in the public sector, roles are being combined for efficiency reasons: for example, in nursing, the ward sister and the matron are being replaced by the new job of nursing officer. This movement is likely to accelerate in the coming years as global competition intensifies. That said, many firms are still organised on traditional lines with strong demarcation of authority.

SUPERVISION DIFFERENTIATED FROM MANAGEMENT

Supervisory management differs from other branches of management in many ways, including the degree of authority and the degree of daily contact with employees. Generally speaking, supervisors have less authority than managers and are likely to spend more of their time dealing with employees. Managers, on the other hand, will perform activities other than supervisory ones such as long-term planning, and typically will have less contact with employees.

Betts (1983, p. 6) in the following quote explains clearly the difference between the supervisory and the management function:

> The supervisory function is concerned with the day-to-day running of the group, which will entail a certain amount of attention to detail depending upon the size of the section. If the section is large the supervisor will need to master the art of delegation, passing on the minor tasks to his colleagues, thus giving him more time to plan and control the work effectively. The managerial function, on the other hand, should be concerned with thinking ahead on questions of policy, programmes of expansion, new products, new markets and so on, thus leaving the detail and less important tasks to managers' subordinates.

Despite the eloquence of Betts, it should be clearly understood that the supervisory function and the managerial function differ in degree more than kind. Indeed, as Evans (1995, p. 115) points out, "every manager is a supervisor, and every supervisor is a manager". Further, within supervisory management there is, as noted earlier, a great deal of variation. Some supervisors will deal almost exclusively with employees, others have minimal contact with employees. In addition, it is widely recognised now that a knowledge of management theory is essential to a supervisor and that supervisors must see themselves as part of a management team, and behave accordingly. Chapter 2 deals extensively with the managerial role of supervisors.

THE RESPONSIBILITIES OF SUPERVISORS

Because of their unique role in the organisation, supervisors are often seen as the link between employees and management.[2] This is wrong in the sense that it portrays the supervisor as somehow different from both employees and management. Also, it fails to

---

[2] Keys et al. (1990, p. 6) make this point. The origin of the term dates back to Likert (1967) who saw supervisors as the "linking pins" between senior management and employees.

recognise that supervisors have wide responsibilities. Finally, distinctions in organisations are, as noted, slowly being eroded. The development in manufacturing towards teamwork is premised on removing job demarcations. In the financial sector, as in the manufacturing sector in general, there are movements to remove this distinction between manager and employee.[3] It should be stated clearly: supervisors are link people in just the same way as there are links between different levels of management.

FIGURE 1.2: THE MANY RESPONSIBILITIES OF SUPERVISORS

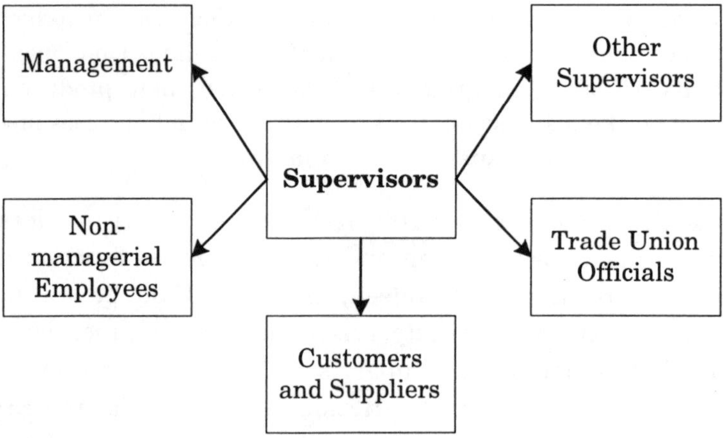

As Figure 1.2 shows, supervisors have many responsibilities. Their first, and primary one for most supervisors, is towards employees. As their manager, supervisors have to develop a working relationship with employees based on trust and commitment: they have to be responsive and understanding of employees as well as demanding of them. Secondly, supervisors have to co-ordinate with other supervisors and staff specialists such as personnel managers. The development of teamwork and the focus on decentralising authority has made inter-departmental co-operation

[3] Stone (1988) makes this argument for the financial sector. I have written elsewhere about the current attempts in the metal engineering sector in Germany to remove this distinction between blue- and white-collar work (see Harvey and von Behr, 1994).

particularly important. Thirdly, supervisors have responsibilities towards higher management, especially ensuring that the work entrusted to them is carried out in the manner envisaged by senior management. In addition, supervisors provide an important communications link between non-managerial employees and senior management. Fourthly, some supervisors have dealings with trade unions, especially in regard to industrial relations procedures and custom and practice. Grievances, that is, complaints by employees, are generally dealt with initially by first-line management. Finally, many supervisors increasingly have responsibilities to customers and suppliers. In regard to the former, with changes in product market strategies, there is increasing awareness in both manufacturing and services firms of the need to be more responsive to customers. In the office or on the shopfloor it has meant dealing with customers' complaints and needs in an immediate and responsive way. The appointment some years back of a national ombudsman, and the installation of watchdogs in some sectors, such as the banking sector, has made customer awareness extremely important.

In sum, the supervisor has responsibilities to employees, staff specialists and fellow supervisors, management, union officials, customers and suppliers. Not surprisingly the job of the supervisor is a complex and varied one. It can also be a demanding position. Tasks that supervisors can perform, among others, include the following:

- Advising and working with management
- Conducting interviews (employment, performance appraisal, counselling, disciplinary, etc.)
- Controlling costs
- Delegating work
- Giving directives
- Introducing new employees
- Motivating and leading employees
- Planning the work of the group
- Rewarding and disciplining employees

- Scheduling and assigning work
- Training employees
- Writing various documents (letters, reports, forms, etc.)
- Making presentations
- Being responsible for health and safety.

The performance of these and other tasks can make the job of the supervisor a challenging and rewarding one. Supervisors who do their jobs well can experience a great sense of satisfaction.

CHAPTER SUMMARY

A supervisor is a person at the level of first-line management who has responsibility for the work of others. Some jobs reflect the term supervisor in their title; others make a passing reference to it; still others have no reference to it all. People in supervisory positions, regardless of their specific job title, perform the supervisory function. This infers a managerial responsibility to manage resources and responsibilities to employees, management, fellow supervisors, staff specialists, union officials, customers and suppliers.

Developments in technology and law, new management practices, and new ways of organising production increase the need for change. The influx of multinational companies into Ireland, first American, and later Japanese and to a lesser extent German, is ensuring that these changes are affecting all firms, both public and private, domestic and international. The increasing emphasis on people as a firm's best resource, skill shortages in some sectors in Ireland, the advent of contract work along with the increasing participation of women in the labour force all make demands on managers to manage in a new way.

As noted earlier, one outcome of all this change is that the exact nature, or role, of the supervisor may not be entirely or adequately defined in a firm. Even people who have worked for years in supervisory positions are questioning their own position in the face of great change. Among the many questions supervisors have to ask are:

- Should the supervisor be consulted when an organisation recruits a new employee?
- What is the best way to handle change?
- What powers should a supervisor have over employees?
- Should supervisors be friendly with employees, or use first names?
- What relationship should supervisors have with their staff, especially outside work?
- How does one get promoted to a supervisor?
- Who is the best person to be a supervisor (the most senior, the best employee or the most educated employee)?
- What sort of training should a supervisor receive?
- Is there a difference in supervision of same-sex and mixed (male and female) groups?
- How does one motivate employees who work on fixed contracts?
- Should a supervisor belong to a trade union?

It is impossible to answer all of these questions. Rather, this book provides an overview of supervisory management and in so doing lists the skills and knowledge a person needs to have to be an effective supervisor. It is up to the reader to apply this knowledge and these skills. As every supervisor's job differs, there are no hard or fast rules about supervision: sometimes a supervisor needs to exercise authority for a job to be done; other times, gentle persuasion is all that is needed. That said, there is nothing magical about the supervisory function; anybody can become an effective supervisor. Training, knowledge, understanding and the right attitude, along with dedication and effort, are, however, very important.

References and Further Reading

Adair, John (1988) *The Effective Supervisor*, London: The Industrial Society, London.

Betts, P.W (1983) *Supervisory Studies*, London: Pitman.

Bittle, L.R., & J. Newstrom (1990) *What Every Supervisor Should Know*, New York: McGraw-Hill.

Bolton, W. (1986) *Supervisory Management*, London: Heinemann, 1986.

Evans, D. 91995) *Supervisory Management: Principles and Practice*, Fourth Edition, London: Cassell, 1995.

Harvey, N. and M. von Behr (1994) "Group Work in the American and German Non-Automotive Metal Manufacturing Industry", *International Journal of Human Factors in Manufacturing*, Vol. 4, No. 1, pp. 1-16.

Keys, B. and J. Henshall (1990) *Supervision: Concepts, Skills and Assessment*, New York: John Wiley & Sons.

Mosley, D., L. Megginson, P. Pietri (1993) *Supervisory Management: The Art of Empowering and Developing People*, third edition, Cincinnati, Ohio: South-Western Publishing Company.

Likert, R. (1967) *New Patterns of Management*, New York: McGraw-Hill.

Stone, Brian W. (1988) *Supervisory Skills*, London: Pitman.

Chapter 2

The Managerial Role of Supervisors

THE OBJECTIVE OF THIS CHAPTER

A number of points can be made about the managerial role of supervisors. First, the managerial aspects of the supervisor's position have, in the past, been played down. Partly to blame for this is the fact that most supervisors have been promoted from the ranks of employees and still tend to wear the hat of an employee. Worse still, when appointed no training or induction programme was forthcoming. In other words, little was done to help these individuals cope with the managerial aspects of their new supervisory jobs. Second, as noted in Chapter 1, the trend in recent years has been to either to eliminate or expand the role of the supervisor. Supervisors in the leading-edge firms have become team leaders and facilitators and have taken on far more responsibilities such as dealing with customers or interacting more with higher-level management. Hence there is increasing awareness of the need for supervisors to see themselves more as managers, which in turn places pressure on them to learn more about management.

After reading and studying this chapter, the reader should have the following:

- A knowledge of the supervisor's managerial role
- a broad understanding of the functions of management.

The next chapter deals with the changing nature of supervisory management.

WHAT IS MANAGEMENT?

The term "management" is an ambiguous term. Tiernan et al. (1996, p. 1) point out that it can refer to a process which managers undertake to achieve organisational objectives, to a stock of knowledge about how to manage, to the people who manage and finally to a career in itself. The job of management is equally open to debate. As Pettinger (1994, pp. 1–2) has made clear in a passage worthy of full quotation, management has been variously described as an art, a science and a profession. It is a science in that there are:

> precise elements, scientific and exact aspects that have to learned and assimilated. It is a profession in so far as there is a general recognition that there are certain knowledge, skills and aptitudes that must be assimilated and understood by anyone that aspires to be a truly effective manager. Management is an art in the sense that within these confines and strictures there is great scope for the use of creativity, imagination, initiative, and invention within the overall sphere of the occupation.

Not surprisingly, given such disputes over the meaning of the word "management", there exist many definitions. Henri Fayol (1949)[1], one of the earliest writers in the field of management, proposed his famous definition of management as:

> to manage is to forecast and plan, to organise, to command, to co-ordinate and to control.

These are now called the management functions,[2] with staffing and directing being substituted for command (see Figure 2.1). The usefulness of this approach is that it allows one to focus on what managers do, which is planning, organising, staffing, directing and controlling work.

---

[1] See Chapter 3 for more information on Fayol.

[2] There are numerous variations on the management functions, including POMC (Planning, Organising, Motivating and Controlling) and POLCA (Planning, Organising, Leading and Controlling Activities). This book follows the standard "Planning, Organising, Staffing, Directing and Controlling" which is widely attributed to Koontz and O'Donnell (1980).

FIGURE 2.1: THE MANAGEMENT FUNCTIONS

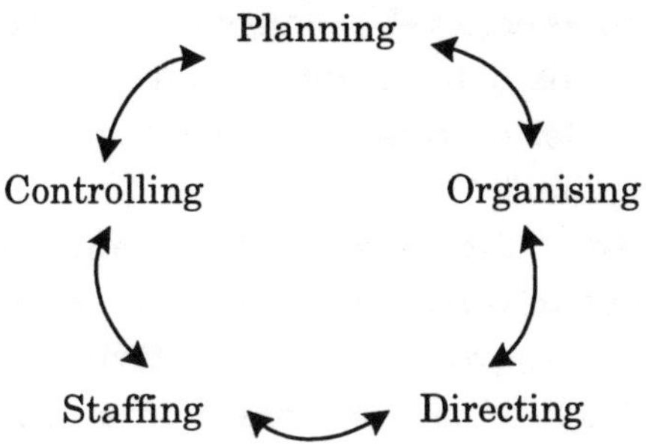

The traditional view is that managers spend different amounts of time on different functions. For example, the higher managers are, the more likely they are concerned with planning, especially long-term strategic planning. By contrast, because of the constant interaction with employees, lower level managers, including supervisors, spend much of their time directing (that is, leading and motivating) employees. That view, however, is being called into question because of the many demands made on all managers. Therefore, regardless of management level, a working knowledge of these functions is essential for all managers. The next section examines each function in detail.

Planning

Planning is one of the most important functions of management, since without plans the organisation has no goals or targets. Most importantly, it allows organisations to make best use of current resources and to anticipate, to the extent possible, future trends and possibilities. It is such an important function that, potentially, every employee in the organisation is involved in planning. However, the degree and type of planning vary according to the level of management. As noted earlier, the job of higher-level management is to plan the overall policy of the firm based on factors such as product market strategy, finance, resources available, etc. This is sometimes referred to as strategic planning. Lower-level management, including supervisors, is more concerned with what is referred to as tactical and operational planning. These deal with the day-to-day running of the firm and, in effect, put in place action that will achieve the broad strategic objectives set by higher level management. Finally, employees themselves have to plan to ensure that the work prescribed is carried out in the allotted time. Time management is, for example, an aspect of planning.

What is required of the supervisor in planning? The supervisor, very simply, has to think out a course of action for the future based on available resources — time, material and people — so that the job entrusted to the supervisor gets done in the way it was envisaged. In some instances the supervisor may get support from middle-level management, and at other times involve the employees in the decision-making and planning. With or without support, the responsibility for planning for the work group lies with the supervisor.

Organising

Simply put, *organising* has to do with scheduling work. Speaking in broad terms, supervisors are often allocated overall responsibility for a particular task and the authority to delegate work. In delegating work, the job gets done by employees. This is a very simplistic view based on the traditional view of work, namely, that management plans the work and employees do it. Supervisors, being the link between the two, oversee the work. Such a view does not do justice to the important work of supervisors and managers, particularly in the area of organising.

As noted, organising, from a work perspective, refers to the way work is arranged among the employees of the organisation. To be more specific, organising is the process of scheduling work so that it can be accomplished most effectively using the firm's resources, including people, material, machinery and money. This may mean deciding the exact mix of people and machinery, or more likely, allocating tasks to individual employees. Because people bring different skills to the workplace, supervisors have to be able to assign work according to each individual's capabilities within the framework of the group's overall capacity to get the job done. To do this requires a broad range of skills on their part. They have to ensure that the work is carried out as envisaged, that there is no duplication of work, and that no employee has too little or too much to do. In all, organisation involves much co-ordination to achieve the right balance.

To give an example: supervisors are typically in charge of a number of employees. It is their responsibility to determine, firstly, what activities have to be done, secondly, how these activities are to be grouped together, thirdly, who is to carry them out, and fourthly, how they are to be carried out. This necessitates providing employees with the authority to carry out their tasks, and the training and the tools necessary to accomplish them. It further involves putting control mechanisms in place to ensure that the work is carried out according to plan and taking corrective action if necessary. In all, organising involves the setting up of processes and controls and the establishment of an effective work group. Central to the latter is the building of a culture which promotes close interaction and allows the group to achieve its target. Group or teamwork is thus the essence of the management function of organising.

Staffing

The management function of *staffing* refers to the issues affecting the employment of people. This means more than just hiring employees. Selection, placement, training and development of employees are all part of the staffing function, as are performance appraisal, compensation, and promotion. Staffing is essentially a management activity. It is a function which every manager and supervisor must do, not just the personnel or human resources manager.

Staffing, as a result, is a complex activity. It begins with the recruitment of staff. Recruitment is essentially concerned with analysing existing staff levels, forecasting the supply and demand of staff and, finally, establishing and implementing manpower plans. Despite what may seem, in Ireland, a declining workforce, there is, in most organisations, a continual need for firms to attract talented staff. This is because employees will leave for personal reasons (retirement, another job, etc.) or move between jobs in the same firm. Some of these employees have to be replaced. Thus recruitment entails not just an understanding of the numbers and skill levels of people leaving the firm, but also the ability of firms to attract new and qualified candidates. Once in the organisation, new employees often have to follow an induction programme and/or be trained. While supervisors do not always get involved in the recruitment of staff, they do get involved in welcoming new employees. An interview may have to be held with new employees to make them aware of department rules, procedures and customs. To introduce new employees to existing staff, supervisors may have to organise meetings or make one-to-one introductions.

Training often has to be provided to prepare new and existing staff to do their jobs properly. Supervisors have to consider whether it is better to do training themselves in-house or should they arrange for external or off-the-job courses. Training is important to the extent that it facilitates the movement of staff to jobs where they can exercise greater, or different, responsibilities. However, training can also be expensive, disruptive and time-consuming.

The supervisor's concern with staffing varies from organisation to organisation, and even within an organisation. Some supervisors may have authority for staffing, others not. Some are heavily involved in training, others deal only with trained people. Regardless of the degree to which supervisors are involved in staffing decisions, it is the area where supervisors have to follow certain procedures and legal requirements (employment law is dealt with in Chapter 19). However, suffice it to say that there has been considerable legislation passed in recent years, both a new law regulating industrial relations and another dealing solely with part-time employees, which has had a bearing on how employees are managed. In this area more than any other, a knowledge of the law is crucial.

Directing

Just because a person is hired to do a particular job does not necessarily mean that it will be done. Rather, the employee has to be instructed on what is expected of them and often further motivated to perform that job with maximum effort. This is called *directing* in management terms.

Directing is an important aspect of the supervisor's job. Rather than simply telling a employee what to do — or disciplining them for not doing it or rewarding them for doing it well — the supervisor must be able to coach employees to reach their full potential. When channelled towards a constructive goal, people's energies can be extremely productive, and when not channelled properly they can be extremely disruptive. It is the supervisor's job to bring out the potential in each person they supervise, and to direct or channel it towards a constructive outcome.

More than any other management function, directing is considered an action. There are two elements to this. The first concerns the issuing of orders and instructions (directives). The second concerns motivation and leadership — building an effective workforce that will work willingly and enthusiastically towards the accomplishment of the desired objectives. It is, of all the management functions, the one supervisors are most concerned with. Top management, by contrast, usually spends a relatively small amount of time directing.

Controlling

As noted, supervisors are entrusted with the responsibility of managing resources, mainly materials and people. This, as pointed out, means planning and organising work as well as directing employees. However, mechanisms have to be put in place to ensure that work is carried out in the way it was planned. This is referred to in management terms as *controlling*. Specifically, controlling refers to the process of ensuring that employees do what they are supposed to do. Without controls, the actual output of a work group may have little bearing on what was planned.

Everyone in the organisation from the Chief Executive Officer (CEO) to the production operative is involved with some element of control. The CEO, for example, may establish control measures, such as budgets which limit the spending of departments, or objectives which function as targets or controls for departments to meet. The production operative, by contrast, is concerned with control in terms of clocking in or out, or meeting a standard in a job, or building a product to the right specifications. All of these activities imply control in one form or another.

The supervisor, like the CEO or the production operative, has to set up some form of control. These controls can affect employees or they can affect the output. A simple example of the former is the time clock, which is used to control the number of hours worked. An example of the latter would be Total Quality Control, which is dealt with in Chapter 16. When employees do not meet whatever standards have been set, the supervisor must accept at least some of the responsibility.

Although there are a variety of control mechanisms, most follow certain basic rules. First, they should indicate deviations without delay, and show who or what is responsible for the deviation. They can then be corrected quickly and effectively. Second, control mechanisms should be relevant to what is being controlled. Third, controls must be economical, that is, they must be worth the expense involved. Finally, control mechanisms should be adaptable to the changing demands of firms. As organisations become larger, control mechanisms should be capable of being modified rather than scrapped.

Cole (1993, p. 191) has outlined the stages to control, as follows:

- Establish standards of performance
- Measure performance
- Compare actual results against standards
- Take corrective action where required.

Control thus begins with setting out targets that must be met. These establish standards which function as benchmarks to judge performance. Once standards are in place, the next two stages are to measure performance and compare it against the standard. A comparison between the expected result and the actual result will indicate the extent of any deviation. That deviation should be corrected as soon as possible, which is the fourth stage. Some problems are corrected easily, others not. For example, if a machine is faulty, or if parts are not being produced to the right tolerances, then steps to correct the problem can be easily taken. If, on the other hand, a problem is related to an employee not performing their job properly, the supervisor must determine the appropriate action.

The controlling function is undergoing some change these days as there is a trend towards placing greater trust and responsibility on employees. This draws into question certain control mechanisms and, in particular, the degree of supervision a manager exercises over employees. The supervisor must make a judgement as to how closely to supervise a work group, taking into account such factors as the willingness and ability of employees to work unsupervised, the degree of difficulty of the task, and the supervisor's comfort with self-supervision. With the general rise in educational standards, along with the trend towards empowerment, supervisors should give employees as much freedom as possible to perform their jobs.

THE SUPERVISOR AND THE FUNCTIONS OF MANAGEMENT

Research would indicate that supervisors are increasingly being called upon to assume higher-level management duties, such as planning, and are finding themselves taking on more responsibility or just simply more work. In addition, in interviews conducted for this book, supervisors pointed to the increasing demands of their work, and to the need to find a balance between operational duties (participating in employee's work) and managerial ones (overseeing employee's work). A working knowledge of management functions can help greatly in finding that balance and in responding to new demands. To quote from Haimann (1994, p. 12):

> The benefits that you as a supervisor will derive from learning to be a better manager are obvious. First, you will have many opportunities to apply managerial principles and knowledge to your present job. Good management as a supervisor will make a great deal of difference in the performance of your department. It will function more smoothly, work will get done on time, you will probably find it easier to stay within your budget, and your workers will more willingly and enthusiastically contribute toward the ultimate objectives.

It should be understood that despite the rhetoric about management — the importance of strategic planning or the role management plays in the development of modern society — much of managerial work is chaotic and variable, and many of the activities performed by managers are reactive and up to a point boring. Understanding the management functions may help one be a better supervisor, but there are times when supervisors have to perform repetitive and dull tasks.

CHAPTER SUMMARY

Planning, organising, staffing, directing and controlling are the functions of management.

Planning deals with some very basic aspects of business, such as what is to be done, when it is to be done and who is to do it, and what resources — employees, materials, facilities, etc. — have to be used. Effective planning allows supervisors not only to prepare for the future, but also to make better use of the resources available, as well as their own time.

Organising refers to scheduling or allocation of work. Because supervisors have so much contact with employees, they will spend a great deal of time organising work. The basic premise is to ensure that work is evenly distributed among employees, and that the best use is made of resources.

Staffing refers to a host of factors relating to the employment of employees, such as recruitment, selection, training, staff development, compensation, performance appraisal and the like. As noted, despite having daily contact with employees, supervisors by and large do not have full authority for staffing. Rather, that is handled by the human resources or personnel department.

Directing refers to motivating and leading employees. It is one of the most important functions for supervisors since they have direct responsibility for the performance of a work group. The managerial role of supervisors is to channel the energy, enthusiasm and commitment of employees, as individuals and as members of a work group, towards the attainment of agreed goals, rather than necessarily to participate in the work itself.

Controlling, the final managerial function to be examined, refers to the methods and systems used to check performance and to ensure that plans are working the way they were intended to work. From the supervisor's perspective, control tends to consist of monitoring employees' performance. It is widely accepted now that less control is better and that employees should be given more freedom and responsibility in the jobs they perform.

References and Further Reading

Betts, P.W. (1993) *Supervisory Management*, sixth edition, London: Pitman, chapters 7 & 8.

Cole, G.A. (1993) *Management: Theory and Practice*, fourth edition, London: DP Publications, p. 191.

Evans, David (1995) *Supervisory Management*, fourth edition, London: Cassell, chapters 3, 5, 6 & 7.

Haimann, T. (1994) *Supervisory Management for Healthcare Organizations*, Iowa City, IA: Wm. C. Brown Publishers.

Koontz, H., C. O'Donnell and H. Weirich (1980) *Management*, seventh edition, New York: McGraw-Hill.

Lynch, John J. & Frank W. Roche (1995) *Business Management in Ireland: Competitive Strategy for the 21st Century*, Dublin: Oak Tree Press.

Pettinger, R. (1994) *Introduction to Management*, London: Macmillan.

Tiernan, S., Morley, M. & Foley, E. (1996) *Modern Management: Theory and Practice for Irish Students*, Dublin: Gill and Macmillan.

Chapter 3

SUPERVISORY MANAGEMENT IN HISTORICAL PERSPECTIVE

THE OBJECTIVE OF THIS CHAPTER

Organisations today value the important contribution supervisors make to organisational effectiveness, and demand from those individuals greater personal skills and qualities.[1] This was not the case in years past when the ability and willingness to exercise authority was considered the hallmark of a successful supervisor. This chapter examines why this change occurred. It begins with an account of the history of supervision, traces the development of management thought, and concludes with an understanding of today's changing business environment.

After reading and studying this chapter, the reader should have the following:

- An understanding of the historical role of the supervisor
- A broad understanding of theoretical approaches to the study of management
- A knowledge of the constraints under which supervisors have to work today.

HISTORY OF SUPERVISION: THE SUPERVISOR AS AUTHORITY FIGURE

The development of the factory system in the late 18th century changed both the meaning of work and the way work was organ-

[1] See Chapter 4 for a discussion of the skills and qualities of supervisors.

ised. Prior to industrialisation most people earned their own living, either from farming or from craft work. The invention of the steam engine, among other things, increased the pace of factory production, and over the course of a short time the factory system became more profitable than the home-based, cottage system. Society went from an agrarian to an industrial one. Ireland, for historical reasons mainly having to do with colonisation, remained largely an agricultural society, but in the North East and around Dublin, industrial life soon overshadowed farm life.

In the space of 100 years or so, the factory system became relatively commonplace. However, this growing size and complexity gave rise to numerous problems, notably those of co-ordination and control. The solution was to recruit a new breed of people called managers. This, in turn, gave rise to a need for supervisors to oversee workers. These tended to be the most skilled and senior of the workforce, hence the origins of the term "senior or superior operative". Most supervisors were selected partly on their ability to work hard, and partly because they possessed certain characteristics, notably that were able both to take and give orders.

The factory of old was considerably different from today's. There was, for a start, far less order. Most workers worked reluctantly and were poorly treated. There was no science or theory of management, and no books a person could read which would enlighten them on how to manage. Worse still, managers were selected, much like supervisors, for all the wrong reasons. Social class became the defining feature of management, in the same way as seniority and being a "company man" became the hallmark of the supervisor or foreman. Authority became the defining feature of the supervisor. He, and the early supervisor was usually male, directed workers, assigning work and often disciplining workers as the need arose. He controlled work, hiring and firing at will.

The reaction of individual people to the demeaning and harsh nature of work was to organise into unions. Hence, from the late 18th century, unions started to form, first for skilled craft workers, and later for unskilled workers[2]. The factory became, in time,

---

[2] The Regular Carpenters of Dublin, the first Irish union, met, as recorded, for the first time in 1764. Unskilled workers did not organise until late into

a battleground between workers, on the one hand, forming and joining unions for their own security, and the owner-capitalist, on the other, who subjected workers to increasingly harsher conditions. As Gunnigle et al. (1995, p. 96) note, the concept of "sweated labour" came into being to reflect the atrocious factory conditions of the time.

TAYLORISM: A SOLUTION TO THE PROBLEM OF CO-ORDINATION

As noted, the earliest factories lacked a system of organisation. This was particularly the case in the US, where different ethnic groups worked alongside each other often with considerable language difficulties. In Britain, the class system necessitated the development of the gang system in which the owners contracted with foremen, termed chargehands[3], who in turn employed the workers. The owners, for class reasons, did not therefore interact with workers. Ireland would have mirrored the British case.

One of the first major inventions to apply to manufacturing was Eli Whitney's concept of interchangability. Whitney's invention, which essentially allowed for parts to be produced in great quantities, revolutionised the face of manufacturing. For the first time, parts could be made in mass quantities, easily transported by virtue of the advancements in transport, and sold to an ever-increasing population. Despite the far-reaching developments, changes in the science of managing lagged far behind. People were working together in greater numbers in factories doing jobs which were very restrictive and narrow. As factories grew the need to co-ordinate and control became greater still. The person who addressed himself to this question was Frederick Taylor (see biographical note).

The time in which Taylor worked was most important. Factories grew immensely in size, labour was plentiful, and new technology was coming into vogue. The problem was how to organise these factors of production properly. Taylor's primary interest

---

the 19th century. The Irish Transport and General Workers Union, ITGWU (now, after amalgamating with the Federated Workers of Ireland, SIPTU), was formed in 1909. Unions were not legally recognised until 1871.

[3] In Germany, a supervisor is still called a *Vorarbeiter* (literally fore-worker).

was in efficiency (followers were later to be known as "efficiency experts" or, more correctly, industrial engineers). Taylor believed workers "soldiered", that is, intentionally slowed the pace of work. He further split this into "natural soldiering" and "systemic soldiering". The former is the natural tendency to slow things down and take it easy, the latter is the conscious attempt to restrict output. Soldiering could be explained, in Taylor's view, for three reasons: first, by workers' fear that if they worked hard they would do themselves out of a job; second, by what he called the "rule of thumb", that is, the lack of an established method; third, by poor working methods, that is, management. Taylor's answer to this problem was scientific management, reflected in his principles of management.

Biographical Note: Frederick Winslow Taylor

An American by birth and engineer by profession, Frederick Winslow Taylor (1856-1915) was primarily concerned with how the shopfloor of a factory was organised. He began his working life as an apprentice and rose to be chief superintendent of the Midvale Steel Company. He later moved to the Bethlehem Steel Company, and concluded his working life as a consultant. In the process he perfected what he was to term "scientific management".

He published his first book, *Principles of Scientific Management*, in 1911.[4] However, it was his testimony before a special US government hearing which made his ideas extremely popular. This testimony, along with an updated account of his ideas, was published posthumously in 1947 as *Scientific Management*.

These were Taylor's four principles of management:

- Development of a true science of work
- Scientific selection and training of workers
- Bringing together science of work and the training man
- Co-operation of management and workers.

[4] The book is now out of print although his ideas are summarised in a variety of books. For further information on Taylor, and particularly change, see Chapter 16 on world class manufacturing.

A true science of work would replace rule of thumb. Using scientific methods, each job was analysed and, through a combination of trial and error and science, the best way of doing the job was determined. Second, only the best workers, that is, the most productive, were to be selected and trained. Generally speaking, the most productive worker's job was analysed and this set the standard for all other similar jobs to follow. Thus, by dividing and subdividing work, the scientific manager could minimise the likelihood of error. Moreover, the speed at which work could be performed was increased dramatically because of the concentration on, and perfection of, one simple task. Finally, workers and management were to work together with workers sharing in the gains of work. Effectively, the latter meant a piece rate system:[5] by working harder workers were entitled to higher wages.

Taylor maintained that employees should profit from any gains in productivity. Piece rates were thus used as the way of getting workers to perform repetitive tasks. In reality, Taylorism did provide for real gains in wages, though at a cost. Scientific management led to simplified jobs with each worker going through the same few motions over and over again. The end result was a boring but efficient process. Moreover, workers, voicing their concern through trade unions, resented the fact that their skill and knowledge were taken away from them.

Despite such criticism, Taylorism was very influential. As noted, the concept of mass production, particularly in the US, is based primarily on a concept of Taylorism. Henry Ford, adopting Taylor's ideas to the fullest, implemented the first $5-a-day wage at his River Rouge plant in Detroit. Disregarding monotony, workers were more than content to suffer for a high wage. By the 1930s Taylorism had arrived. Mass production was seen as the most efficient way of manufacturing products.[6]

---

[5]A piece-rate system, usually associated with assembly work, is where workers are paid by the amount (or piece) they produce. The more pieces (parts or components) made or assembled, the more one is paid.

[6] For an understanding of the influence of mass production on the development of the world's economies, see Piore and Sabel (1984).

Taylorism and the Supervisor

Under Taylorism, factory work, while highly paid (relative to farming), became very demeaning and repetitive rather than self-fulfilling and enjoyable. Taylor showed no consideration for the effect that alienating work would have on workers and on society at large. The job of the supervisor became more difficult still. Supervisors needed to be authority figures and to carry out orders; they were promoted from the ranks of the workers, typically though not always being either the most senior or most productive worker, or both; finally supervisors had to closely supervise their employees in order to ensure that they actually did what they were supposed to do.

The trend today is towards more complete jobs. For example, Chapter 17 describes the development of job enlargement and job enrichment in the workplace. The former means increasing the variety of tasks to be performed and the latter refers to expanding the degree of skill and responsibility of a job. Thus many jobs in industry are now being broadened, making greater demands on the worker's time, skills and energy. Much of this is in response to pressures in the marketplace, that is, for firms to survive in the global environment more work has to be done by fewer people.

Supervisors are at the forefront of change in this regard. Going against the grain of what Taylorism prescribed, self-supervision is becoming very popular. In many instances, the supervisor of today "manages" more people, not by standing over them and issuing orders but by giving them more responsibility, in effect allowing employees to be their own supervisors. Far from making the supervisor's job easier, this places extra demands on the ability of supervisors to manage. That is, supervisors need to know more about the human element and when to direct work and when to let employees direct themselves.

HENRI FAYOL AS THE FATHER OF MANAGEMENT THEORY

Taylorism, it must be understood, is primarily an engineering discipline and therefore lacked a managerial aspect. That gap was filled by Henri Fayol (see biographical note), a French citizen, who was the first person to write about a theory of management.

Until then there was very little written about management, and certainly no attempt to produce a grand theory of management.

> **Biographical Note: Henri Fayol**
>
> Fayol (1841-1925) began his working life at age 19 as a mining engineer for the firm of Commentary-Fourchamboult-Decazeville. Working all his life for this company, he reached the position of managing director at age 47. Near bankruptcy when he took over, by his retirement, at age 77, the company was extremely successful. He became, as a result, very popular in France, much sought after for his advice. Based upon his managerial experience he wrote *General and Industrial Management*. Originally published in French in 1916, under the title *Administration Industrielle et Générale*, the English edition came out in 1949.

Fayol argued that there were three aspects of management:

- The activities of the enterprise (what firms do)
- The elements of management (the job of management)
- The principles of management (guidelines or rules for better management).

The activities were:

- Technical (concerned with production)
- Commercial (concerned with buying and selling)
- Financial (concerned with funding the organisation)
- Security (concerned with the protection of property)
- Accounting (concerned with bookkeeping and financial matters)
- Managerial (concerned with the management of the organisation).

Fayol argued that five of these activities — technical, commercial, financial, security and accounting— were well-known and accepted as important to the functioning of any organisation. Far less well-known and lacking in available information were the management activities. According to Fayol, to manage is "to forecast and plan, to organise, to command, to co-ordinate and to control". As noted in the previous chapter, this provided a standard definition of management and today we refer to these as the functions of management, though often substituting the words "staffing" and "directing" for "commanding" and "co-ordinating". Fayol's contribution to the study of management was that he was the first to recognise that management was a separate activity and he provided, in the form of principles, certain guidelines or rules to manage. More importantly, he argued that the ability to manage was not a divine right, or something innate, or limited to a small number of people, but rather could be learned and improved upon by the application of his principles of management.

Fayol's Principles of Management

Drawing on his long experience of management, Fayol outlined fourteen principles of management, occasionally referring to them as rules (Table 3.1). These principles were to provide guidelines for managers. The list is not exhaustive and each principle should be applied only if relevant to the situation at hand. Fayol, however, believed that by following these a manager could successfully manage any type of organisation. Many, as we shall see shortly, bear relevance to supervision.

Fayol and the Supervisor

What is the relevance of Fayol's fourteen principles of management to management in general and supervision in particular? The first thing to be said is that Fayol should be seen in the light of the times in which he wrote. That is, Fayol believed very much in order and thus the supervisor to him was one who controls workers, largely by following the principles outlined in Table 3.1. Authority was therefore extremely important. Moreover, the individual was subservient to the company and work was extremely specialised. Many of these principles, notably unity of command and direction, are structural or bureaucratic in nature. Many do not tie into a modern, complex world where change is constant. Still, some have relevance to today's organisations, notably the focus on initiative and *esprit de corps*, both of which are central to team or group work.

Table 3.1: Fayol's Fourteen Principles of Management

1. Division of Work	Jobs are minimised both for the worker and for the manager. The latter should only manage what he or she is capable of managing.
2. Authority and Responsibility	This is the right to give orders.
3. Discipline	Employees should obey rules.
4. Unity of Command	Each person should have one and only one superior.
5. Unity of Direction	There should be one superior and one plan for a group of activities.
6. Subordination of Individual to the General Interest	The general good should prevail over the interest of the individual.
7. Remuneration	Pay should be fair for the employee and the firm.
8. Centralisation	All activities of the firm should be centralised.
9. Scalar Chain	The line of authority should extend clearly from top to bottom.
10. Order	Everything and every one should have their proper place in the firm.
11. Equity	Employees should be treated with fairness and justice.
12. Stability of tenure and personnel	Employees, particularly managers, need to be given time to fit into their jobs.
13. Initiative	All employees should be encouraged to show initiative where possible.
14. Esprit de Corps	Managers should foster harmony and encourage employees to work together.

BUREAUCRACY: A MANAGEMENT APPROACH TO THE CIVIL SERVICE

Max Weber (see biographical note), a German sociologist, ranks alongside Karl Marx and Emil Durkheim as one of the founding fathers of sociology, a discipline commonly referred to as the science of society because of its concern with how society, rather than individuals, functions. Weber's particular concern, among many, was how authority is exercised in large organisations. To him, the essence of effective and democratic management was bureaucracy. Though the term "bureaucracy" has taken on a negative connotation of late, in Weber's view bureaucracy was beneficial because it helped to avoid managerial abuses, particularly nepotism and favouritism. Like Fayol, therefore, Weber has to be seen as a product of his times. Then (in the late 19th century) abuse in one form or another was common. There was, as we have seen, no written knowledge as to how firms should be run. Managers ruled by decree, often using and abusing employees. There was little limit on the powers of management. Often, jobs went to family members, and it was by no means certain that the best employees were selected. Rules were lax, and people were more likely to be promoted to managerial positions due to their standing in society rather than their training or special skills for managing. What was needed, according to Weber, was a set of rules that would ensure that managers operated efficiently, competently, and fairly — in short, bureaucracy.

This may seem strange to a lot of people. Indeed, the modern connotation of the word "bureaucracy" is "red tape" or officialdom, that is, an excess of paperwork and rules leading to inefficiency and inaction. Yet, to Weber, bureaucracy was an intelligent and democratic way of running businesses with a system of rules at its core. Rules ensured that authority was exercised in a controlled and acceptable way by subjecting officials to published standards and accepted practices. In so doing it legitimised authority. By having rules to be followed, an organisation avoided arbitrary or discriminatory action on the part of management and legitimised authority in the eyes of employees.

Biographical Note: Max Weber

Born in Germany, Max Weber (1864-1920) trained as a lawyer but later turned his attention towards the emerging discipline of sociology. Aside from his work in the field of the sociology of organisations, he wrote widely on religion and on the development of capitalism. He was a professor at the University of Berlin for most of his academic life. His most well-known books are *The Protestant Ethic and the Spirit of Capitalism* (1930) and *Economy and Society* (1968). The latter contained his analysis of bureaucracy.

These are some of the features of bureaucracy that Weber outlined:

- Each job has a written job description
- Rules are recorded in writing
- Jobs are hierarchically arranged where one level of jobs is subject to control by the next higher level
- Official positions have permanency; job holders do not
- Officials are appointed to the office because of their technical ability
- These officials are not the owners of the organisations
- Work is highly specialised with each employee performing a set task.

These features, Weber went on to argue, would mean that a bureaucratic organisation was capable of attaining the highest degree of efficiency and was, in that sense, the most rational way of controlling people.

The Problem of Bureaucracy

As organisations grow in size, rules tend to attain an importance of their own that can counteract their original intention. This is because, as organisations grow, specialisation increases, new jobs are created and old jobs redefined or made redundant. New staff are recruited, and existing staff are retrained. When flexibility and informality are required, the bureaucratic rules, put in place when the organisation was begun, often have negative effects. Instead of regulating people, rules are used to control and discipline people. Inefficiency often results.

Increasing size almost inevitably implies complexity. Rules, however, are less suitable to complex organisations. In particular, rules have a tendency to lead to predictable and standard behaviour. Furthermore, supervisors, as others have argued, can end up spending their day implementing rules rather than getting work done. A case in point, familiar to many organisations, is the necessity to fill out forms to achieve something. Rules thus become overbearing and a restraint on one's job and the overall efficiency of the organisation.

Complex organisations need to be more adaptive and flexible, and more responsive to customers' needs. This is particularly the case for firms which operate in the global market, where competition is fiercest. But even domestic firms have their problems. They too are exposed to increased competition. Unions in the ESB, for example, are well aware of the need to move away from restrictive practices. Their fear is that members' jobs will be lost to international companies who have the potential to provide electricity cheaper in an open market.

In all, bureaucracy has its problems. Though originally perceived as the democratic solution to managing large organisations, bureaucratic organisations tend to take on a meaning of their own. As a result, most large organisations nowadays, including the Irish civil service, are implementing plans to debureaucratise. The movement towards decentralising, that is, moving public offices outside of Dublin, is designed in part to personalise departments. Now it is possible to contact individual civil servants by telephone, and queries and complaints are handled in a more professional, yet personal manner, with the respondent giving their name. Supervisors in particular have been trained to handle complaints, often by speaking directly to the person making the complaint and then following up the issue until it is resolved. Most of these changes are in response to increased competition and the need to meet customers' needs. In the process, the supervisor's job has changed.

Weber and the Supervisor

What lessons can be learned for supervisors from studying the Weberian concept of bureaucracy? Firstly, and perhaps most importantly, it focuses attention on the positive side of bureaucracy. As noted, rules are designed to limit arbitrary action by management and to promote competent behaviour. Thus rules have a use: they provide for orderliness and consistency. Without rules there would be disorder: people would be unsure what to do, and how to interact with others. Similar to Fayol's principles of management, supervisors can follow rules and perform their job in accordance with what has been laid down. Indeed, one could say that today, with the influence both of labour law and health and safety regulations, supervisors need to be more aware of, and follow, rules.

Rules, however, can easily be abused, or misused, and can promote rigid behaviour. This is the downside of bureaucracy. Many jobs nowadays require more flexibility. In office work today it is not always a case of turning up at 9.00 a.m. and going home at 5.00 p.m. Rather, employees are asked to contribute more and to be more responsive to the customer. The corollary to this is that employees themselves may demand greater flexibility from employers. If they require an hour off during the day to run an errand, supervisors should be able to show flexibility. In all, rules are becoming less important, being overshadowed of late by demands for greater flexibility and trust. Ultimately, Weber, like Fayol, may be seen as a product of his times. But a knowledge of Weber at least helps to place bureaucracy in its proper place, though rules, the core of bureaucracy, should be used sparingly.

THE 1930s: THE GROWTH OF PERSONNEL MANAGEMENT

Even before Taylorism took hold, there was, from the early part of the century but accelerated in the war years, a new development in management called *welfarism*. Some employers, influenced by religious beliefs, notably Quakerism, took great steps to improve the harsh conditions of factory life. Welfare departments, as they were then called, were set up to co-ordinate what would now be called personnel issues. In Ireland, from early on this century, both Guinness and Jacobs (now Irish Biscuits) established strong reputations for a caring approach to employees. Other companies quickly followed suit, and during the 1914-18 war, when employment was high in Britain, more welfare departments were established. These played a large part in offsetting the pathetic conditions workers toiled under. After the war, when demand for products decreased, and as high employment gave way to unemployment and despair, many firms abolished welfare departments.

It was not until the mid-1930s that a new school of thought, referred to as the Human Relations approach,[7] emerged which argued that employees had important social needs, particularly the need to be treated well in work. Organisations were thus encouraged to be more attentive to people's needs, and this would in time translate into higher productivity. Many of the earlier writers in this school, particularly Elton Mayo, were psychologists with the result that industrial psychology began to exert greater influence in the field of management. Mayo's pioneering work gave way in time to the groundwork of various motivation theorists, including Abraham Maslow and Frederick Herzberg, both of whom are examined in detail in Chapter 13. It was around this time that personnel management began to grow. Issues of concern to the personnel managers were the selection, induction, training, compensation and development of employees. From the end of World War II on, as trade unions became a force to be reckoned with in society, the personnel function eventually took over responsibility for managing industrial relations. In the process, personnel managers took over many of the staffing duties previously the concern of line managers, including supervisors.

HUMAN RESOURCE MANAGEMENT (HRM)

Personnel management has been overshadowed in recent years by what is now called Human Resource Management (HRM). Human resource management, as Gunnigle et al. point out (1995, p. 238), arose with two very distinct American perspectives: one focused on the individual, the other on broader strategic issues. Taking the former first, a HRM view argues that people are a firm's best resource, and that the company must attract, retain

[7] See Chapter 13 on the human relations approach.

and develop the most qualified and suitable people. Procedures, policies and practices need to be put in place to secure the commitment and involvement of individual employees. The second strand stresses a more strategic role for personnel and industrial relations issues in management and aligns personnel policy with company strategy. Hence, a company with a strategy to become a world class competitor needs to discuss personnel issues at board level. Therefore, issues that would have normally been the responsibility of line management are now more likely to be considered as part of a broad HR strategy decided by senior management. This is to ensure that HR policies are centralised and apply to the whole organisation. Hence supervisors needs to be more attuned to the overall organisational strategy, just as senior management needs to be cognisant of what is happening at the shopfloor level.

Human Resource Management and the Supervisor

HRM in general demands a more professional approach to management with strong implications for supervisors. To begin with, HRM has introduced a whole new range of management practices including, among others, performance appraisal and teamwork.[8] Supervisors not only have to be familiar with such practices, but may in some cases have to implement them. There is, in addition, inherent in HRM the important focus on the individual. Supervisors, therefore, need to be more attentive to both the individual and group needs of employees.

While the development of personnel management has in many ways diminished the job of supervisory management, HRM has to a large extent reversed that process. That is not to say that supervisors will resume the authority of hiring and firing employees, but the job of the supervisor is changing qualitatively with the result that supervisors are becoming facilitators and coaches rather than managers. More is demanded of supervisors, both in terms of what they bring to the job and what is done on the job itself. Finally, an emerging view is that supervisors are becoming

---

[8] Performance appraisal is the system whereby employees' work is appraised, typically by their immediate supervisor (see Chapter 15). Teamwork is discussed in detail in Chapter 17.

more important now because of the central thesis of HRM: people are the most important resource in the organisation.

THE CHANGING BUSINESS ENVIRONMENT OF TODAY

HRM is just one of many changes affecting supervisors today. The increasing use of technology, and in the way it is being used, is changing the face of work. The way work is organised is changing as rapidly. Teamwork is becoming the norm in manufacturing firms, and to a lesser extent in service organisations. Teamwork places new demands on supervisors, especially if supervisors become the team leaders or team facilitators. Finally, the way firms do business is also changing. Product quality has become the defining feature of competition. This is reflected in market trends with a far wider choice of high-quality products being offered to consumers today. It is reflected in organisational practices in terms of the implementation of new techniques like Total Quality Management (TQM)[9] and in the customer-oriented focus of the modern firm. Firms are becoming, to borrow a computer term, more user-friendly. What is causing this change?

Competition can account for much of it. With the rise of multinational companies, coupled with the breaking down of trade barriers as is happening in the European Union, many firms are doing business on a global basis. The overall result is that firms, domestic and international, small and large, have to make radical changes simply to survive. Employers in particular are looking at ways to increase production or improve quality or both. These changes have placed new demands on all categories of workers, but none more so than the supervisor. In many instances, supervisors have taken on new roles, becoming leaders, trainers and motivators of people. Less relevant now (though perhaps still demanded) is the need for supervisors to discipline and control employees. In other cases, layers of supervisory management are being done away with, as employees themselves take on the role of self-supervision. Supervisors, as a result, are being made redundant or, alternatively, being transferred to different jobs where they themselves become team members. Finally, many

[9] See Chapter 16 on TQM.

employees are seeing their job responsibilities expanded to include many tasks that were previously the domain of the supervisor (and not always accompanied by an increase in wages!), and supervisors themselves are performing higher-level management duties.

Increasing competition has brought with it change which is not always accepted by people. Rationalisation in the public sector, such as the recent CCR (Cost and Competitiveness Review) in the ESB, has brought early retirement for some and more work for others. New agreements also allow for new work practices such as contract work, job-sharing and part-time work, all of which can be subsumed under the heading of "atypical work". The latter, along with words like rationalisation and downsizing, have become the buzz words of the 1990s. They greatly affect supervisors, largely because many of the changes that are taking place occur at the workplace level where supervisors operate. Hence supervisors have introduced change to, at times, a sceptical workforce, or manage greater numbers of contract employees.

Change, finally, takes places against a background of increasing diversity in society. With the advent of the EEC (now EU), and with many emigrants returning to Ireland with new ideas and different perspectives, the face of business is changing in one way or another. The Chinese have an apt saying, namely that "out of ten fingers, nine are different". Thus, society is far more diverse now, with different people, different ideas and different views all having to co-exist together.

Pressure for Change from Employees

Aside from competition and the manner in which it forces firms to introduce new work practices and change existing ones, there is another front from which change is being demanded. This is from employees themselves. The awareness and expectations of people, from employees to shareholders to customers, have increased dramatically due, in no small part, to increased educational opportunities and the influence of the media. Many people are undertaking educational courses in their own time and on their initiative. In some cases, firms are providing encouragement, often in the form of reimbursement, for students who do well in external examinations. The ESB and An Post, for example, as well as numerous private sector firms, pay for approved educational courses because they now recognise the importance of education in providing a skilled workforce. One consequence of this is that standards and expectations have risen. People nowadays not only expect more from work, but know what to expect. They know something about human resource management, what motivation is, or how to lead. They expect their supervisor to know, too. Many employees may want to see flexitime or job-sharing implemented. They may want the latest and fanciest computer available or they may claim a right to do something, or that their rights are being infringed. To cope with these new demands, the supervisor has to be more knowledgeable than ever before. Further, the option to refer a decision to someone else is less available now.

CHAPTER SUMMARY

The job of supervisory management has come full circle in recent years. The origins of this level of management suggests the need for an authoritative and commanding person. Today that individual is more of a coach or mentor to people rather than a director (or dictator). To perform the role of the coach that individual has to be more confident and knowledgeable and more attuned to individual needs. Certainly the development towards human resource management has demanded a more professional approach to all levels of management and has also provided some of the tools for this. But HRM is just one of many changes affecting supervisors today. Others include the increasing use of technology supported by new work practices such as Total Quality Management and teamwork; new legislative requirements, particularly in the area of employee relations and safety and health; greater expectations from shareholders and employees, along with change in the demographics of work, and, in particular, the increasing participation of women in the labour force; increasing competition in the marketplace, especially of a global nature; and the continued focus on quality. Alone or in combination, these factors continue to force change as a matter of priority, in the private as much as the public sector. Hence the following classification of today's business environment by Tiernan et al. (1996, p. 307):

> Instead of a stable and certain environment, organisations are now faced with complexity, uncertainty and dynamism, all of which demand change.

These changes in one way or another have changed the very skills demanded of supervisors. In today's highly competitive business environment, working often in a constraining manner, supervisors must resolve problems and make decisions, in a timely and effective way. This requires new skills and a new way of managing, which is the subject of the next chapter.

References and Further Reading

Betts, P.W. (1993) *Supervisory Management*, sixth edition, London: Pitman, chapter 2.

Bittle, L.R., & J. Newstrom (1990) *What Every Supervisor Should Know*, New York: McGraw-Hill , chapters 1 & 2.

Boyd, Andrew (1985) *The Rise of Irish Trade Unions, 1729-1980* (second edition), Dublin: Anvil Books.

Gunnigle, P., McMahon, G., & G. Fitzgerald (1995) *Industrial Relations in Ireland: Theory and Practice*, Dublin: Gill & Macmillan.

Piore, M. & C. Sabel (1984) *The Second Divide: Possibilities for Posterity*, New York: Basic Books.

Tiernan, S., Morley, M. & Foley, E., *Modern Management: Theory and Practice for Irish Students*, Gill and Macmillan, Dublin, 1996, chapters 3 & 14.

Weber, M (1968) *Economy and Society*, New York: Bedminster Press.

Weber, M. (1930) *The Protestant Ethic and the Spirit of Capitalism*, London: Allen & Unwin.

Chapter 4

THE EFFECTIVE SUPERVISOR

THE OBJECTIVE OF THIS CHAPTER

Much of the change that is happening in businesses today is occurring at the level of the workplace. These changes include the increasing use of new technology, the implementation of a variety of new management practices, the broadening of job responsibilities, the creation of new jobs as others vanish, and increased accountability. Supervisors are at the forefront of these changes: they have to introduce change and their own jobs are changing too.

This chapter examines the skills required to deal effectively with change, as distinct from being swamped by it. More specifically, it argues that in performing both people and task duties, supervisors need a variety of skills, not all technical, to meet adequately the many demands made on them. The chapter begins with a description of "the effective supervisor", which is followed by discussion of the skills and qualities required of supervisors.

After reading and studying this chapter, the reader should have the following:

- An understanding of skills required to be effective in a supervisor's position
- A sense of the importance to supervisory management of self-development.

IS THERE AN IDEAL SUPERVISOR?

There is no such thing as an ideal supervisor. A good supervisor, however, is an individual who is able to encourage and lead other people to higher performance and has the broad range of skills and knowledge necessary to perform the job competently, and to change as new demands are made on them. Bad supervisors, on the other hand, cannot get on with people, do not understand and motivate others, are not good at managing and cannot carry out higher-level tasks. They may have the training and knowledge to be good supervisors, but are unable to apply them properly. Finally, someone who makes for a poor supervisor is typically an individual who cannot respond to change or is unable to deal with the varied and chaotic pace of work today.

Effective supervisors, however, are individuals who are good at doing their job, and at getting other people to do theirs. Indeed as Gillespie (1994, p. 12) comments:

> the supervisor get the people in his department to do what he wants done, when it should be done, and the way he wants it done, because they want to do it.

This is achieved in part by creating a work culture based on trust and respect, that is conducive to hard and rewarding work rather than standing over employees. And it entails an ability to deal with the increasing diversity and individualism of today's workplace. Effective supervisors therefore:

- Know what their role and responsibilities are
- Attempt to further themselves
- Are excellent communicators
- See themselves as part of a management team
- Are able to lead and motivate staff to higher performance
- Are content with their jobs and comfortable and open in dealing with staff
- Are sufficiently qualified
- Are able to balance both task and people duties
- Are aware that employees do want to do their jobs properly and conscientiously, and that they take great pride in their work.

Table 4.1 attempts to portray the changing nature of supervisory management. Gone, or at least slowly going, is the day when supervisors stood over workers while issuing orders. In its place is the arrival of a new breed of supervisor, the person who is a facilitator, there when needed but out of sight when workers are doing the job they are well capable of doing.

TABLE 4.1: THE OLD SUPERVISOR VS THE NEW LEADER

Old Supervisor	New Leader
Thinks of self as a supervisor or boss	Thinks of self as facilitator, sponsor, coach, or internal consultant
Follows chain of command	Deals with anyone necessary to get the job done
Works alone	Works as part of team
Most senior member of work group	Rotates leadership
Hoards information	Shares information
Tries to master one major function	Tries to understand whole process
Demands long hours	Demands satisfied customers
Supervises workers	Lets workers supervise themselves

Source: Adopted with modifications from Peppard & Rowland (1995).

THE SKILLS REQUIRED TO BE AN EFFECTIVE SUPERVISOR

Supervisors, like all managers, have to perform both people and task duties. People duties means looking after the needs of people and includes such duties as assigning work to employees, ensuring that they have the proper skills and tools to perform that work, and creating in addition an environment conducive to high productivity. Task duties refer to the tasks or items that have to be done by supervisors in order to ensure that the work that is done, such as conducting interviews, making phone calls, writing letters, etc.

In order to perform both people and task duties, supervisors, as a rule, need a variety of skills. These include:

- Technical skills
- Interpersonal skills
- Administrative skills
- Communicative skills
- Conceptual skills.

Technical skills are the certified skills necessary to perform a particular task, such as nursing, driving, plumbing, machining, etc., and include in addition, knowledge of equipment, processes, systems, etc. Generally speaking, supervisors who are able to perform employees' jobs make for better supervisors.

Interpersonal skills (also called human or people skills) are the skills necessary to manage people, such as leadership and motivation.

Administrative skills are the skills necessary to handle the administrative and paperwork components of the position, including the ability to plan and control work.

Communicative skills deal with the ability to communicate with others, particularly employees and management. This includes, from a practical perspective, the ability to make written and oral presentations.

Conceptual skills include a host of intellectual skills such as the ability to analyse, reason, synthesise, and interpret information. Analysing means the ability to divide a problem into its constituent parts, while synthesising, its opposite, means seeing a particular problem in whole terms. Reasoning means the ability to solve a problem in logical steps, either from the particular to the general (induction), or the general to the particular (deduction). It is these conceptual skills that allow a supervisor to problem-solve and make decisions.

The supervisory function will differ from organisation to organisation and even within organisations. Therefore, the degree to which each skill is required will vary. Some supervisors will spend a lot of time dealing with employees, hence the importance of "people" skills. For other supervisors technical skills are paramount. Indeed, some supervisors have to be more skilled than operators in the performance of manual work. For others, the opposite prevails. Managers who supervise office staff, for example, generally do not know how to type or do shorthand, but a supervisor of a post-graduate student needs, in theory at least, to be more knowledgeable than the student. Still others need both people and technical skills in equal proportion. A nursing supervisor, such as a matron, is likely to be a SRN (state registered nurse), that is, have the technical skills, and will also need many people skills in managing nurses. Similarly, a Garda Sergeant has both the technical skills (of a qualified Garda) and the people skills to manage.

As was pointed out in Chapter 1, there is a view, which has much validity, that the management of people is of paramount importance to most (but not all) supervisors, hence the importance of interpersonal skills. Stone (1988, p. 25) makes this clear:

> In so far as you are judged at all in the purely supervisory aspects of your work, it will be how you obtain the best possible work from your staff for your organisation. There is certainly no question that such is the way in which those staff will judge first and foremost; and the fact that you may be technically superb, or have other qualities in life which are admirable, will always rank second or lower to how you are as a manager of people, as far as they are concerned.

Stone calls this management style, which basically means creating the atmosphere of openness and democracy in the way one manages. It is a point which we will return to in Chapter 14 (on leadership).

UNDERSTANDING SKILLS AND KNOWLEDGE

Skills are often thought to be innate, that is, something we are born with (or without as the case may be). However, a skill, by definition, is also something that can be learned and improved upon. Management skills are built up from experience and training, and the occasional error. In principle, management means knowing how to deal with people, how to get the job done, and how to cope with new demands. The skills to do this, like those in sport, can be taught. Students can and do come to colleges, learn about management, and go on to be better managers. Similarly, with dedication and effort, and a talent for management, you can become an effective supervisor.

There are, however, a number of points that must be noted about this view. First, managerial skills are difficult to enumerate and therefore difficult to teach, in part because they are human skills that are dependent on the situation at hand. Skills and knowledge thus have to blended with experience. To complicate matters, no two experiences are exactly alike. A supervisor may have to respond with authority in one situation, and openness in another. Equally, advice may be given with the best of intentions in a classroom or a book but is not applicable to every situation. Knowing how to apply knowledge and how to use the skills appropriately are what matters. That is, experience as much as training and knowledge is important in responding to constant change.

The second problem with management skills has to do with the changing nature of the job and particularly the importance of a new breed of knowledge which is coming into demand. Knowledge from a broad perspective can be either of two kinds: codified or tacit. The former refers to knowledge which is factual and expressible. Supervisors should know what is expected of them by senior management, they should have a good understanding of the mission of the organisation and their contribution or potential contribution to it, they should have knowledge of the law, etc. Tacit knowledge, on the other hand, is that which is known yet not capable of being expressed (or at least difficult to express). It is the sort of knowledge which is gained through experience, such as the knowledge skilled workers have of their craft. It is argued now that tacit skills are becoming increasingly important in the management of business today (see Ainger et al., 1995). A person can learn about personality and interpersonal behaviour, but never quite understand how to manage people. The latter is to a large extent an innate skill, and part of the tacit skills that an individual brings to the workplace and builds upon through experience.

THE QUALITIES OF A SUPERVISOR

Research would indicate that, almost without exception, people enter the ranks of supervisory management through promotion. Referencing their own research in America, Bittel and Newstrom (1990, pp. 7-8) make an insightful point:

> Three out of every four supervisors are promoted from the ranks of the organisation in which they serve. Typically they are long-service employees. They have greater experience, have held more different jobs in the organisation, and have significantly more education than the employees they supervise. Usually, it is apparent that supervisors are chosen from among the best and most experienced employees in the organisation.

They go on to highlight what they see as the most important qualities in a supervisor, which are:

- Energy and good health
- Ability to get along with people
- Job know-how and technical competence
- Self-control under pressure
- Dedication and dependability
- Ability to stay on course
- Teachability
- Problem-solving skills
- Leadership potential
- A positive attitude toward management.

Chapter 5 of this book includes a survey of supervisors and managers in Ireland which, like Bittel and Newstrom, indicates that supervisors are held in high standing and that senior management is demanding more of the supervisor: a better educated and better skilled manager.

CHAPTER SUMMARY

People in supervisory positions often occupy precarious roles in organisations. They are first and foremost managers, but spend much of their time dealing with rank and file employees. While their primary management responsibility is dealing with people, they many have many administrative tasks to do. These tasks can tie up much of a day's work. Much of the change that is occurring today — from the introduction of computers to the implementation of new management practices — directly affect the supervisor. Finally, the supervisor in the 1990s works under a series of constraints; the lack of training is one, the lack of managerial recognition another. Taken together it can be said that the job of the supervisor is a varied and important one which demands many skills.

The effective supervisor needs to learn how to approach each situation, and select from a body of skills and knowledge. Knowledge gained from training and experience, and in particular an understanding of people, processes and the law, are the keys to successful supervision. The art is in applying them.

References and Further Reading

Ainger, A., Rukesh K. & R. Ennals (1995) *Executive Guide to Business Success through Human-Centred Systems*, London: Springer

Bittel, L.R. & J. Newstrom (1990) *What Every Supervisor Should Know*, New York: McGraw-Hill .

Gillespie, K. (1994) *Creative Supervision*, New York: Harcourt Brace Jovanovich.

Malone, S. (1996) *Learning to Learn*, London: CIMA Publishing.

Malone, S. (1997) *Mind Skills for Managers*, London: Gower.

Mosley, D., L. Megginson, P. Pietri (1993) *Supervisory Management: The Art of Empowering and Developing People*, third edition, Cincinnati, OH: South-Western, chapter 2.

Peppard, J. & P. Rowland (1995) *The Essence of Business Process Re-engineering*, London: Prentice Hall.

Stone, Brian W. (1988) *Supervisory Skills*, London: Pitman.

Tiernan, S., Morley, M. & Foley, E. (1996) *Modern Management: Theory and Practice for Irish Students*, Dublin: Gill and Macmillan, chapter 1.

Chapter 5

THE CHANGING NATURE OF SUPERVISORY WORK IN IRELAND[1]

THE OBJECTIVE OF THIS CHAPTER

This chapter reports on research work conducted by the author. Using a detailed survey, the author interviewed over a period of two years (1996–97) a range of personnel in a variety of public and private sector organisations. In all, 18 organisations were visited. Those interviews were taped and the information transcribed. The survey was designed on the basis of desktop research of existing material on supervisory management.

The aim of the survey was to gain a broad understanding of change in the work of supervisors. The sample of people interviewed was not meant to be statistically representative, but there was an attempt to study a diverse group of organisations. That diversity included all branches of the military, the Garda Síochána and a wide range of public and private sector organisations. In the past, organisations like the military and the police have often been omitted from study, although the change process has affected them greatly.

SUMMARY OF RESULTS

Tradition has it that supervisors deal with issues as they arise, and interact almost constantly with employees. Recent events draw into question this traditional assumption. Organisations have been downsizing, in the process reducing layers of manage-

---

[1] A version of this paper was presented at the Second Conference on Management Research in Ireland, Dublin City University, 18/19 September, 1997.

ment and introducing new technologies, new techniques and new forms of work organisation such as teamwork and employee empowerment. These developments, accelerated in recent years, carry wide implications for supervisors. In particular, the notion of the supervisor as a "people manager" is changing as they assume more managerial responsibility, are working less with people, and are increasingly higher-skilled.

In addition, the increasing willingness of employees to pursue (part-time) educational opportunities (in many cases in order to gain promotion), the increased incidence of hiring supervisors from outside the organisation as distinct from promoting within (indicating the growing importance of technical qualifications) and finally the increase in responsibilities for supervisors all serve to indicate a trend towards the growing professionalism of supervisory management.

However, the results were not conclusive. In the public sector, excluding the military, nurses and the police, there is strong recognition of change but little movement in that direction. It is noted, of course, that the military is currently midway through the policy of employing soldiers on five-year contracts, and the consequences of this are not yet known (this may be extended to twelve years of service provided that certain military criteria are met). Similarly, the PDR (Personnel Development Review) because of current difficulties with the Representative Associations, who seek to have the PDR linked to pay and productivity issues, has not yet been implemented in the Garda Síochána. Finally, the Nursing Commission may in time bring about major changes in the nursing profession. But it is in the private sector, notably in the manufacturing and financial sectors, that, not unexpectedly, change is greatest. However, as there is considerable variation in the role of the supervisor, both within and between organisations, generalisations are difficult to make. Also, movements towards professionalism of supervisory management may be only a trend for the leading-edge organisations, and is brought about by a range of factors, notably downsizing, teamwork and an increase in educational standards.

Change in the Work of Supervisors

In discussing change, many commentators pointed out that it was not primarily the job of the supervisor which has changed, but rather that technological, legal and organisational developments, many of which are beyond the control of the supervisor, have brought tremendous change to their work. Undoubtedly, the increasing use of computer technology has created its own set of problems. Similarly, legal changes, including health and safety considerations, as well as standards such as ISO 9000, have created a greater need for documentation and accountability. Finally, supervisors are at the forefront of the new changes such as downsizing and delayering, and the move into teams, in which they have both to manage and to experience change. Also public accountability is greater now for organisations such as the Garda and the military. Accountability has also increased as an indirect result of computers: data is available to a wider range of people, problems are more likely to show up and are more easily traced to the source. In all, keeping abreast of change — new processes, new systems, new technology, and legal requirements — is a major problem for supervisors. Change is complicated by developments in staffing: supervisors are having to make do with less staff, as well as more diversity in the workplace (for example, more women in the workplace) and new employment systems (more use of casual labour, for example).

The following section examines four major factors of change: rising educational standards, new legal requirements, new technology and teamwork.

Educational Standards as a Force of Change

One factor that was mentioned in interviews as causing change was the rise of educational standards which both facilitates and encourages change. An increasing number of supervisors have sought educational opportunities outside the workplace. Significantly, this was seen as the key to achieving promotion. This is particularly the case in the public sector where promotion, by government edict, has been severely limited. Managers in the private sector also noted that they looked favourably in terms of promotion on individuals who pursued outside courses.

Some organisations, by far in the minority, were demanding, encouraging and facilitating higher educational and training standards in the provision of in-house courses and support for outside courses. One factor motivating this change was the need for higher-skilled supervisors. In manufacturing, for example, the difficulty of getting engineers to work on night shifts, along with new process technology, necessitated higher-skilled supervisors who could fill in for them. Indeed, as a result of technical developments one organisation took the step of recruiting supervisors directly from colleges.

Many organisations also pointed to the cost of training, the opportunity costs as much as the real cost, and the fear of poaching in a tight labour market, as restrictions on their ability to train. Fear of poaching was mentioned as a particular problem in the hotel industry where labour mobility is traditionally high and where there is a severe labour shortage. It was mentioned that increasingly new entrants to the labour force with certified training would enter directly to supervisory ranks, while contract labour provide the rank-and-file employees. Aside from the hotel sector, as has been well reported, electronics companies reported difficulties in recruiting employees due to skill shortages.

Administrative Duties: Legal Requirements

Despite the emphasis on people management, administrative duties remained an important, and indeed increasing, aspect of most supervisors' work. These administrative tasks were extremely varied in scope and included the planning and scheduling of work, writing reports, and recording technical, legal and production data. These requirements were seen to have increased in recent years —for example, the recording of health and safety or quality data in electronic form —adding fuel to the view that supervisors have more paperwork to do.

These developments affected supervisors in a variety of industries, including manufacturing, the hospitality sector, construction as well as the military and the Garda. However, there was variation both within and across industries. In hospitals, for example, reports are now becoming more important, especially with safety procedures and the potential threat of litigation. In positions which are extremely technical, such as those in the aviation industry, the keeping of records brought about by increased accountability has risen dramatically in recent years. It was mentioned by fire brigade personnel that more work now has to be quantified, and that standards are constantly increasing, hence the importance of time management, writing and computer skills. Further, there is increasing supervision or accountability of the fire-fighter's work. In the Garda also, legal changes and public accountability have resulted in their increasing administrative role, fuelling the public debate about the role of the police in the modern society.[2] Similarly, in the financial sector, legislative and accounting changes were demanding higher-level skills on the part of the supervisor.

Many supervisors criticised the rise in paperwork, notably in the writing of reports with respect to health and safety issues that gave rise to the essential reactive nature of their work. Many pointed to, in addition, the lack of time and skills necessary to perform these duties. Managers pointed to an additional problem: supervisors, they felt, were often unwilling to take on new responsibilities, especially in regard to health and safety.

In concluding this section it is worth quoting in full from a fire officer as to the increasing administrative demands:

> A station officer often does not have the time to do all the administrative duties he is required to do. They have a lot of administrative duties, with the result that important duties like problem-solving, etc., don't get done. They have more administrative tasks to do, not only health and safety considerations, but also for the first time, they are moving in the direction that health and safety has to be quantified. There are constant improvements being introduced and these have to be written down. Standards have to come to a higher level now. That protocol is being monitored by

[2] Since 1984, there has been an accelerating volume of new legislation affecting the Garda. Some, such as powers of detention, custody regulations for prisoners, Garda Síochána (Complaints) Act and more recent anti-drug and organised crime legislation, are addressed directly to the first-line supervisor, i.e. the sergeant, thereby producing a change of role in which management had little influence. This in turn has produced greater legal risk and a much greater administrative work volume for sergeants.

> committees who watch to see that every station meets the proper standards. There is more accountability now, and there is a problem with this because of the fact that the tools were never given.

The Technical Context of Change

New technology includes not just stand-alone computers, but, more importantly, advanced computer-controlled equipment and an increasing emphasis on process technology. Managers pointed to the increased use of computers in the workplace, and more use of software packages from word processors to spreadsheets to e-mail, to complete "packages". In the services sector, for example in the insurance industry, image-processing technology is seen as the key to the future with whole departments being organised in teams. In the Garda, £26 million has been set aside for information technology upgrading. In the Air Corps, there is now a store inventory system, and all branches of the military are linked by electronic mail. In the hospitality industry, a cash register is now a computer in disguise, and increasingly computers are being used for stock inventory and rostering. In hospitals, the influence of technology, coupled with broadened job responsibilities, are demanding higher technical skills for nurses.

Of the various problems mentioned by interviewees regarding technology, most likely to be mentioned was the difficulty of getting training, or when trained, being fully able to use computers. Taken to its extreme, one manager pointed out that:

> training in computers is a lot of trial and error, with people asking someone how they did something. Computer packages just appear, with no training forthcoming. They teach themselves.

One explanation for this is the degree of work intensification which leaves little time for learning. Supervisors themselves in the course of interviews often pointed to computers that sat on desks without being used, having neither the time nor, in some cases the inclination, to learn about them. It was felt that the lack of training costs organisations in the long term. Indeed, the ability to exploit technology to its fullest was mentioned in a number of interviews. Certainly it can be said with much justification that competitiveness will depend on the ability of organisations to exploit technology that is supported by new work practices, for example as noted in the insurance industry, where image processing and teamwork seem to go hand in hand. Many of the organisations studied were in the midst of continuous change, with the results inconclusive. Supervisors were at the forefront of these changes, but expressed some concern at the ability of organisations to meet this challenge.

Another difficulty mentioned was that new employees arrived on the job without the necessary training. Supervisors then had to take time off to train these employees and money had to come out of the budget. Other problems included getting the training but never using the computers to maximise the training. There was strong criticism of the training methods. In the hotel industry, the lack of training in team skills was considered a major shortcoming. It was stated that the RTCs and CERT needed to change their training methods and move away from the old directional method to one which emphasises participation and teamwork. A human resources manager in a process industry made a similar point, namely, that workers should have the appropriate skills for teamwork prior to entering the workplace.

Restriction of access to technology, rather than just the training, was cited as another problem. While computers are now commonplace in the military and the Garda, their use is restricted to commissioned officers and NCOs in the case of the military, and individual specialists in the Garda. A similar trend occurs in the manufacturing and services sector where supervisors preferred to deal with people directly rather than, say, by e-mail. In regard to e-mail, however, it was stated in many organisations that it was becoming a standard way of communicating, hence the need for greater technical and computer skills.

Technology also places restrictions on organisations. For example, in the broadcasting industry, new technology usually has a lifespan of about three years, hence the need for constant training. This presents two very different types of problems: one in which current employees cannot cope with constant change, hence early retirement is widely practised; another is that, given the investment in training, employment contracts have to be lengthy to maximise the return on training. The "greying" of the labour force was cited as causing great difficulty in bringing about change.

Teamwork: Problems and Concerns

The trend towards teams, combined with downsizing, impinged greatly on supervisors. While in some manufacturing firms there was a preference to retain the title of supervisor despite the new team environment, others have introduced the title of team leader and/or facilitator to replace the supervisor of old. With new titles came new responsibilities — notably the shift from managing to facilitating — and with it a host of problems. Supervisors felt uncomfortable with the new title and thought they lacked the training to be facilitators. Supervisors — now team leaders — in these industries were the most vocal in their complaints about overwork and reactive work. Also mentioned was the problem of dealing with team members who failed to reach the standard of the group, employees who refused to participate in teams and employees who were not acceptable to the team.

Generally, it was felt that when problems occurred, the (now) facilitators reverted to their old supervisory style of managing. Some supervisors predicted the demise of supervisory management with the advent of teamwork. In manufacturing, supervisors were seen as the people to provide leadership to a team, hence any question of the demise of supervisors was likely to happen in the future when self-supervision becomes the norm rather than the exception as it is now. In the financial sector, which has had similar experiences with teams, selective downsizing was practised and it was by no means guaranteed that the supervisor (or superintendent to use the proper term) became the team leader. Rather, many of these organisations showed a willingness to use psychometric tests, despite their dubious value, to select, what they felt, were the best team leaders.

Problems Faced by Supervisors

In the course of this research many supervisors expressed uncertainty about the future. Most often mentioned was the difficulty of dealing with contract employees, complicated by the loss of permanent staff and, generally speaking, less staff doing the same amount or, more likely, extra work. This was a view mentioned in well-established (and well-known) organisations that have experimented with atypical work in recent years, and have experienced some degree of industrial relations problems. The current supervisory staff in these organisations entered in a time of growth and future prospects. Today, as those organisations downsize and delayer — very often with negative consequences in terms of promotional opportunities — these staff have experienced real problems with motivating incoming and contract labour, if not also themselves. It was mentioned that in organisations like the Garda and the military the culture of the uniform and the strong vocational ethos maintained high morale. In well-established organisations which have gone through, and in some cases are still experiencing, major restructuring programmes, demotivation was seen as a major problem. The lack of control over compensation, that is, the authority to reward employees, was cited as a major barrier to supervisory work. Supervisors noted that they were being shouldered with increasing responsibilities, but yet lacked the authority to perform that new role effectively. Budgetary restrictions were noted as causing great difficulty, as well as the problems associated with attempting to manage employees outside their own work group, despite the advent of teamwork. Work intensification — not surprisingly mentioned by many supervisors — gave rise to other problems, notably the inability to plan ahead, leaving supervisors to their usual fire-fighting, reactive mode.

In some of the organisations, labour turnover was sharply on the increase, especially where the dominant view was that terms and conditions of employment had deteriorated rapidly in recent years. Wages, or the prospect of promotion, were not seen as the incentive to work they used to be. A shortage of labour in certain industries, notably the hospitality sector, the construction industry and, indeed, all branches of the military, were causing problems in terms of supervisors having to make do with limited resources. There was also some criticism of the lack of awareness by senior management of these problems which supervisory management are now facing, and many supervisors felt that trade unions lacked either the willingness or the ability to represent their views.

Industrial relations was not cited as a significant problem area, except in organisations where there were current conflicts. In the military the growing influence of representation, and in the Garda difficulties relating to representation, complicated the problem and, in some cases, has changed the character of the employment relationship in these organisations. Similarly, at the time of conducting this research, the nurses were involved in a serious industrial relations dispute. However, as stated, it was supervisors in well-established organisations who were, by far, the most vocal and the most critical of recent changes. In the Army, the expansion of duties, from border security to providing armed escorts and guards of honours was seen as stretching already limited resources. Similarly, in the Garda, as in the Navy and the Air Corps, public accountability to provide a presence was felt to be distracting from what they saw as their proper role.

There was a strong feeling among supervisors that there existed a glass ceiling which affected promotion for both men and women. This issue is dealt with in a later section.

Senior Management: Problems Mentioned

Senior management pointed to a different set of problems facing supervisors. Among these managers, mainly human resources managers, there was the perception that supervisors were less willing to assume higher-level management duties, such as problem-solving and planning, as well as taking responsibility (as distinct from avoiding it) that came about as a result of changes in work practices. For example, one interviewee, a human resource manager in the financial sector, commented that "people have to learn to confront problems, instead of making do or packing them over to someone else". This problem was compounded by the fact that in this organisation internal transfers were quite common, hence, as supervisors moved from department to department, more training was required. However, the idea that current supervisors were less willing, and indeed in some cases unable, to take responsibility was mentioned by a number of managers. This was a view expressed by all three branches of the military. Strictly speaking, in the military, officers have responsibility for a platoon and all authority emanates from them. However, in interviews with officers, many felt that the corporal and/or sergeant should take more responsibility for a platoon, in effect, should exercise leadership. Thus, despite the trend in the military towards rising educational standards, more responsibility is not necessarily being taken by first-line management, that is, the NCO level. This is also true of the Garda Síochána. The rise in the standard of education has not been matched with an increase in the willingness to take on responsibility. It was suggested that this anomaly is probably related to a mismatch between modern management structures and the established rank structure. Under the newly implemented Strategic Management Initiative, there is a general aspiration in the public sector to get all workers to be more responsible and accountable. It remains to seen, however, how successful such a programme will be.

The age-old view that supervisors spend too much time doing operational work and too little on management was mentioned frequently. A variation of this problem was that some supervisors got bogged down with administrative work, rather than spending more time coaching and managing workers. Again to quote a manager:

> They should probably spend more time doing the managing job rather than the operating. The culture here is that they would work very closely with the people they supervise, and if someone was missing, they would stand in and become a working supervisor.

Partly at fault for this was the fact that supervisors were often still promoted on the basis of technical rather than managerial (that is interpersonal) skills. In their supervisory jobs, they continued to perform their old jobs rather than taking on the mantle of a manager. The Garda recently set up a two-day seminar for newly promoted sergeants, entitled Your New Job, which specifically sought to address this problem.

It should be noted that supervisors themselves pointed out that they lacked the resources and, in some cases, the skills to undertake higher-level tasks and, in particular, to deal with crises. Interviewees also noted that they were given responsibility, but not necessarily the authority, to make decisions, that they lacked control over resources, and that they were subject to the control of others: "the accountants are dictating more" as one supervisor cleverly put it.

One interviewee made the following observation:

> The major barrier is the lack of training, and an understanding of what he has to do. The officers have bought into this thing of exchanging negatives. It is up to each individual every day he is on duty, to do what he sees fit (within certain parameters), but he has never been given the tools. Everybody talks about changing, but nobody has quantified what needs to be done. A job gets done, good, bad or indifferent, and we have got by for years, with the job being done.

In all organisations studied there was a view emerging of the acceptance of the need for change. For example, one commentator noted: "There is a lot more emphasis on performance. Excuses are not accepted now". Such a view typifies the feeling, directly or indirectly, that came across in interviews.

THE MANAGERIAL ASPECT OF SUPERVISORY WORK

This section of the chapter deals with the change in the managerial aspect of the supervisory work in regard to job descriptions, promotion, training and skill formation.

New Titles

The term "supervisor" is a blue-collar, factory term. It predominates most in manufacturing, least in the service sectors. Even though the term is used in the hospitality sector, it appears that hotels are now preferring the term "head of" (department, bar, restaurant, etc.) or simply "manager" rather than supervisor.

Supervisors in manufacturing, as indeed in the hotel and construction sectors, have a strong craft orientation. In the hotel industry, supervisory terms include assistant manager and head of department, whereas in the union houses at least, entry is by way of a craft qualification (head chef, barperson, etc.). The construction industry, bearing a strong orientation towards craft work, employs the term supervisor who is, by training, a fully qualified craftsperson. More crucially, a supervisor on a small construction site needs far more all-round skills. Both these industries are currently experiencing major skills shortages with the result that people entering these industries through a craft or educational route are entering directly to the ranks of supervisor.

The financial sector, including banking and insurance, favours the terms Executive Officers or Senior Executive Officer; in the latter cases recruitment requires graduate qualification with holders of that office performing more high-level managerial functions such as planning. Generally speaking, the preference in the services sector is for the all encompassing term "first-line management" (and less often front-line manager). A first-line manager is, as noted, an executive officer, where clerical officers, despite movements towards the broadening of job contents, are not considered managers. It is worth noting that in organisations such as the Central Bank, where there is a manufacturing wing, the term supervisor still persists, reinforcing the notion that supervisor is a blue-collar term.

Despite the advent of a variety of management practices, from teamwork to empowerment, few organisations have changed what they called supervisors. Where new titles have come into vogue they reflect change and, in particular, a broadening of job responsibilities. In nursing, for example, the term nursing officer (assistant and chief nursing officer depending on rank) is taking over as the amalgamation of the charge nurse and ward sister. Nursing is also being affected by the introduction of the new category of nurse's aide, as well as the fact that increasingly nurses were being asked to perform higher-level management and medical duties, as well as to participate in the training of student nurses.

More likely to change were greenfield organisations, whereas in established organisations, changes in titles were less frequent. In one manufacturing organisation, new terminology was avoided in order to deflect any claim by the trade union for increased pay. The most far-reaching change was in the insurance industry where the movement to teams and the adoption of image processing carried wide implications for (to use the correct term) first-line management. In one company, regarded as the leader in innovation in the industry, supervisors, or team leaders as they are now called, were responsible for a number of teams, and the role changed from one of supervisor to facilitator.

Entry to the Ranks of Supervisory Management

Promotional procedures have changed greatly in recent years, with an increasing emphasis on merit rather than seniority, as was often the case in years past. Promotional systems were most elaborate in the public sector including, in one organisation, awarding points on the basis of an interview, aptitude test, service and performance in the job. In the Garda Síochána, applicants for promotion to sergeant must pass an examination, and are then interviewed (by a board consisting of a chief superintendent, a superintendent and a civilian) and promoted as a vacancy arises (candidates are interviewed first at regional level and then centrally for those selected). Public accountability was seen in the Garda as a strong influence on its management practices.

The lack of promotional opportunity for supervisors, particularly in the public sector, but complicated in the private sector by rationalising, downsizing and contracting, was cited as a major problem, potentially giving rise to industrial relations problems as reflected in an increasing number of grievances. Not promoting women to supervisory positions in nursing was, and continues to be, a major bone of contention for female nurses. In the military, as is well-documented, the entry-level qualifications have risen in recent years (between 60 and 70 per cent of new entrants have a leaving certificate qualification, and a small number have primary degrees). Younger people are coming through the system with more educational qualifications than the commanding officers, with the imposition almost of a glass ceiling (for male and female officers). There was a strong feeling in the military that pay and conditions of employment have deteriorated relative to the civilian sector. The problem is compounded further by the advent of representation (PDFORRA for the enlisted ranks, and RACO for commissioned officers). It is worth noting that all branches of the military saw a huge decrease in the number of applicants for cadetships, though this drop was not seen as affecting the overall high level of candidates. It cannot be denied, however, that in the public sector, despite the adoption of elaborate promotional structures, the lack of promotion, expanded job responsibilities and job embargoes have caused widespread unease.

Training

Despite increases in administrative work, along with the need to assume high-level management duties, supervisors still maintain the primary management focus of dealing with people. However, there was a recognition in certain cases of the need to manage people better. With the exception of the aeronautical industry, including the Air Corps, where technical skills are uppermost, and a few isolated jobs where supervisors tended equipment, the vast majority of respondents saw the ability to get along with people as the most important skill, along with, in the military and the Garda, leadership skills. The focus on people skills received renewed emphasis with the move to teams: supervisors were receiving training in facilitation skills in order to lead teams.

Most organisations therefore stressed the importance of management training in the area of human resources, or "people management" as it is more commonly called. As one interviewee put it, "people are more complicated to deal with than equipment", hence the emphasis on "soft" training. There was a strong feeling in many organisations that supervisors were trained to "do their jobs", but lacked the important management skills. This is particularly the case for occupations where there is a high degree of technical competence required, for example in nursing. When respondents were asked to explain what they meant by people skills they included such areas as problem-solving, conflict handling, and confronting problems, or what in one organisation was referred to as coaching skills.

Only in the Garda was it seen that people skills were adequate, and that the focus of attention has shifted to legal and technical training. Garda training, for example, has changed in recent years. Training is longer and after an initial training stint in Templemore gardaí are then sent to stations for more training, before returning to Templemore. The ability of these organisations to attract high-calibre individuals in the first instance, along with new legal changes and increasing use of technology, was seen as one reason to reduce management training in favour of a more legal and technical focus.

Finally, it should be that noted that health and safety requirements, especially under the 1989 Act, along with fear of litigation and the new quality parameters make for a greater need for increased training in the manufacturing field.

Qualities of Supervisors

As noted earlier, many supervisors are recruited on the basis of certain qualities, usually technical, which prove of little value as supervisors. An open-ended question[3] soliciting what managers thought were the qualities most valued to be a supervisor brought an array of responses. Those responses are worth mentioning in full here, in part because the responses show the high opinion managers have of supervisory work. Responses included:

> "Personal qualities [include] the ability to operate as an individual."
>
> "Qualities are high standard of professional behaviour and accountability and a high standard of technical competence."
>
> "Supervisors have to be decisive and they have to have a sense of responsibility."
>
> "The personal qualities are to work as part of a team."
>
> "Primarily the ability to listen, rather than being dogmatic."
>
> "Good clear communications. Employees have to be clear about what you said, and be able to come back to you if they

---

[3] The question on the survey was: "What personal qualities do you see as important to the job of supervisory management?"

do not. If you are in any way ambiguous, the situation could get dangerous."

"The number one quality that we look for is the capability to draw the line and tell people what to do. Very old fashioned. Strong individual."

"Liking people. A certain amount of flexibility will do you good. You need to be fairly tenacious now. If you have a good idea, you will not necessarily get it through. You need to be quite organised and make a clear case."

"Important qualities are willingness, proper attitude of mind, good team leader and capable of integrating".

CHAPTER SUMMARY

It is still the case, to a large extent, that supervisors deal with people. In response to a question soliciting information on the degree to which supervisors worked alone or with others, the responses leaned sharply towards the latter. Nurses work with others, rarely alone. A Garda sergeant's work very much still revolves around people, not desks. The primary responsibility for supervisors in manufacturing organisations and in the services sectors, with some notable exceptions, is the management of people. The exceptions are the supervisors who have responsibility for equipment.

There are, however, important developments which are changing the face of supervisory management. There is an acknowledgement from human resource managers that supervisors need to show more initiative, work alone more and rely less on the threat of disciplinary measures to manage people. Similarly, as was pointed out by supervisors, their work is becoming more reactive rather than proactive in this age of downsizing and delayering. Hence the need for more planning and training in (what is perceived to be) higher-level management skills, such as problem-solving, negotiations, scheduling, etc. Finally, the increase in technology, along with legal and social changes, have brought a new dimension to the work of supervisors with, in particular, increased accountability.

Part Two

The Development of Personal Skills

Chapter 6

THE SUPERVISOR AS COMMUNICATOR

THE OBJECTIVE OF THIS CHAPTER

Speaking and writing are the main forms of communicating messages. However, body gestures, particularly facial expressions and hand movements, as well as silence and listening, are also used to transmit and receive messages. Together, the various forms of verbal and non-verbal communication allow us to communicate more than just our ideas, but also our feelings, thoughts, and desires. Communicating also depends on the manner in which people perceive messages, however, as it is perception, the way another person interprets our actions and words, which gives meaning to communication.

Communication is therefore a complex process. It is also, from a business perspective, an extremely important yet misunderstood function. There is the tendency to assume that communication is informational, that is, simply getting a message across. But it is also inspirational in the sense of getting people to take the required action. This means following up on messages to see that they are properly understood. Similarly, there is the tendency to focus on active communication and to ignore the importance of passive communication.

Clearly, because supervisors deal directly with people, face-to-face communication is very important and increasingly so in light of the changing demographics of the labour force. But today the increasing technical sophistication of work, coupled with legal developments, is creating a multi-faceted picture of communication in organisations. Supervisors need not just to be able to communicate with people, but they need to be able to use a variety of media, including computers, fax machines, voice mail, cellular telephones, etc., and to communicate more technical and legal information. Communication, therefore, is not something which should be taken for granted.

After reading and studying this chapter the reader should have:

- A knowledge of how communication works
- An understanding of the importance of communication to the organisation.

The following chapters deal with specific aspects of communication, including interpersonal communication (Chapter 7), public speaking (Chapter 8), and writing (Chapter 9).

UNDERSTANDING THE PROCESS OF COMMUNICATION

The communication process is often described in terms more suited to the early forms of the transmission of radio signals: a sender encodes a message, transmits it through a channel (such as a telephone) which is then decoded by the receiver (see Figure 6.1). In work terms, the communication process begins with the supervisor having an idea or message that needs communicating: a job has to be done, so the supervisor must issue a directive. Next, the directive is formed, choosing the language and the medium which best suits the message. Thirdly, the message is transmitted, often in supervisory work by speaking directly to employees. The message is reinforced by body language and tone of voice, by pointing to something, and by stressing important facts such as the time of day and the urgency of the task. Fourthly, the message is received and interpreted by employees who, in response to the message, take some form of action. Ideally, that action will be the execution of the directive as issued by the supervisor. In practice, it may not be, possibly due to various barriers as discussed below.

Barriers to Effective Communication

For a variety of reasons, many organisations lack effective communication systems. In some cases, the system is poor: the telecommunication or the computer network may be out of date or simply not functioning as well as it should. Alternatively, employees may not be sufficiently trained, or have access to the technology. A particular complaint mentioned by supervisors in various organisations in Ireland was the difficulty of using electronic mail (or e-mail for short). Supervisors felt that e-mail, rather than helping, actually reduced linkages between people. A similar argument can be made against, say, fax machines or voice mail. Despite its obvious benefits, technology can distort messages as well as give the perception that face-to-face communication is not important.

FIGURE 6.1: THE COMMUNICATIONS PROCESS

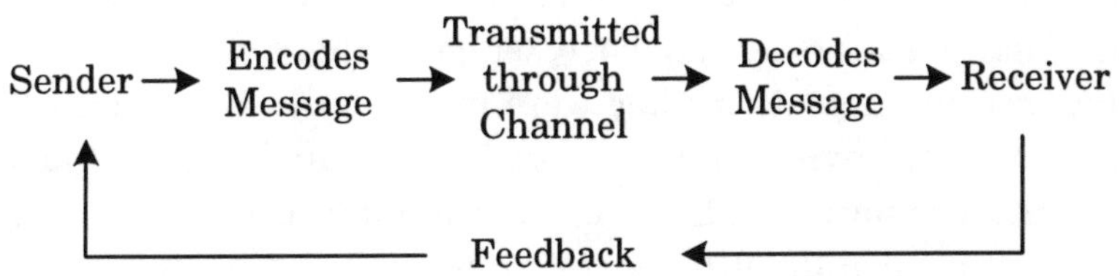

Interpersonal differences between people — class and status differences, poor listening skills, personality differences, lack of trust — give rise to a variety of communication problems. It is commonly pointed out that the differences between various grades of employees, such as managerial and non-managerial employees and between white-collar and blue-collar employees, can make communication more difficult. For example, due to these status differences an employee might not feel comfortable in communicating with a manager, or vice versa. One manager interviewed pointed to the difficulties supervisors have with senior management: "They find higher-level management the most difficult to communicate with. They feel intimidated by them, and they can be abrupt".

Language is not always understood (in the way it was intended to be understood). Words carry different meanings when used in different situations and one person can interpret a message very differently from another. A lack of knowledge or a lack of interest can, equally, hinder the successful transmission of messages. Interpersonal differences can be complicated by organisational problems. Excessive levels of hierarchy, for example, can function as a barrier to communication between management and rank-and-file employees. A board of management may issue a policy on quality or employment equality with specific guidelines. However, the message may not get communicated to the area where it is needed most: the office or the shopfloor.

Clearly the barriers to communication are many. However, in interviews for this book many managers were adamant that supervisors, by and large, were good communicators and were particularly adept in getting messages across to employees. Not surprisingly, in the Garda Síochána and in branches of the military, it was felt that the system of recruitment and training weeded out bad communicators at an early stage. Where difficulties were noted in communication, they were primarily in the technical aspects, that is, having access to, training in and a willingness to learn and use multi-media forms of communication. Complicating these technical difficulties were problems relating to the downsizing of organisations and the increasing use of contract labour, as well as changes in the age profile of workers. Supervisors in these organisations mentioned that it was more difficult communicating with transient staff and more care had to be shown to the framing of messages when dealing with older workers.

Overcoming Barriers to Effective Communication

The primary way to improve communication is to put more thought into the message, especially how it will be interpreted by the receiver. The use of feedback and repetition are also simple methods of ensuring compliance. A supervisor may include on a memo sent to an employee a request for feedback, or in a face-to-face interview request that the employee send a memo outlining what was said at the meeting. This is a way of checking that the message was understood. Similarly, in meetings a person can repeat the message: "correct me if I am wrong, but this is what I think you said". After sending a written message a supervisor can always telephone a person and ask was the message received and understood? Repetition can be used to reinforce ideas. Very often in communication, there is one central message to be got across. This should be stated at the beginning and repeated as necessary. This way the receiver (the reader or the listener) knows exactly what the message is. Similarly, a supervisor should be specific when issuing directives: say "I would like the order completed by 4.00 p.m. today", rather than "I want the order done by today". By being specific, stating clearly the purpose of the message, repeating it, and asking for feedback, a message is much more likely to be understood.

There are also other ways in which a supervisor can work at being a better communicator. The first is to give attention to listening skills. Sometimes people hear only what they want to hear; they may be tired or simply have little or no interest in participating in the discussion. Thus it is easy for a listener to allow the mind to wander and daydream. Facial expressions can tell whether a person is listening. In some instances, people are so overburdened by a particular issue, usually a problem, that they have great difficulty in concentrating. In such instances, a supervisor should schedule a private appointment with the employee.

The establishment of a proper climate in work, with trust at the centre of the employment relationship, can go a long way towards ensuring that messages are received, understood and, most importantly, acted on. Maintaining an "open-door" policy, being on a first-name basis and being responsive to individual needs are some of the many ways in which a supervisor can convey an employee-centred approach to managing. This helps to get rid of the barriers between employees, and makes employees feel comfortable in expressing their thoughts and feelings.

COMMUNICATION SYSTEMS IN ORGANISATIONS

Organisations have communications systems which effectively mirror their organisational structure (Figure 6.2). This is the formal channel, which needs to be distinguished from the informal channel or "grapevine". The latter is reflective of people's need to develop social relationships at work, and can function either to solidify the culture at work or as a barrier to the official communication system.

FIGURE 6.2: COMMUNICATION SYSTEMS IN ORGANISATIONS

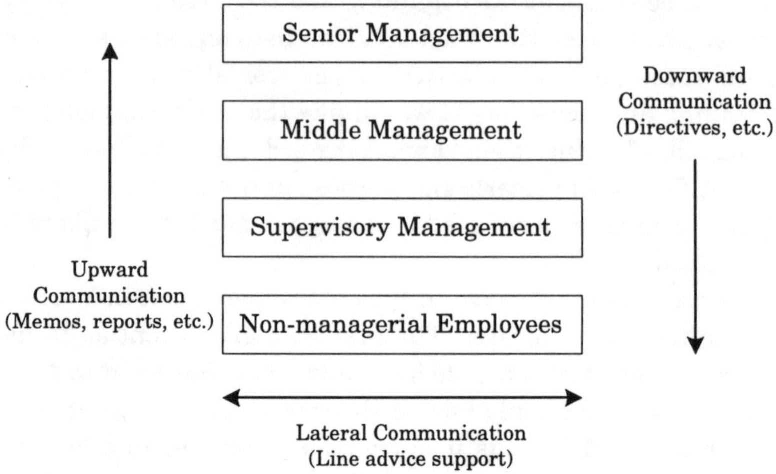

A message may be communicated in many ways: downwards to employees, upwards to senior management, laterally to fellow supervisors (see Figure 6.2) and externally to union officials and customers (see Table 6.1). Lateral and external communication are becoming more important for the supervisor of the 1990s. As firms are re-organising employees into teams, including multi-departmental (or cross-functional) teams, the need for lateral communication increases. Further, senior management now requires departments to work more closely together, particularly in such areas as quality control.

TABLE 6.1: WAYS OF COMMUNICATING

Type of Communication	Explanation	Examples
Downward Communication	Typically occurs when someone at the top, for example a senior manager, communicates a message to someone below, say a supervisor. Top management uses this channel very frequently.	• issuing directives • soliciting and listening to employees' views • employment, appraisal, counselling interviews • communicating standards to employees • rewarding and encouraging employees • making management policy known and accepted.

Upward Communication	In the same way as a manager may send a message downwards, a employee may send a message up to management. This is referred to as upward communication. This not only allows employees to air dissent, but also functions as an important source of information and ideas.	• progress reports • airing employees' opinions • making suggestions and recommendations • clarifying management policy.
Lateral Communication	Communication from one department to another by people at the same level, say supervisor to supervisor, is referred to as lateral communication. Lateral communication is extremely important for co-ordinating and in helping to remove any duplication of tasks.	• meetings between departments • problem-solving and project teams
External Communication	This category include communication between a supervisor and a trade union official and/or customers or clients.	• meetings between union officials and employees (collective bargaining, joint consultation etc.) • meetings between employees and customers (cross-functional teams, etc.)

A particular problem raised in research was the difficulty of communicating across shifts between different supervisors. As organisations reduce in size, co-ordination becomes more important. Similarly, supervisors are now required to keep staff better informed of impending change, and of the management of progress in achieving that change. The use of Just-in-Time production and Total Quality Management[1] in manufacturing requires constant information that must be communicated to all employees of the firm. Finally, with delayering, i.e. the removal of layers of management, and downsizing, i.e. reduction of staff levels, or-

[1] See Chapter 16.

ganisations are under pressure to get more productivity out of all employees and to work more closely with customers. In other words, communication is not three-dimensional (management, supervisor and employees), but multi-dimensional and interactive. It is complicated further by the fact that all parties could be in contact with each other using a variety of means, from face-to-face meetings (including team briefings) to the use of fax machines, tele- or video-conferencing, electronic mail, etc.

FORMS OF COMMUNICATION

Ideas can be communicated by words (verbally) or action (non-verbally). "For many (although not all) supervisors and indeed managers", Evans (1995, p. 180) notes, "verbal communication is by far the most frequently used medium". It is not difficult to see why: the central feature of supervisory management is usually dealing with people and issues as they arise. Hence the need for a supervisor to perfect the art of face-to-face communication. The spoken word is used also because of the many advantages it has over the written word. For one, it takes far less time to speak than to write and there is much less concern with formality (spelling, grammar, etc.) when speaking. Further, one can convey more (especially non-verbally), and if an employee is unsure of the message, the meaning can be clarified, thus ensuring that the message is better understood. Feedback can also be given immediately. Further, employees prefer to see and hear their supervisor rather than receive written messages which can appear cold and convey the wrong message entirely. Finally, most people prefer talking to writing. It is not just quicker, but easier.

Despite the many advantages that speaking directly with people has, a supervisor should not lose sight of the written word. Indeed, writing is one medium which is often under-used, yet has many advantages. Notably, writers can take time to compose their thoughts. Also, important messages, especially those relating to legal matters, have to be written. Generally speaking, more thought goes into writing, hence the usefulness of the written message for communicating important information. Finally, face-to-face communication is not always possible for a variety of reasons: the supervisor and employee may work on different shifts or in different areas. Finally writing is the best form for communicating to a large number of employees.

Non-Verbal Communication

The term non-verbal communication is extremely wide in scope. It includes various forms of behaviour such as body language (see Table 6.2), listening (or not listening), behaviour (such as style of managing) or non-action (such as silence). Non-verbal communication, according to Pettinger (1994, p. 94): "either gives an impression of ourselves to someone else without our saying anything, or else it reinforces what we are saying". In other words, how we act reinforces or negates a message. Laughter, a handshake, even a glance has meaning and is subject to interpretation, regardless of one's intention. Hence, supervisors in issuing a directive to employees can further emphasise certain aspects of the message by the choice of language, by altering the pitch or volume or by particular actions. They can also negate the intention of the message by not behaving in a manner which is consistent with the message.

TABLE 6.2: FORMS OF BODY LANGUAGE

- Proximity and territory (personal space and closeness)
- Orientation (the way we angle our bodies towards people)
- Bodily contact, appearance
- Gesture, posture
- Facial expression
- Eye contact, head nods
- Paralanguage (how we say something).

Source: Daunt, 1996, pp. 24-35.

CHAPTER SUMMARY

Communication is both an active and a passive process. When we talk to someone, or send a letter, we are actively communicating., A good deal of communication, however, is passive and is reflected in our action which accompanies the words we use. Hence how we say something — that is, the signals we send with messages — is as important as what we say.

Communication is a crucial aspect of the supervisor's job. Indeed, there is an important obligation on supervisors to communicate well, upwards to managers, downwards to employees, and laterally to other supervisors. Communication is enhanced by framing a message in a form which the receiver is more likely to understand — usually by being clear and specific — and, secondly, by asking for feedback or confirmation. Repetition can be used to make sure a message is understood. Though messages may be communicated in many ways, the best way depends on the situation at hand and the resources available.

Non-effective communication can make it difficult for supervisors to perform their job. If employees have difficulty in receiving and/or understanding messages, directives are less likely to be obeyed, and employees will be less motivated to work at the standard they are capable of. Effective communication, though partly an art, is also a skill. Like all skills, it can be learned and improved. A supervisor can become an effective communicator, largely by recognising, firstly, the importance of communication to the organisation, and secondly, by giving more attention to it.

References and Further Reading

Bennett, R. (1994) *Personal Effectiveness*, second edition, London: Kogan Page, Chapter 3.

Betts, P.W. (1993) *Supervisory Management*, London: Pitman, London, 1993. Chapters 14 and 15.

Cole, G.A. (1993) *Management: Theory and Practice*, fourth edition, London: DP Publications Ltd.

Daunt, S. (1996) *Communication Skills*, Dublin: Gill & Macmillan.

Evans, David (1995) *Supervisory Management, Principles and Practices*, fourth edition, London: Cassell.

McClave, H. (1986) *Communication for Business in Ireland* Dublin: Gill and Macmillan.

Pettinger, R. (1994) *Introduction to Management*, London: Macmillan.

Stanton, N. (1996) *Mastering Communication*, third edition, London: Macmillan.

White, J. (1986) *Successful Supervision*, second edition, London: McGraw-Hill, Chapter 10.

Chapter 7

INTERPERSONAL SKILLS AND THE ASSERTIVE SUPERVISOR

THE OBJECTIVE OF THIS CHAPTER

Interpersonal behaviour refers to the interaction between two or more people, and includes not only the words we use (i.e. what we say), but the non-verbal actions that accompany such words (i.e. how we say it), such as body language (facial expressions, gestures, hand movements, etc.). Most managers and supervisors feel that by far the most important skill a supervisor should have is the ability to get along with people, broadly referred to as interpersonal (or people) skills. This includes the ability to understand oneself and others, and to know how one's behaviour affects or is interpreted by others. Thus, to manage effectively, supervisors need an awareness of people — their backgrounds, status, and attitudes to and expectations from work — and supervisors themselves need to behave in an appropriate manner. Supervisors need to be knowledgeable and assertive, not ignorant and aggressive; and they need to convey in their behaviour what is expected of employees. Table 7.1 contains of a list of activities in which interpersonal skills are required.

After reading and studying this chapter the reader should be able to:

- Understand interpersonal behaviour
- Recognise behaviour as either aggressive, passive or assertive
- Ideally, act in an assertive manner.

It is important to realise that learning about interpersonal behaviour is essentially an experiential exercise. This means that, like public speaking or writing or conducting interviews, only so much can be gained from reading. The reader is encouraged to seek further training in this field, and to put into practice the ideas expressed in this and other chapters.

TABLE 7.1: THE NEED FOR INTERPERSONAL SKILLS

Interpersonal skills are needed in a variety of activities in work including:

- Speaking to groups
- Disciplining employees
- Negotiating
- Handling requests
- Conflict-resolving
- Interviewing
- Mediating
- Coaching
- Dealing with customers
- Communicating
- Facilitating
- Working in teams.

TYPES OF BEHAVIOUR

Broadly speaking, behaviour can be classified as being of one of three main types:

- Aggressive behaviour
- Passive (or non-aggressive or non-assertive) behaviour
- Assertive behaviour.

These are explained in detail below. It should be understood that people can and do change from one type of behaviour to another, depending on the situation and their mood. However, for most people, a certain type of behaviour tends to dominate their dealings with other people.

Aggressive Behaviour

Aggressive behaviour is defined as infringing on other people's rights. The aggressive individual generally fails to take account of what other people think or do. In the work environment an order delivered aggressively typically indicates to the receiver that they have nothing to contribute and that their views or feelings are not important.

Aggressive supervisors are likely to interrupt employees when they see fit and to call meetings when it is most disruptive to staff. Rarely seeking input, aggressive supervisors are slow to give praise. If they do, it tends to be done grudgingly or without enthusiasm. Instead, the aggressive supervisor presents the image, in some instances very real, of being tough and uncompromising. They are, by nature, forceful and hard-headed, and rule by decree, with little input asked for, or allowed, from employees.

Aggressive behaviour is an affront to others. It infringes employees' rights and causes great stress. More than that, aggressive behaviour tends to be counterproductive. When employees are told to do something, and given little input into the decision, and little choice thereafter but to carry out the task, they will do only what is required of them, and sometimes even less.

Aggressive behaviour can be effective in the short run. Employees can be forced to work hard to achieve short-term goals. However, the costs are high, particularly in terms of employee morale and turnover. Productivity in the long term nearly always suffers. Furthermore, aggressive behaviour can be mentally draining both on the aggressor and the person on the receiving end. An aggressive supervisor often finds it difficult to establish working relationships with others, especially fellow supervisors. The element of inter-departmental co-ordination, so crucial to organisational success, will be lost.

Passive Behaviour

Passive behaviour, not surprisingly, is almost the exact opposite of aggressive behaviour. It means not standing up for one's rights and not dealing with people in an open, honest and appropriate manner. Holland and Ward (1990, p. 3) refer to it as:

> the doormat syndrome, where we allow ourselves to be trampled on by other people. It is characterised by a feeling of powerlessness and inability to take control of our lives.

Aside from an inability to stand up and air one's feelings, a passive supervisor typically pays little attention to staff and lets the organisation run itself. Because they cannot handle pressure well, passive supervisors expect little back from employees. In other words, the behaviour of the leader tends to carry over to the people who are being supervised. They see themselves as poor performers, rarely stretched to the limit and do little to further themselves. The organisation as a whole suffers.

Organisations that have passive supervisors tend to be slow to respond to external pressure. They lack dynamism and stress the status quo. Employees who dislike this approach will move on or else put up with passiveness and themselves become passive. In many organisations, conflict is rarely dealt with properly. Decisions that have to be made are not made. In all, change will be far less well handled.

In sum, passive supervisors tend to avoid issues, rarely seek out extra challenges and responsibilities and accept the status quo as if it were normal and unchangeable. Being afraid to express their feelings even when they are in the right, they tend, at meetings, to be quiet and usually go along with the majority view. If they come under attack, they tend to retreat entirely. They may see themselves as inadequate in the job, giving rise to feelings of low self-esteem. Employees tend to disrespect the passive supervisor. In all, passive behaviour leads to inertia in the work environment. Inertia in turn leads to, at best, acceptable performance, at worst, sub-standard work.

Assertive Behaviour

Holland and Ward (1990, p. 2) list the following definitions of assertiveness:

- The ability to express our ideas and feeling, both positive and negative, in an open, direct and honest manner

- The ability to stand up for our rights while respecting the rights of others
- The ability to take responsibility for ourselves and our actions without judging or blaming other people
- The ability to find a compromise where conflict exists.

The foundation of assertiveness, from an individual perspective, is self-esteem, that is, being positive or happy about oneself. Being assertive is particularly important for any supervisor, not least because supervisors spend considerable time interacting with employees and the demands of the job increasing. Supervisors who are assertive are able to handle situations at work in a rational, mature and controlled manner, keeping emotions, their own and others, under control. Assertiveness means not giving in to others, such as, for instance, a boss who makes unreasonable demands or employees who refuse to do work. It also means recognising that one has rights as do others and that both sets of rights have to be accommodated.

Types of Behaviour and Management Styles

Behaviour is related to management styles.[1] Aggressive behaviour is often linked to a management style referred to as "management by intimidation". Some supervisors are, by nature, aggressive and successful at that. The image often presented of the "successful manager" is one who is commanding and direct. Orders are given and expected to be carried out. Aggressiveness leads to a style of supervision which entails close monitoring of staff and which is focused largely on getting the job done. Hence the expression "close supervision" and "task-oriented management".

Passive behaviour is associated with a style of non-management. A non-manager is a person who fails to take charge, rather like a ship without a rudder. Such individuals tend to avoid responsibility or, if forced to accept it, do so without a murmur.

Assertive behaviour is associated with what can be referred to as an employee-centred approach to management. This is a style

---

[1] See Chapter 14 for further discussion of management styles.

of management which takes account of people's needs. Being more confident and self-assured the assertive supervisor will take on responsibility and show more initiative and thus win respect.

People are often afraid to be assertive. Sometimes they are shy, which is a natural response, or else they are not aware of their rights in a situation. Still others opt not to be assertive, in part because they confuse aggression with assertiveness. Finally, the skills and, particularly, the ability to analyse situations are sometimes lacking. However, none of these reasons — shyness, preference for not being assertive, or the lack of skills — is an adequate excuse for not being assertive. Rather, the supervisor, to be effective, should take the time to learn the skills of assertiveness and put them into practice.

The next section deals with recognising different types of behaviour, which is followed by a section on how to be assertive.

Recognising Different Types of Behaviour

Assertive behaviour tends to be recognised verbally by statements beginning with "I" or "my". Examples include:

- "I believe that this is how we should do it."
- "My view on this matter is . . ."
- "I am of the opinion that . . ."

As can be seen, aside from being clear and to the point, assertive statements indicate that it is the person who is speaking and not some other entity, and hence is in full control of the situation. Though specific, assertive statements also leave open the possibility that the speaker may not be correct. Thus stating "it is my view . . ." signifies that this is one's opinion and that, being an opinion, it may or may not be correct. It further invites listeners to contribute their own opinions on the matter. Assertive statements usually give explanations for the views and even suggest alternatives, such as:

- "I did this job this way before. It worked. It would be best, I believe, to do it that way again."

Rephrased aggressively, the above statements would appear as follows:

- "This is the only way to do it."
- "Do the following or else."
- "I am in charge here and this is the way it is done."

The aggressive person tries to dominate the other, largely by being overpowering in the choice of words and the accompanying action, such as waving a finger or making strong eye contact. Such dominance may take the form of exploiting weaknesses in the other person whether that be the individual's personality, position or view.

Passive statements, by contrast, tend to be long-winded and rambling. These show uncertainty in the speaker. Hesitancy, denoted by long pauses, and poor framing of words, even more so, are signs of passive behaviour, such as:

- "Well, ah, I thought maybe we could do it this way, but you probably know more than I do."

This response indicates a lack of clarity and confidence. Assertive responses, by contrast, are very specific. Specific questions are usually used to garner information:

- "What are sales expected to be this month?", or
- "What days will I be working this week?"

Typically such questions elicit clear responses. Rambling and long-winded questions and the use of indecisive words (e.g. maybe, probably), and indecisive expressions (er, ah, etc.) are a sign of unassertiveness and should be avoided.

Non-Verbal Forms of Communication

As was learned in the previous chapter, we communicate both verbally and non-verbally. Behaviour, whether aggressive, passive or assertive, can also be communicated non-verbally.

A person who is aggressive tends to take an aggressive stance. They appear unfriendly and wear a face to denote as much. By contrast, assertiveness can be signified by friendly and non-threatening gestures. Whereas aggressive people will likely raise their voice to accentuate a point, usually a negative or threatening one, the assertive person keeps the tone consistent and pleasant. The assertive supervisor appears relaxed and inviting, and keeps all hand and body movements co-ordinated and consistently friendly and inviting. The aggressive person, by contrast, can engage in finger-pointing or fist-thumping, even folding the arms to convey the image of unfriendliness, and can move about to intimidate and harass the listener.

Establishing Understanding and Common Ground: Conversational Skills

Being assertive also means establishing a rapport or common ground with others. Common ground refers to the interpersonal relationships between people as individuals. It is based on empathy, which means understanding the other's point of view.

Good conversational skills are essential to supervisory management. They allow a supervisor to establish rapport which in turn permits greater understanding. In this regard opening a line of communication is often the most difficult to do.

Questioning skills play a major role in supervisory communication. There are numerous categories of questions including:

- Open questions
- Closed questions
- Leading questions
- Specific questions
- Reflective questions.

An *open* question is one which cannot be answered yes or no, and which encourages respondents to answer in their own words. They generally begin with how, why or what. Examples include:

- "How are you feeling today?"
- "Why did that happen?"
- "What's up with John?"

A *closed* question, such as

- "So you are not feeling so good today?"

can be answered with a cold yes or no. Further, it usually receives a short reply and is used by non-talkative people. In all, closed questions do not lend themselves to furthering the art of conversation. By the same token, it is a good idea to avoid what are termed *leading* questions. Leading questions are questions that often force a person into an expected reply, such as

- "You don't feel so well today, do you?"

When people expand on a question, giving back more than was asked, this is usually referred to as free information, such as:

- Q: "Do you feel well today?" (closed question).
- A: "No, not at all. My stomach is a little upset and I did not sleep very well last night" (free information).

Free information is also referred to as self-disclosure. It is the essence of good communication. Speakers disclose information openly and honestly and are at ease with the other person.

Listening

Perhaps one of the most underrated interpersonal skills is listening. It is commonly pointed out that people hear but don't listen. That is, we hear what people are saying, but rarely concentrate on or take in what is being said. For supervisors, listening is very important. In principle, supervisors should be attentive to the employees they supervise. In reality, many supervisors have difficulty with listening.

In order to improve listening skills, try the following:

- Listen carefully and to all that the speaker has to say, withholding judgement until they are finished. Avoid interrupting the speaker and don't get distracted by the surroundings.
- Try to ascertain what are the main points the speaker is making. Give the speaker your full attention and try to make sense of what they are saying and of any bias the speaker has.

- Maintain eye contact with the speaker but avoid staring.
- If in doubt, ask questions to clarify what the speaker has said, or alternatively paraphrase what the speaker has said to make sure you understood it.

Being Assertive: Examples from Work

This section gives some examples of how to be assertive at work. These include handling requests and conflict (particularly dealing with aggressive people), speaking up at meetings, handling and giving criticism, and in general asserting one's rights. All are based on the same principle: knowing one's rights, and standing up for them without infringing other people's rights.

Handling requests is an important aspect of a supervisor's job. A knowledge of assertiveness can help in this regard. The supervisor has a right to say no. More important is how it is phrased. As noted earlier, the response should be specific and direct and be accompanied by reasons. Besides, it is always a good idea to offer a suggestion or a way out that is respectful of the other person's needs or rights. This way, a constructive agreement can be reached which is fair to both sides.

Handling conflict is another area where assertiveness can help. It deals with two elements. The first is dealing with a superior and sticking up for one's rights, the second is dealing with employees and being firm with them. In both cases the same rules apply, namely, decide what one wants to say, stick to it, repeat the assertion if necessary and deflect any statement that may take away from one's aim. At all times, be specific and to the point, and do not be distracted from the main goal. Sometimes in the event of unexpected criticism or attack, it is better to pause, analyse the situation and then carefully and slowly respond in an assertive manner. Remember the earlier points: choose one's language carefully and keep body movements consistent. Further, it is important at all times to be factual. Try not to get carried away by emotions and be cognisant of other peoples' needs. That way one can defuse the situation and work towards a better solution for all. Table 7.2 offers advice on how to achieve a win-win solution.

TABLE 7.2: HANDLING CONFLICT: A WIN-WIN APPROACH

- Have mutual respect for each other
- Look for common ground
- Establish needs, wants, worries
- Redefine the problem
- Focus on a result acceptable to all
- Give options and remain flexible
- Keep your mind open
- Be positive, not negative
- Work together to solve a problem
- Delete "but" from your vocabulary
- If your approach isn't working, change something
- Take a deep breath.

Source: Cole, 1993, p. 44.

CHAPTER SUMMARY

The three types of behaviours can be understood in terms of rights: non-assertiveness is not standing up for one's rights, aggressiveness is infringing another's rights, and assertiveness is acknowledge one's own rights and the rights of others. Of the three, assertiveness is clearly the most appropriate for supervisory management. A supervisor can be assertive by phrasing messages in a tone which is not considered aggressive or threatening to others, and that respects other people's rights. Assertive supervisors, by and large, are not afraid of change and welcome challenges. They tend to be more content in the job and win respect from others.

The alternatives to assertiveness are either passiveness or aggressiveness. Being too passive or too aggressive can affect one's ability to function as an effective supervisor. Each tends to result in poor performance and affects one's own sense of well-being as well as staff morale. Individuals who are unassertive tend to feel that their contributions are minor. Individuals who are aggressive aggravate others. In the long run, they are likely to experience problems. Therefore, aim to be assertive.

References and Further Reading

Back, Ken. & Kate Back (1982) *Assertiveness at Work, A Practical Guide to Handling Awkward Situations*, London: McGraw-Hill.

Bennett, R. (1994) *Personal Effectiveness*, second edition, London: Kogan Page, Chapter 2.

Betts, P.W. (1993) *Supervisory Management*, sixth edition, London: Pitman, Chapters 9 & 10.

Dickson, A. (1982) *A Woman In Your Own Right; Assertiveness and You*, London: Quartet Books.

Harris, T. (1973) *I'm OK. You're OK.* London: Pan Books.

Holland, Stephanie, & Clare Ward (1990) *Assertiveness: A Practical Approach*, Bicester, Oxon: Winslow Press.

Chapter 8

MAKING PRESENTATIONS

THE OBJECTIVE OF THIS CHAPTER

Supervisors are often required to address groups of one sort or another. For example, a supervisor as team leader may have to present the results of a project to another group of workers or management; or address staff to effect a change in group behaviour; or make a presentation to someone who is leaving. In the latter, there is a stress more on spontaneity than preparedness, but it is, nonetheless, public speaking. And speaking in public is a vital management skill which supervisors should have. It is achieved in part by using the following techniques: speaking slowly, clearly, and making eye contact with the audience. In addition, preparation and, particularly, repeated practice make for good speakers.

This chapter will use the terms "public speaking" and "making presentations" interchangeably. Basically, the latter is the modern term for public speaking, especially at work, where the use of modern aids, from overhead projectors to computers, is common. However, the basis of any presentation, and especially the type made by supervisors, is being able to speak effectively in public, hence the use of the old-fashioned term "public speaking". The primary focus of this chapter is on public speaking rather than technical presentations. However, it should be noted that, increasingly, multi-media presentation formats are becoming more available in workplaces today, and the supervisor should be familiar with the technical aspect of public speaking.

After reading and studying this chapter, the reader should:

- Have an understanding of the techniques and skills involved in making presentations
- Be able to put these ideas and skills into practice.

WHAT IS A PRESENTATION?

A presentation serves many functions. It could be designed, for instance, to impart knowledge or information, to inspire people to a particular view or course of action, or to entertain. Presentations given at functions tend to fall into the latter category, though in every presentation there is, hopefully, some element of entertainment. A supervisor's presentation is more likely intended to inform or to motivate. This requires that the supervisor deliver a presentation clearly and effectively, and that the content — the message — be understood and remembered. This chapter explains how that is done.

Some presentations are given impromptu, others memorised. Some are read from a prepared manuscript, others given with the aid of notes or visual aids. In all cases, the same basic rules apply: speak clearly and slowly, be as brief as possible, and make eye contact with the audience. How one delivers a presentation depends largely on how often and how well one practises. Practice helps to improve the content of the presentation, as well as to build confidence.

MAKING PRESENTATIONS AS A PROCESS

Making formal presentations as a process can be broken down into three parts:

- Preparing the presentation
- Writing the presentation
- Delivering the presentation.

The first two parts are examined in detail below, while delivering a presentation is dealt with in the section on "practical tips".

Preparing for the Presentation

The first rule in preparation is to know all the details about the practicalities of the presentation. This includes the following:

- The time and place where the presentation is to be delivered
- The length of time allocated to the presentation
- The audience.

Where and when the presentation or presentation is to be made is of paramount importance. In many cases the speaker knows the venue very well, in which case plans can be made without too much fear of anything going wrong. In instances where the speaker has never been to the venue, then the necessity to enquire about the room and the type of facilities available is greater. Speakers have been known to go to the wrong place, turn up with slides but no slide projector, forget their notes, or bring the wrong ones. Problems, especially simple, unforeseen ones, put great stress on an individual. The general rule is: arrive in good time, test the equipment if necessary and have a backup plan for unforeseen events.

One suggestion is to make a list of exactly what one needs. Such a list may include:

- Notes
- Manuscript
- Overheads/slides
- Name of person to meet
- Time it takes to get there
- Time of the presentation, etc.

The supervisor should go over the list just before leaving the house or office.

The final aspect of preparation is to know the audience. All presentations have to be tailored to suit the audience. Giving a presentation to the local residents' association, for example, is far different than giving a presentation to a group comprising senior management. The content will differ, as well as, possibly, the method of presentation. Generally speaking, the more formal the group, the more formal the presentation has to be, and vice versa. Informal presentations, such as a presentation to an employee or a contribution to a meeting, also have some element of preparation. So prior to making their presentation, supervisors can jot down on a piece of paper what they intend to say.

Writing the Presentation

There are several tasks involved in producing the written material from which one delivers the presentation:

- Gathering the information
- Writing it up
- Improving or editing the presentation.

The general rule is to gather as much information as possible, make the presentation concise by editing and cutting material and then adapting it to the audience.

Gathering the Information

An individual may be required to research information from various sources: the library, government departments, newspaper offices, etc. In researching, the important thing is to gather as many facts as possible. The next step is to remove any unnecessary, irrelevant and/or duplicated information. In writing a presentation, one has to be able to read the minds of the audience and ask "is this relevant and interesting?" Better still, ask oneself, "if I were part of the audience, would I want to listen to this?"

The Sections of the Presentation

Typically, presentations have three main sections:

- Introduction
- Main body
- Conclusion.

Simply put, in the first part, the introduction, you tell them what you are going to say; in the second part, the main body, you tell them; and finally, in the conclusion, you tell them what you told them.

The Introduction. The introduction should both relax and stimulate the audience. For this reason, it is best kept short, and spoken slowly and clearly so that the audience's attention is held. Some speakers, especially experienced and professional ones, often begin with a joke or a story. Such an introduction serves to welcome the audience to the issue, and, once attention is assured, the speaker then indicates what the presentation is all about.

As stated, the purpose of the introduction is to make the listener aware of what the presentation is all about. This is achieved by stating concisely and clearly the central theme of the presentation. The introduction is thus short and to the point — in some cases no more than a few sentences. An introduction may also serve to introduce the speaker. In that way, the introduction gives some biographical details, such as:

> My name is John Smith. I am the plant superintendent. I started work with Crawley and Sons twenty-two years ago as an apprentice. Three years ago, I was promoted to plant superintendent. Today, I am going to talk about supervision. I will begin with a brief description of the workers I supervise.

The Main Body of the Text. The main body of the text is the core of the presentation. This is the most difficult part and often takes the most time to prepare. It is best to begin with key points and expand the text thereafter. Brainstorming can be very helpful in this regard as it helps to overcome the initial blank wall one meets when starting to prepare the main body.

There are two examples given next where the main ideas are jotted down initially in an outline format. These can be expanded into full text at a later stage.

Example Number One: How to Motivate Staff

- (Introduction)
- What is motivation

- Ways of motivating people
- Pay as a motivator
- Non-pay issues as a motivator of people
- (Conclusion)

Example Number Two: Quality Control in a Factory

- (Introduction)
- What is quality control?
- Methods of ensuring quality control
- The role of workers in quality control
- (Conclusion)

Concluding the Presentation. As with the introduction, the conclusion should be short and to the point, and ideally should be memorised. Mostly, the conclusion should concern itself with summarising the main points, in some cases repeating the introduction.

Protocol sometimes dictates that the speaker concludes the presentation by thanking the audience. This may be an expression of gratitude for the time and patience of the audience, as well as a signal to all concerned that the presentation is over. By memorising the conclusion, one can be more assured of finishing on a good note. Also, in the event that the presentation is running over time, the speaker can jump to the conclusion earlier than expected and finish the presentation on time.

PRACTICAL TIPS

Practical Tips One: Writing the First Word

The Chinese have an old saying "the longest journey begins with the first step". In writing a presentation the first word is often the most difficult to write. This is particularly the case for people who have little experience with writing and who may have been out of school or college for a while. As with speaking, following a few basic rules can help immensely.

The first rule is: do not be overcome by the daunting task of writing and delivering a presentation. Nothing comes immediately. It takes time, a little practice and often a lot of mistakes before one succeeds. Try to begin the task with a positive attitude and a goal in mind. Most people who are asked to give presentations are asked to talk about something they already know about. The Greeks have an appropriate saying: "begin with the lemma (what one knows) and work through to the dilemma (what one does not know)". Presentations are usually not written in one sitting, but are rather worked on over a span of time. However, they must be begun, and it may help to remember the old Irish saying "Bíonn gach tosú las" — every beginning is weak. Therefore, don't lose confidence at the start.

Save for offensive or inappropriate words, there are no hard or fast rules regarding the words one uses. However, it is best to aim for simplicity as well as clarity. As stated earlier, be yourself. Do not try to use overly complicated words, since your audience may not understand or appreciate them. As the quip from *Alice in Wonderland* goes, "say what you mean, and mean what you say". Thus, choose your words carefully and with meaning in mind.

Oscar Wilde, in his own defence, once said that there was no such thing as a moral or an immoral book, just good writing or bad writing. Following that logic, it may be said, there are no moral or immoral words, just good words and bad words. Thus words convey certain meanings which can be either positive (good) or negative (bad). Examples of short words that are more effective are:

- *Buy* rather than *purchase*
- *Send* rather than *transmit*
- *Rooms* rather than *accommodation*
- *Begin* rather than *commence*.

The surest way to avoid jargon is to keep a dictionary and thesaurus at hand. Many computer software programs now come with a spell-checker and a thesaurus built in. Some even have grammar checkers. An alternative is to have someone proofread the presentation for errors and wrong use of language.

To reiterate an important point: be natural. Use words you would yourself use in daily conversation save for jargon, slang or foul words. The rule is: know the audience, and tailor the presentation to suit them. Then carry out the presentation with minimum interruption.

Practical Tips Two: Practising the Presentation

The less experience one has with public speaking, the more important it is to practise. The best way to do this is to try the presentation out on a family member, making adjustments both for delivery, time and content.

Hearing one's voice out loud can sound strange, making the planned experience of speaking a bit intimidating. This is normal. Over time, however, you will grow accustomed to it. There is little danger of over-practising. However, sometimes in practice, you lose confidence and try to change. It is a good idea, therefore, to perfect the content of the presentation early on, and stick with it.

When practising a presentation one tests not just for delivery but also time. Keep within an agreed time limit. Where there is no time limit, use your initiative. As a rule of thumb, most presentations should not last more than one half-hour, some even no more than a few minutes. Presentations which are long tend to be dull. The audience shuts off, and stops listening. Therefore, plan always to finish early, or at least on time. This may mean saying less but often, in saying less, more is remembered.

The rule then is: keep a presentation short, speak slowly and say it with effect. This way the presentation will be remembered, for its content rather than for problems with delivery.

Practical Tips Three: Delivering the Presentation

As noted, plan to arrive in good time, with a contingency plan in hand in case of any problems. Start on time, since people value punctuality. Also, waiting around or rushing to get to the appointed venue merely makes one nervous.

The opening sentence or sentences are often the most important for two reasons. First, they set the tone for the audience as to what is to come later, and second, hearing one's voice can seem strange. Moreover, there may be no response from the audience and the words seem to drift into the oblivion of the room. This again is quite commonplace and to be expected. Your voice will sound different, you may be nervous and the audience may, equally, not be at rest. The important thing is to maintain your composure and deliver your presentation as planned.

The only thing different you should do is to project your voice. This is because, even with microphones and public address systems, the voice needs to be raised to ensure that everyone can hear you. In fact, a rule of thumb is to aim your voice at the person at the back of room and assume further that the person's hearing is not great. Speaking too softly, as if in conversation with someone else, is the most common mistake made in public speaking. Therefore, always remember at large gatherings to lift your voice. Not excessively, but enough that you can be heard. And remember to keep the volume consistent save for stressing important points.

Nerves can be controlled in many ways. Arriving late can often unnerve a speaker. Arriving too early can have the same effect. Allow, say, a half hour before the presentation. Make sure everything is ready and prepared. Do a routine check: are my notes in order? Is the public address system in operation? What about the overhead projector, is it set up properly? Once these checks are made, it is often a good idea to chat with the audience and/or chairperson. This serves many purposes. In the first instance, it helps to settle nerves and gets you in the mood for speaking. Talking with someone beforehand prepares the voice for the main event to follow. Finally, relaxation techniques and deep breathing can help to ease a person.

Enthusiasm is important. It comes from a belief in one's subject and comes across in the manner in which one delivers a presentation. Examples include pausing where appropriate (typically between major points so as to give ideas time to sink in). Or raising one's voice to stress a point. Finally, the speed at which one talks can illustrate how much a speaker feels about a particular subject. Speak too fast, and the audience may think that the speaker, like the subject perhaps, is uninteresting. Speak too slowly, and the audience falls asleep.

It is important to bear in mind that the speaker should not move around, nor keep their hands in their pockets. The latter indicates carelessness, while walking around invites the possibility of turning one's back on the audience. Be aware of any peculiar mannerisms you possess, such as scratching your head, putting your hand over your mouth, etc. Such actions, while perfectly harmless ordinarily, are a distraction when speaking. One possibility here is to videotape yourself speaking (in the privacy of your home preferably), and study the tape afterwards for any unusual mannerisms.

Practical Tips Four: Memory and Visual Aids

Speakers often make use of some form of aid, whether it is reading from a prepared script or, more likely, reading from notes scribbled on pieces of paper.

This is perfectly acceptable. Even for presentations that are given at short notice, the speaker has some form of notes written on a piece of paper, a napkin or whatever is handy. When preparing notes, it is generally better to write on each note the sections or subsections of the presentation. The presentation is not fully written out, rather key words, phrases or sentences are written down as cues. Hence the term "cue cards". To use cue cards, follow these rules. Buy more than is necessary, since, in the course of preparing the presentation, you will discard many. Second, organise the presentation into many sections or subsections. Finally, practise giving the presentation, discarding, refining or adding cards where necessary.

Aside from writing thoughts down on a card, a speaker may make use of a slide projector, an overhead projector or even a computer. This is particularly the case in businesses where such devices are commonplace. Projectors have many advantages. For a start they add professionalism to a presentation. Second, they take attention away from the speaker, perhaps putting them at ease while focusing attention on more important information, the presentation. Third, they operate as cue cards for the speaker. Fourth, in the case of an overhead projector, notes can be written on the side of the transparency, visible to the speaker but not to the audience.

Slides and overheads, while having many advantages, also have the potential to cause problems. Slide projectors have been known to malfunction, especially in the middle of a presentation. Further, both slide projectors and overhead projectors need either a screen or white wall, and, for slide projectors, a dark room. They also need more preparation, and are more costly.

The latest invention is images projected from a computer to a screen. Such equipment, though a marvellous development, is extremely expensive and only likely to be found in large firms or universities. Moreover, it requires some technical expertise, along with presentation software, such as Powerpoint, to prepare the slides.

At the other end of the spectrum lie the old fashioned blackboard and, more lately, the flip chart. Both are wonderful devices for making presentations, but less useful in formal presentations. Both are advantageous for making points as the presentation progresses but are disadvantageous in a few ways. Firstly, the speaker may turn their back to the audience; secondly, they can prove disruptive to the flow of the presentation; and, finally, they depend much on the ability to use and, if not prepared in advance, to write effectively on a board in front of an audience.

The last aid to the speaker is the handout. Some speakers distribute beforehand a full copy of the text of the presentation. This is both good and bad. On the one hand, it means that the audience can follow the presentation, missing out very little. Also, people can take home the full copy of the presentation, without having to worry about taking notes. The downside is that the audience has the tendency to read the notes, ignoring the speaker in the process.

Visual aids should be used when appropriate rather than for the sake of it. Excessive use of visual aids takes the personal touch away from presentations. Moreover, visual aids are typically more expensive and time-consuming to prepare. Furthermore, they are prone to mistakes. They are, however, particularly useful for presentations which are to be repeated many times over. This justifies the time and expense in making them.

CHAPTER SUMMARY

Public speaking, not being a daily activity for most people, often seems daunting to them. As a result of both their lack of experience and training, most people shy away from public speaking. However, supervisors need to learn how to deliver presentations competently and practice is the most effective way to learn.

Public speaking is largely a skill, albeit a learned one. The techniques that were outlined in this chapter should help an individual to speak competently and professionally to others. However, as pointed out, to speak in public one needs to practise a good deal. Visual aids such as overhead projectors or slides can help but they are secondary to the art of delivering a presentation.

References and Further Reading

Bennett, R. (1994) *Personal Effectiveness*, second edition, London: Kogan Page, chapter 1.

Daunt, S. (1996) *Communication Skills*, Dublin: Gill & Macmillan, chapters 4 & 5.

Evans, David (1995) *Supervisory Management, Principles and Practices*, fourth edition, London: Cassell, chapters 34 and 35.

McClave, Henry J. (1986) *Communication for Business in Ireland*, Dublin: Gill and Macmillan, chapters 8 & 9.

Tierney, Elizabeth (1994) *Show Time! A Guide to Making Effective Presentations*, Dublin: Oak Tree Press.

Chapter 9

WRITING SKILLS

THE OBJECTIVE OF THIS CHAPTER

For some supervisors, writing, save for the odd form that needs filling out, or the much required signature on a slip of paper, is not a frequent job requirement. For others, writing is a crucial aspect of their daily work routine. In the latter category, for example, fall supervisors in administrative and clerical positions. In general, however, writing is an important managerial skill for all supervisors to learn. Legal requirements and increased bureaucracy, along with staff reductions, are demanding more of the supervisor in the modern organisation. As one supervisor put it: "Everything has to be recorded now, and orders have to be justified". And this has to be done on a computer rather than by hand.

Writing at work covers a multitude of areas, including writing letters, memos and reports. Still other documents that need writing are forms such as applications and performance appraisal forms. Despite such variation, this chapter will use the term document to include all forms of writing including letters, memos, forms and reports.

After reading and studying this chapter, the reader should have an understanding of:

- What is required in writing letters, memos and reports
- How to write quickly and effectively.

The next chapter deals with time management.

EFFECTIVE WRITING

Effective writing should be clear and to the point. It should be free of all (or almost all) grammatical mistakes and bad punctuation. It should convey to the reader the intended message, no more, no less. It may be designed to inform and/or to promote action. Either way, it has to be communicated and understood. The acronym KISS or "Keep it Short and Simple" denotes the core of effective writing. Effective writing, like public speaking, is a product of preparation and practice. In writing terms, the latter is referred to as revision. Thus, after preparing, writing begins and then is revised, revised and revised.

TABLE 9.1: SHORT RULES FOR EFFECTIVE WRITING

- Be clear about the subject being investigated
- Be clear about the purpose
- Be aware of your readers, what they know and do not know.
- Be accurate
- Be objective
- Be relevant
- Be concise
- Be ordered
- Be comprehensible
- Be wary of technical jargon
- Avoid too many personal opinions and "I" statements

Preparation

Preparation essentially involves building a framework or plan for what is to follow. The writer must be able to answer a series of questions: what is the purpose of the writing, to whom is it addressed, why I am writing it, and finally when and where is it to be sent?

The most important question by far is: what is the purpose of the letter, memo or report? Here are some examples:

- To arrange a meeting

- To hire an individual
- To order goods
- To find out information about a product
- To sell a product or service
- To invite someone
- To explain a recent action.

State the purpose at the beginning of the document, such as:

> "I am writing to inform you about our company's product, the Deluxe range of lawnmowers."
>
> "This report is a summary of the performance of Department B for 1997."
>
> "This memo outlines the job duties of the forklift driver."

This serves two purposes. First, it makes it easier for one to start writing, and second, it informs the reader from the beginning what the document is about.

The second question is to ask oneself: why am I writing this document? It may be that a phone call is more appropriate and more effective, or that it is someone else's job to write this document thus freeing up your time for more important tasks.

The third question is: who is going to read this? Asking who is the reader opens a Pandora's box of responses. For example, am I writing to the right person? Do I have the right name? Will they understand the terminology and language I use? Better still, will they understand the message I hope to get across? Will they react to this document in the way I want? All of these questions should be considered at an early stage, and repeated as necessary while writing. As noted previously, effective communication is a product of transmission and understanding. That is, the intended individual or individuals must receive and understand the message. Framing the message in terms and language with which the reader is familiar will improve the chances of understanding.

Talking on the telephone is a spontaneous task; writing is not. A supervisor must plan in advance, get down to the matter at hand, and revise the draft document constantly. Therefore, allocate time for writing, put effort into it, and work away without interruptions.

THE WRITING ITSELF

There are two broad ways of composing any document. The first is to follow a set pattern. This could begin, as stated earlier, by listing the names and addresses of the sender and receiver, and by stating unambiguously the purpose of the document. Then one can begin writing paragraphs, one after the other, until the concluding or final paragraph is reached. This is a methodical approach to writing and has relevance for business documents.

An outline is particularly helpful in this regard. If faced with writing a report on how your department performed for the last three years, one could begin by stating the main headings. These could be as follows:

- Introduction (stating what is to be said)
- Body:
  - ◊ Year One
  - ◊ Year Two
  - ◊ Year Three
- Conclusion (stating what has been said)

This can be further developed by adding subheadings to the body of the text as follows:

- Year One:
  - ◊ Financial Performance
  - ◊ Staff Performance
- Year Two:
  - ◊ Financial Performance
  - ◊ Staff Performance
- Year Three:
  - ◊ Financial Performance
  - ◊ Staff Performance

Once having completed the outline the writer can then begin the process of writing. Basically, this means adding the text to the headings, a process to which we will return later.

A second approach, more the domain of the creative writer, is to write as one feels, that is, write whatever comes into your head. This is the free-wheeling approach, which is enhanced by brainstorming. Brainstorming is a wonderful technique in getting one on the path of writing and especially useful at breaking mental blocks. Furthermore, it ties in with the view of seeing writing essentially as a creative task. Finally, brainstorming is aided by computers where documents can be drafted and refined over time. That said, most writers use a pen and paper when brainstorming and later transfer the output to the computer.

Either approach is effective and their usefulness depends on the situation and the individual. I tend to begin writing in the free-wheeling way, writing down thoughts as they come into my head. It is often much later before I bother to rearrange the material to follow a set pattern. Others, however, prefer to organise their writing in regimental fashion, by beginning at the beginning and ending at the end. The point, however, is not which method is best, but rather which method best suits the individual and the situation.

Structure

Memos begin usually with a heading, such as:

To:	James Kitchener
From:	Mary Sinclair
Ref:	Work Schedule
Date:	July 15, 1997
cc:	Joan Fletcher

Memo styles vary, depending on the organisation. For most it is a matter simply of stating the names of the sender and the receiver, the date and what the memo is referring to. It is common courtesy to inform the receiver that the memo is being routed to someone else, hence the customary "cc:", meaning "carbon copy".

Reports are more difficult. They are customarily not written in any set way, though some organisations may have a particular style to which they adhere. However, most reports begin with an executive summary or short introduction. Again, this is designed to convey to the reader what the report is all about.

Introductions should state clearly the purpose of the document and who is writing it. In addition, in the case of a memo or letter, it may acknowledge any previous communication, such as:

> "This memo is in response to your memo of January 10, regarding holiday arrangements."

The body of the document is, generally speaking, the main part. It is typically the longest part of the document since the main argument or arguments of the document are contained there.

The conclusion closes the document. Not surprisingly, conclusions tend to be short and often repeat in a few sentences what was stated previously. A letter should be formally closed with either "Yours faithfully" if addressing the receiver by name, or "Yours sincerely" if addressing the receiver by title such as "Dear Sir or Madam". The sender's name and title should follow. Examples are:

> Mr. John Smith
> Allied Drive,
> Dublin
>
> Dear Mr. Smith,
>
> Yours sincerely,
>
> James Jones
> Plant Supervisor

The Irish form of this is "A chara", and "Mise, le meas". Public bodies sometimes use the Irish form, private organisations less so.

Revision

The final stage in writing, and often the most important stage, is revision. This entails going back over the earlier drafts and proofreading for mistakes as well as for the flow of the argument. When revising:

- Look for excessive repetition
- Check that the ideas flow from one paragraph to another and that they are coherent
- Confirm that what is in the document is factually, legally and organisationally correct.

Revision takes time and should not be skipped. Too often, people write letters and memos, even reports, and are so drained at the end, and so fed up with the task of writing, that they don't bother to check their document. Still others, at the final stage, spot a mistake, make the corrections and post the document without actually checking to see if they corrected the mistake properly. This is why it is a good idea to have someone else do the final proofreading.

WRITING AIDS

There are many aids available to the writer, or potential writer as the case may be. These range from the old-fashioned but indispensable dictionary to the ultra-modern, and some say almost indispensable, computer. In between are books which teach how to write, and books which provide sample letters. All aids, in one form or another, are useful to writing. None do the writing, just make it easier to do.

A dictionary, quite clearly, is a must for anyone writing, whether professionally or as part of a job. It confirms proper spellings as well as the meanings of words. Less important, but useful nonetheless, is a thesaurus. It suggests, among other things, synonyms. So, for example, instead of writing "useful" continuously, the thesaurus would suggest "advantageous" or "beneficial" or "essential" or "invaluable". Use the dictionary and thesaurus at the revision, not the composing, stage. Otherwise, one loses the flow of writing. Similarly, if using a computer, spell-check after the first draft, and always after the final draft.

There are many books available to help the process of writing. These include self-help books on how to write better, books which give sample letters and, finally what are called style books. The latter abound with information on how to write properly, including rules on grammar, punctuation and the like.

Computers are fast becoming a way of life for many employees. In the area of writing, in particular, computers offer much. Data can be stored and retrieved almost instantaneously. One can rush out a draft copy, and then do the editing at a later stage. If that were not enough, modern word processors offer many options that assist in writing. Clearly, the most important is the spell-checker, but now the latest programmes include a thesaurus and a grammar-checker as well. Even indexes and table of contents generators are standard features. Therefore, if available, use a computer.

PRACTICAL TIPS ON WRITING

1. Check which medium is the correct one. Writing is a time-consuming activity and sometimes, though certainly not always, it is advisable to telephone or visit instead.

2. Ask yourself a whole series of questions, the so-called who, what, where, when and how outlined earlier. Writing involves much thought. The supervisor who thinks first about writing and who sets out to write with a plan usually does the better job. However, do not think too much to the point of procrastination. Writing is something that has to be done rather than thought about.

3. In terms of the writing itself, begin with a draft, preferably on a computer. Brainstorm and write quickly, removing later any negative suggestions. Alternatively, or indeed in combination, build a draft copy using the outline method. This means to create the main headings (introduction, body and conclusion) and then break the main body of the document down into subheadings. With a pen and paper, make the argument flow from one subheading to the next. Then fill in the main body of the text.

4. Be consistent with style. Avoid repetition, and unnecessary statements and words. Begin with an introduction and summarise in the conclusion. State your case clearly using language that everyone can understand.

5. Consider the reader at all times. Couch the memo in language that they will understand. If necessary ask for replies. And follow up.

6. Use computers and use them effectively. This includes using the spell-check, glossary, thesaurus, outliner, grammar-checker, etc. The time taken to learn these features will more than pay off. Maintain a standard format which can avoid unnecessary typing.

7. In addition to computers, there are books — dictionaries, thesauruses, style manuals, self-help books and books with sample letters and memos — which can help the writer in the daily chore of writing. As with computers, use them to the fullest.

8. Seek advice if necessary, particularly on legal matters. Ask others to proof your writing, particularly for mistakes, inconsistencies and repetition. Even with spell-checks and grammar checkers, computers are far from perfect. Neither are people, but a combination of human and computer checks goes a long way towards producing the perfect document.

9. Finally, take as much time as is needed. However, it is best to begin writing as early as possible, take a break and return to it with a fresh mind. However, for short documents, such as memos and letters, complete the task in one sitting. This may mean allocating time during the day to do this, and putting a hold on telephone calls and visitors to the office.

CHAPTER SUMMARY

This chapter concentrated on two aspects of writing: the first is getting started, the other is getting the composition right. In terms of the first issue, one should waste less time in writing memos, letters and reports by either using the brainstorming method or by outlining. Both methods can be combined for maximum effectiveness.

In terms of composition, one should seek help, either from writing aids, such as computers and books, or from people who can proof-read. Follow the acronym, KISS (Keep it Short and

Simple). Documents should be written in a clear, concise and unambiguous language.

References and Further Reading

Daunt, S. (1996) *Communication Skills*, Dublin: Gill & Macmillan, chapters 8-12 .

Evans, David (1995) *Supervisory Management, Principles and Practices*, fourth edition, London: Cassell, chapter 30.

McClave, Henry J. (1986) *Communication for Business in Ireland*, Dublin: Gill and Macmillan, chapters 3-6.

Chapter 10

Making the Best Use of Your Time

THE OBJECTIVE OF THE CHAPTER

A supervisor's job, like that of a housewife, is never done. Often one plans to arrive in work early to write an important memo, or to do certain tasks, only to be met by a problem which demands immediate attention. Other tasks, as a result, get put on the back burner. Suddenly the morning is over, with little accomplished. The situation is repeated in the afternoon, and soon the day is gone, with little achieved and much to do. This was the typical scenario put to me by many supervisors: broader job responsibilities, coupled with shortages of staff, make for a situation in which overwork is the norm rather than the exception. A particular problem mentioned centred around delegating work to contract staff. Some supervisors felt that it was not worth investing the time and energy training contract staff who would soon be leaving the company. So these supervisors did the employee's work themselves. Another difficulty frequently raised was dealing with problems outside the control of the supervisor and particularly where emergencies of one kind or another disrupt a planned schedule.

In addition to the real problems of work overload and dealing with emergencies, many supervisors simply lack the ability to manage time. Time management is basically learning how to structure one's day so that all aspects of the job get done the way they should — on time and effectively. It is something which supervisors should learn, yet many supervisors ignore the issue entirely. And this despite the fact that managing people is a time-consuming activity, and that supervisors have to carry out many administrative tasks, such as writing memos, making telephone calls, or filing. In interviews, it was pointed out by senior managers that it is only very recently that organisations have started to realise the importance of time management for supervisors. As a result these organisations now provide diaries and training in time management for supervisors. However, it takes more than diaries and training to manage time. As one manager made the point: "supervisors have the ability to manage time, but they don't do it". Self-discipline is crucial.

Managing time also has personal relevance. If time gets the better of supervisors, instead of the other way around, they won't perform their job as effectively as they should. The result will be frustration and despair. Therefore, learn to manage time, not so much for your organisation's sake, but for your own.

After reading this chapter the reader should have an understanding of:

- The principles of time management
- How to get one's job done in an effective and timely manner.

In many instances good time management also requires the ability to solve problems and make decisions quickly: they are the subject of the next chapter.

NOT GETTING THE JOB DONE: THE REASONS WHY

There is nothing magical about time management. It is about prioritising work, and getting each job done in a reasonable time. Time management is a skill, but it is primarily a psychological one. Beyond keeping a diary one has to learn to motivate oneself to achieve specific tasks within a prescribed time. This means prioritising work, sticking to a schedule, and not getting sidetracked. I am reminded here of a German tendency which is to begin the workday with a list of items or tasks that need doing. The manager does not leave until all the tasks are accomplished. Time management is not as drastic as that. However, it does require a commitment to stick to planned schedules.

The next section outlines different ways of managing time, first by dealing with people and then by dealing with tasks.

Dealing with People

One of the problems faced by supervisors is the notion that they are doing everyone else's job, including their own. This includes work that should be done by employees and work that is more correctly the domain of one's boss.

Supervisors doing their operator's work is quite common. Indeed, supervisors may believe that the only way to get a job done properly is to do it themselves. They reason that, this way, the job, especially a once-off task, can be done quicker if not also more effectively. The problem here is that supervisors are doing the employees' jobs and not their own. A supervisor has to learn to delegate work. This requires that the employee understand the job that needs doing, and be given time to accomplish the task. By trusting employees and having patience with them, one will find that they are quite capable of performing many advanced tasks. Delegation can also be enhanced by encouraging employees to show initiative.

A supervisor is well-advised to hold regular meetings with staff. However, meetings should be rigidly controlled with regard to time. Have an agenda prepared in advance and circulate it to all staff. Keep the meeting moving at all times, but be open to and encouraging of employees' suggestions.

Dealing with the boss can be trickier. Many supervisors complain that they must do their boss's job. While this may, on the one hand, be because they have a lazy or inefficient boss or one who is not doing the job right, it may, on the other hand, be an attempt by the boss to delegate more real responsibility to the supervisor. If it is the latter, it should have been discussed and agreed between them. Supervisors have to be assertive and stand up for their right to be consulted rather than have the boss's own job dumped on them. A possible course of action would be to discuss it with the boss or, if unsuccessful, with the next manager above. There is little to lose and much to gain.

Another problem in dealing with people is interruptions — phone calls or unexpected visitors. One supervisor made a very pertinent point: "the big problem with managing time is when the day is planned out, something throws it and I can't pick it up again". Supervisors should learn to block time each day to get the important work done. Phone calls and even visitors to the office can be a nuisance in the sense that they are disruptive and demotivating. Therefore, learn to deal with them by (if possible) restricting calls and visits to particular times of the day. One supervisor told me that she continuously had a problem with her boss coming into her office and requesting her immediate attention. Eventually she learned to say no, and asked him to come back when she was ready. It worked.

Dealing with Tasks

There are numerous tasks, some of a routine nature, that supervisors have to perform. There are phone calls to be made, memos to be written, reports to be followed up on, meetings to be arranged, etc. Though they are minor tasks, collectively, they add up to a headache, particularly when supposedly small tasks take an hour or more to accomplish because of a glitch somewhere. A particular criticism raised by senior management was that supervisors spend so much time on simple administrative tasks that the important issues, like decision-making and planning ahead, don't get done.

The question is how to deal with all the minor tasks, before they become major ones. The simplest approach is to remove unnecessary tasks. Some tasks may not need doing, others can be easily delegated. That will take care of some, though not all, tasks. For the rest of the tasks, learn to prioritise.

Prioritising work involves, first, creating a "to do" list with realistic deadlines. A "to do" list is best created when one has time to think. Basically, it involves writing down on paper, preferably in a diary or calendar, the various tasks one has to do. The next step is to select the order in which the tasks should be undertaken. This is, in essence, prioritising.

There are many ways of prioritising, though essentially it boils down to good judgement. One way is to begin with the tasks which are either the least important or the most important. Another way is to deal first with tasks which require the least or the most time. I generally find it best to start with small tasks which helps reduce the list quickly.

Some tasks, it hardly needs pointing out, prioritise themselves. Preparation for a 10.00 a.m. meeting has to be done before 10.00 a.m. or, more likely, the evening before. Similarly, a job may be so urgent that it goes to the top of the priority list. However, there is often a certain leeway in establishing priorities. The goal with prioritising is not to ensure that certain tasks get done, but all tasks.

A final way of prioritising is to deal with tasks that are best dealt with at certain times of the day. Generally speaking, tasks which require creativity are handled best in the morning when one is alert. Other tasks, such as returning telephone calls, may be best done in the afternoon. People who are nocturnal may find that the afternoon is their most productive time.

Learn to expedite things by spending less time on routine matters. Some telephone calls can be handled in less than a minute. Still, some people persist in spending a considerable amount of time on the telephone. Therefore, learn to make short telephone calls. Write down what to say before the call is made, and then refer to it when making the call. Good time management is not just a matter of ordering the day, but of being more productive with time. Finally, it is a good idea to handle similar tasks together. For example, make all telephone calls at one point or, when feasible, hold one large meeting rather than a series of small ones.

When prioritising it is important to understand that not all tasks will get accomplished. This is perfectly natural. Often time is the enemy. Sometimes the task can get done itself, or just simply does not get done. Learn to accept this, and do not let it affect your performance as a supervisor.

DEADLINES, DISCIPLINE AND DIARIES: THE THREE Ds OF TIME MANAGEMENT

Prioritising is useless unless self-discipline is exercised. Discipline is part method and part will-power. Method refers to establishing deadlines for each task. There is truth in the saying that a bad pen is better than a good memory. Therefore, write every task into your diary. However, there is little point in having a diary unless one is prepared to read it on a continuous basis. This is where will-power comes into play.

There is no shortage of choice available when it comes to diaries. Betts (1993, p. 111) provides the best advice of all:

> Examine the range of diaries available to record information. There are elaborate personal organisers with refills, including a diary, addresses, references, a notebook and subject tabs; electronic organisers with many facilities; and simple diaries, which are often adequate. Avoid overcomplicated systems, choose one to suit your needs and choose large formats so you never run out of space.

Not mentioned by Betts, however, is time management software. Increasingly, firms are provided diaries as part of computer software, which, like Lotus Agenda or Microsoft Mail, can be networked. The advantage of this is that everything can be stored electronically and, in the case of networked software, others can have access to it. However, computer usage suffers from a number of problems, notably that people have the tendency to make appointments but forget, for one reason or another, to record it electronically. The alternative to this is a PDA (Personal Digital Assistant) which can be linked electronically to computer systems. The best known of these are the Apple Newton and the Psion Series. However, experience tells me that Betts is correct: a simple system with the potential to grow is best.

With deadlines the important thing is to be realistic. This means giving oneself sufficient time to complete the tasks, and then some more. I have known people to establish long deadlines, others very short ones. In the case of the former, a long deadline may be listing ten items all of which have to be accomplished in the day. Others are more specific and list a set time for each item, such as:

- Writing memos, 9 to 10 a.m.
- Return calls , 10 to 10:30 a.m.
- Meeting with T. Swift, 10:30 a.m.

and so on.

I prefer to write down all tasks that have to be done in the day. Then I go about carrying out each task. As each item is completed, I scratch it out. At the end of the day, what is remaining is carried over to the next day's work by writing in the diary in the proper date. The advantage of this method is that it gives one flexibility in ordering your day. The obvious disadvantage is that certain items continuously get put on the long finger.

Table 10.1 provides tips for managing your time.

TABLE 10.1 USEFUL TIPS FOR MANAGING TIME

- Learn to prioritise and concentrate on getting the important tasks done.
- Use a diary: write every task down
- Organise effective meetings
- Delegate as much as possible
- Plan your telephone calls (don't waste time on the call)
- Set realistic goals and give yourself enough time to get each task done
- Don't procrastinate: Have the will-power to carry tasks out
- Stick to one task and get it done (avoid switching between tasks)
- Be clear about times and dates
- Begin the workday with a plan and stick to it.
- Limit idle gossip
- Block time each day for yourself (don't take phone calls or see visitors then)
- Avoid distractions and interruptions
- Learn to deal with unexpected visitors and phone calls (ask them to call back)
- Be decisive and stick by the decisions made. Say no.
- Choose the appropriate times and/or place to do contact people.

CHAPTER SUMMARY

Supervisors have to perform their own work and they have to supervise other people's work. Hence the importance of time management for people who feel they are doing two jobs for the price of one. Time management has two objectives: getting all tasks done, and done effectively. Because it is part method and part will-power time management is not a difficult skill to master. Rather, one has to learn first to eliminate unnecessary tasks, and to prioritise those remaining so that they can be accomplished in the time available. As with writing, many aids are available such as diaries, year planners and calendars. However, the best way to manage time is to be more productive. This means making the maximum use of available technology, and forcing oneself to get things done.

References and Further Reading

Bennett, R. (1994) *Personal Effectiveness*, second edition, London: Kogan Page, chapter 4.

Betts, P.W. (1993) *Supervisory Management*, London: Pitman.

Evans, David (1995) *Supervisory Management*, London: Cassells, chapter 31.

Mosley, D., L. Megginson, P. Pietri (1993) *Supervisory Management: The Art of Empowering and Developing People*, third edition, Cincinnati, OH: South-Western Publishing Company, pp. 583-9.

Scott, M. (1992) *Time Management*, London: Century Business.

Chapter 11

DECISION-MAKING AND PROBLEM-SOLVING

THE OBJECTIVE OF THIS CHAPTER

Decisions can be routine or major, made by individuals or groups, and they can be aided by computer programmes or made solely on the basis of human judgement. The distinguishing feature of decision-making for supervisors has been that they often have to make decisions immediately, and usually alone, on the basis of their own intuition. In organising work, for example, a supervisor would have to decide what tasks had to be done, who was to do them, when and how they had to be done. Increasingly, though, with broadened job responsibilities and reductions in staff numbers, supervisors are being called upon to make, or participate in a team that makes, non-routine decisions. Such decisions may have strong financial consequences, and may have been made in the past by middle-level management.

This chapter provides information and advice on how decisions are best made, either by the supervisor alone or acting in tandem with other supervisors or with employees as part of a team. While most decisions, especially routine ones, can be made by the supervisor alone, important decisions are increasingly made as part of a team. For this reason the final part of this chapter deals with a method suitable for group processes: consensus decision-making.

After reading and studying this chapter the reader should have an understanding of:

- The decision-making process
- How to make effective decisions
- Consensus decision-making.

DECISION-MAKING: PROGRAMMED AND NON-PROGRAMMED DECISIONS

Simon (1971) introduced to management science the distinction between programmed and non-programmed decisions (see Figure 11.1).[1] The former refers to routine or day-to-day decisions and the latter to unusual or one-of-a-kind decisions. As was pointed out, supervisors in the past made, in the main, programmed decisions, such as decisions about the allocation of work. Increasingly, though, supervisors are being asked to make more non-programmed decisions or at least participate in processes which lead to the making of major or strategic decisions. The latter could include what technology to buy, what employees to recruit, or how best to respond to customers' concerns.

FIGURE 11.1: PROGRAMMED AND NON-PROGRAMMED DECISIONS

Programmed Decisions	Non-programmed Decisions
Complex strategic problems	Simple tactical problems
Decision-making	Problem-solving
Course of action	Choice of alternatives

As was mentioned in previous chapters, there was a strong feeling among senior managers that supervisors were not willing to undertake higher-level management tasks, notably decision-making. Supervisors themselves pointed out that they either lacked the training, were too caught up with minor tasks to perform high-level tasks adequately, or that, despite the rhetoric, they lacked either the authority or the autonomy to make important decisions. A particular bone of contention for many supervisors was that their ability to make decisions which involved the expenditure of money, such as buying in stock, was very much restricted. In addition, it was frequently mentioned that, because of legal developments, supervisors are now more accountable for decisions and that with computers it is easier to trace the source

[1] Drucker (1966) makes the distinction between "generic" and "unique" decisions. Generic refers to standard decision-making where reference is made to some rule or policy; unique decision-making refers to unusual problems that require creative thought or a new approach.

of any decision. For some supervisors, for example a Garda sergeant, decisions had to be taken in a crisis which can be challenged years later in court, or that could have serious repercussions. Similarly an interviewee in the Air Corps noted:

> The senior NCOs (non-commissioned officers) have to make decisions with respect to aircraft: whether it can be flown, etc. He may have to make the decision that a component has to be replaced, or bought elsewhere. He has to certify that the plane is flightworthy. There is pressure now to do things quickly. Decisions have to be made now by the NCO. In the past, it would be referred to the officer.

Such decisions often have long-term implications with important consequences for supervisors. For a start, higher-level decision-making, as distinct from problem-solving, requires conceptual skills. Secondly, supervisors now have greater contact with senior management and are working more in tandem with other supervisors and staff specialists. Finally, one point frequently made by supervisors was that, in the past, decision-making could be postponed, but it is no longer an option to defer responsibility.

ARRIVING AT A DECISION

Said simply, a decision involves choosing a course of action from among alternatives to achieve an objective or resolve a problem. The method an individual may use to arrive at that decision, however, varies greatly.

Intuition is a traditional method of resolving problems and is particularly suited to routine decisions. Intuition means resolving problems or making decisions on the spot using one's instincts without much deliberation. Supervisors with a great deal of experience are good at making such decisions. However, it should be recognised that more complex problems generally require more thought and effort. Furthermore, intuition does not always arrive at the best decision, and it can be emotionally charged. Finally, intuition is closely related to the view of the classical economists that people are rational and well-informed and capable of reaching the correct decision, which is not always the case. Indeed, Herbert Simon (1979), one of the most well-known writers in this field, has argued that managers rarely make optimal decisions but rather seek solutions that are satisfactory. He terms this process "satisficing" behaviour because it leads to satisfactory decisions rather than the best.

Decision analysis, the second method for arriving at decisions, is the application of a logical or systematic approach to decision-making. Table 11.1 lists the systematic stages of decision-making which can be followed in identifying solutions to problems. It is a time-consuming process, however, with no guarantees that a decision will be made, or that the right one emerges.

Between these two extremes — perhaps between too much thought and too little — lies some form of thinking process. An individual may analyse a situation by establishing, as far as possible, all the facts pertaining to the problem or use some creative thinking method, such as those favoured by de Bono (1992), or, in groups, the brainstorming method.

Regardless of which method is used, or combination of methods, decision-making is a skill which can be developed. Decision-making primarily requires conceptual skills, especially the ability to analyse and synthesise information and to be able to reason, that is, move an argument from one stage to another in logical fashion. Group decision-making requires, in addition, the skills of being able to participate in groups. Involving more than one person in a decision introduces a dynamism that may or may not be conducive to effective decision-making.

THE ELEMENTS OF DECISION-MAKING

Decision-making is a process involving compromise. Even with the best information, or with much effort put into the process, decision-making is rarely perfect. It involves a compromise between following one's gut feeling and following a set of guidelines. For legal reasons, a supervisor should follow, as much as possible, established rules, regulations and policies when making a decision: a decision on hiring, for example, must follow organisational policy and legislative guidelines. However, not all decisions are as clear-cut as that, and some element of judgement is necessary.

Decision-making is also a complex and dynamic process. Rarely these days do decisions have no side-effects. Thus, a decision to take one course of action will often have important implications for other actions. Similarly, decisions that please one group of people may not please another. So a supervisor at all times has to consider the full implications. There is a view which says that non-action is often the best response: Americans often call this "virtual response", which basically acknowledges that some problems have a tendency to resolve themselves. A cold, the old saying goes, lasts seven days if treated, one week if left alone.

While there is some truth in this, in today's competitive environment supervisors must ensure that their work group or department is producing at maximum productivity. Therefore, problems cannot always be left to resolve themselves. Better still, a supervisor should aim to resolve issues *before* they become problems. The insightful phrase, "if it ain't broke, don't fix it", has now been rephrased to read "if it ain't broke, fix it anyway".

The following section outlines a logical or sequential approach to decision-making. Decisions, as noted, can also be made in a creative fashion, and particularly by use of brainstorming and idea-charting. The latter methods are explained in a later section. It should be understood that while certain problems require certain approaches, the supervisor can use a variety of methods or approaches. Finally, decisions which are fairly routine or minor can and should be made quickly and without the necessity of going through the various stages outlined below.

Successful decision-makers recognise that there is more to an effective decision than just choosing one option over another. Rather, one way is to follow certain stages, analysing various bits of information before reaching a decision. The five steps in the decision-making process are shown in Table 11.1. This method is useful for complex or difficult problems and where time is available. This method, while designed to arrive at the best decision, pays less attention to the acceptability of the party or parties affected by the decision. Nevertheless, it is extremely valuable for supervisors who face complex problems alone.

TABLE 11.1: DECISION STAGES[2]

Define and Analyse the Problem	Begin the process by clearly stating what the problem is. If there is no problem, state the objective. For example, a team or group may meet to discuss quality. There is no problem here, but there is an objective, namely how to improve quality.
Identify Alternatives	Any problem typically has more than one solution. It is important from early on to identify as many solutions as possible to a particular problem or problems. Use brainstorming to help identify alternatives and gather all the pertinent facts.
Evaluate and Choose	Once a number of alternatives are identified the next stage involves evaluating options and choosing which is best suited to the problem at hand. It is better to use some form of standard to judge an option. The problem at hand typically determines the standard. To follow the earlier example, quality problems are typically defined in terms of defects to products. Where possible, use established rules, policies or procedures in reaching a decision.
Implement the Decision	Once a course of action is chosen, the next stage is to implement the decision. This should be done quickly, and along the lines planned.
Monitor and Control	Once a decision has been made, and a course of action implemented, the next and most important stage is to monitor that decision. One asks: is the decision working out as planned? Are corrective actions necessary? If the decision looks like a bad one, what other alternatives are available?

[2] There are a number of variations on this model, including Koontz & O'Donnell (1980): set goals, identify alternatives, evaluate alternatives, choose alternative; and Drucker (1967): define the problem, analyse the problem, develop alternative solutions, decide on best solution, convert to effective action. The point to be stressed here is that the supervisor should be aware of, and make use of, the various stages, however many, to reach a decision.

PROBLEM-SOLVING METHODS

There are a number of methods or devices available to help with problem-solving and decision-making, most of which fall into two basic categories:

- Scientific methods (operational research)
- Heuristic models (decision trees and SWOT analysis).

Operational research (OR) is an approach to management developed in the US during the Second World War when scientists of various backgrounds co-operated together to develop methods that better utilised the limited resources of a war-time economy. The success of this military operation led to the adoption of these scientific models in management. Basically, OR means to apply a wide range of scientific and mathematical models which provide the basis for making a decision. Though the approach, as noted, dates back over 50 years, recent improvements in computers have given renewed impetus to its use. The various models or techniques which can run on a computer include network and risk analysis, but clearly the availability and ease of use of spreadsheets and database programs, among others, present greater opportunities for managers to avail of technology to reach better decisions.

While OR has particular application to production and financial data, the basic premise of this approach — using conceptual models and making the best use of what data is available — has wide application to all problems. Further, the use of such techniques can lead to optimal rather than satisfactory decisions. Supervisors should attempt to obtain as much data as possible, build as far as possible conceptual models of the problem and utilise what technical support and hardware is available to them. Bear in mind, though, that models and techniques only support people in making decisions: computers do not make decisions, people do.

The supervisor should also be aware of the limitations inherent in OR. To begin with, OR is best-suited for complex financial and production problems, and less applicable to decisions of the sort supervisors make. Secondly, OR is, as noted, a complex scientific process that requires considerable investment in resources (time, equipment and knowledge), with no guarantee of reaching an optimal decision. Indeed, whereas OR is best applied to specific problems, by definition it ignores the overall context of problems. Like all managers nowadays, supervisors need to be conscious of how their decisions affect the performance of the entire organisation and to consider all aspects of a problem.

A decision tree can be described as a conceptual model that maps out a problem, the alternatives to that problem and finally the possible outcomes of those alternatives. The word "tree" is used because the model is laid out in the form of branches. The use of such a model enables the supervisor to conceptualise the problem and thus reach, ideally, a better solution. Figure 11.2 illustrates the basic format.

SWOT is an acronym for Strengths, Weaknesses, Opportunities and Threats. When faced with resolving a problem or making a decision, the supervisor can fill in the headings of a SWOT analysis: what are the strengths, the weaknesses, the opportunities and the threats of the issue at hand. SWOT analysis is particularly suited to strategic issues and is increasingly being used for tactical planning. For example, SWOT can be used in groups as part of a brainstorming exercise to resolve large problems. Figure 11.3 illustrates how a supervisor faced with the problem of how best to increase productivity could examine options under their relative strengths, weaknesses, threats and opportunities. Options could include overtime, taking on extra staff, changing work practices, etc.

FIGURE 11.2: DECISION TREE ANALYSIS

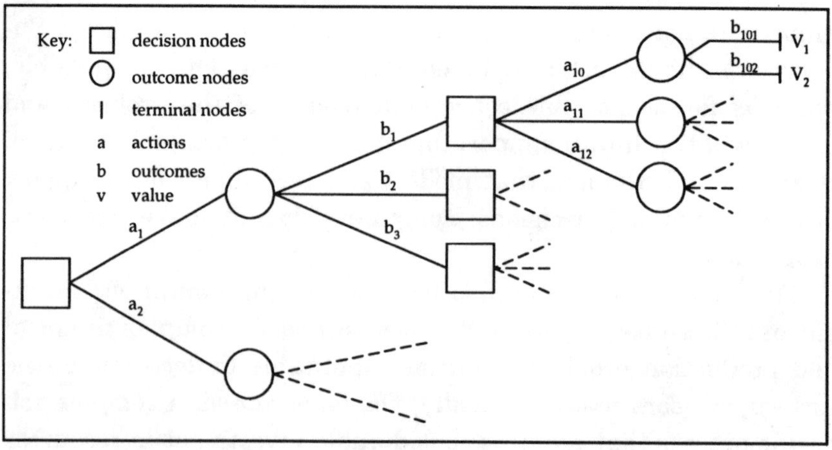

Source: Hamilton (1997).

FIGURE 11.3: SWOT ANALYSIS

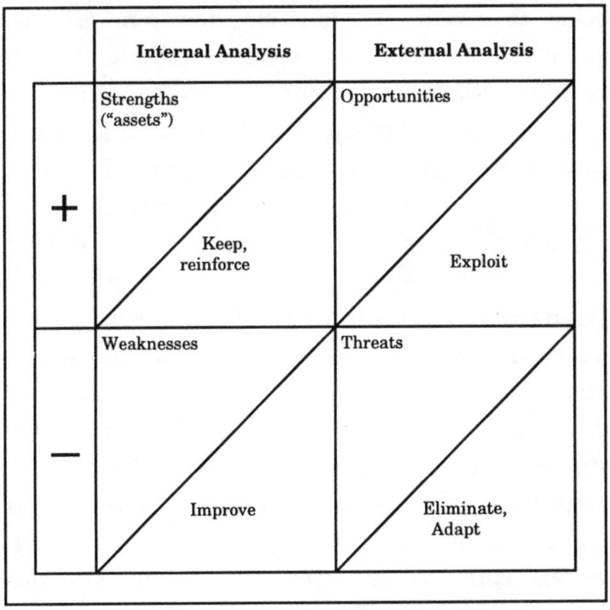
Internal Analysis
External Analysis
Strengths
("assets")
Keep,
reinforce
Opportunities
Exploit
+
Weaknesses
Improve
Threats
Eliminate,
Adapt
–

Source: European Innovation Programme (1996)

Decision trees and SWOT analysis, similar to the decision stages, are heuristic devices in the sense that they allow a supervisor to plot out the stages and development of problem, and to break each problem into its constituent elements. Such models have particular application to large and complex non-programmed problems that are not easily defined. Scientific methods such as operations research have, generally speaking, better application to specific problems, especially those of a programmed nature. Supervisors should be familiar with each of the various methods, and apply each or both as they see fit.

GROUP OR INDIVIDUAL DECISION-MAKING: WHICH IS BEST?

Although in business environments individuals have to make decisions daily, groups are often the best way of making effective decisions for major issues. Group members bring a wide range of knowledge, abilities and experience that no individual, no matter how capable, can match. Indeed, some problems are so demanding, and so difficult that one person alone could not possibly have the expertise to reach an effective decision. Group decision-making has another advantage, namely that decisions reached by groups are more likely to be implemented willingly since they were arrived at openly. Finally, consistent with the argument put forward earlier, the effective supervisor should at all times involve employees in the making of decisions which ultimately effect them so that they may see those decisions as partly theirs.

Despite the good reasons listed above, groups don't always make better decisions than individuals. Instead, group dynamics can work in such a way that a group often reaches a poor decision or no decision at all. The problem is, in many instances, the lack of training in group processes. Said simply, committee members cannot communicate openly and honestly, but instead end up haggling with each other. One method that aids "group-think" is consensus decision-making. This approach was developed in the US for helping committees reach agreement. The next section outlines what consensus decision-making is, and then describes the techniques that can be used in meetings to aid consensus. The terms "team", "group" and "committee" will be used interchangeably.

CONSENSUS DECISION-MAKING

Consensus decision-making[3] is one of many ways groups can arrive at decisions that range from ones based on a lack of response to ones based on unanimous consent (see Table 11.2). It is regarded as an extremely beneficial way of reaching agreement in a group, without friction, and where members will more likely support the decision. It has particular application for teams in the workplace because of the need to generate a culture which is conducive to high performance.

Consensus decision-making can be defined as a process of communication that helps groups reach decisions. It is based on the active and open participation of all group members, where all

---

[3] The author acknowledges the contribution of faculty of the School for Workers, University of Wisconsin-Extension, which developed the material on consensus decision-making.

members are listened to, and the group as a whole values differences of opinion among all group members. Participation means that each member speaks, and expresses their point of view freely and openly. A leader of a team, for example, when chairing a meeting, has to ensure that all members participate. Excessive criticism and interruptions should be kept to a minimum. Listening requires that each member pays attention and gives consideration to what others say. Listening also helps each group member learn from each other.

TABLE 11.2: DIFFERENT WAYS THAT GROUPS MAKE DECISIONS

Decision by Lack of Response	This is where individuals continuously make suggestions until such time as the group finally agrees on one.
Decision by Authority Rule	Groups are often controlled by certain members who, individually or collectively, make all decisions. Typically the chairperson or equivalent uses their full authority to make decisions with little or no input from members.
Decision by Minority	Very often, individuals can combine in small sub- groups to force agreement that suits their interests.
Decision by Majority Rule	Decisions are taken on the basis of majority voting. This is probably the most widely practised method of reaching a decision and often creates a false impression that democratic processes have been followed.
Decision by Consensus	Decisions are reached by consent of most of the participants.
Decision by Unanimous Consent	This is where everyone one in the meeting fully agrees. It is rarely achieved.

Reaching consensus requires that individuals avoid becoming entrenched in their views and be less concerned about their own territory. Instead, the aim is to ensure that the group reaches decisions which benefit it as a whole, not just some individual members.

Consensus does not mean making decisions by a majority vote. Similarly, consensus is not based on true unanimity, something which is rarely achieved in a large group where individuals often fail to speak thus giving rise to false unanimity. Consensus does mean reaching substantial agreement, which is quite different from total agreement on every detail. In some groups, and for some issues, it is almost possible to get complete consensus. With consensus decision-making, the important thing is that members participate in the process and are listened to. A group where only half the members participate is generally not an effective group.

Consensus decision-making is a time-consuming method for reaching decisions and places extra demands on group members. The following section details some methods for reaching consensus.

TECHNIQUES THAT LEAD TO CONSENSUS DECISION-MAKING

Two related techniques can help a team or group reach a consensus are idea-charting and brainstorming.

Idea-Charting

Idea-charting effectively means recording all ideas put forth at a meeting, preferably on a flipchart or blackboard. If a flipchart is being used, the recorder can tear a page when full and tape it to a wall. The advantage of this method is to ensure that all ideas are considered and discussed. Idea-charting is best used in conjunction with brainstorming.

Brainstorming

Brainstorming is a method used to extract ideas from people. It is used primarily to foster creativity and broaden members' points of view. It can be used both within a single group and between groups and has particular application when major problems need a wider view and are not easily solved.

There are few procedures to follow in brainstorming save for the fact that the atmosphere should be relaxed and inviting to the individual. This is important because often some members have an important contribution to make but are too shy to speak. Further, all ideas should be recorded in full view. There should be a "no criticism" rule and no editing. Rather, individuals are invited to give their opinions freely. These are recorded on the flipchart, no further comments are made, and the brainstorming exercise continues until all ideas have been exhausted. It is the facilitator's or chairperson's job to keep the meeting flowing, and to ensure that everyone participates by making a suggestion. When all ideas have been recorded, a second round may be started in which the ideas can be modified by expanding or combining.

Different Roles

When organising brainstorming meetings, three different roles can be identified:

- Chairperson
- Facilitator
- Recorder.

The latter is the easiest to describe and one which we have touched upon already. Basically, it entails recording, in full view, any brainstorming suggestions made by the group. That said, this is an important task, since the recorder has to be able to understand an idea and record it clearly on the flip chart.

The job of facilitators is to aid this process. They should encourage each member of the group to volunteer ideas or suggestions. The aim is to be free-wheeling and unstructured, and, by nipping critical comment in the bud, to help members to use their imagination without constraint. Quantity, not quality, counts; the more ideas the better, and the more variety better still. The facilitator should encourage members to keep going, perhaps by recapping the suggestions so far until they run out of ideas. Finally, at the point at which the team considers the issue to be exhausted, and all ideas have been recorded, the facilitator may arrange for the next stage of evaluating the ideas, preferably after a break. Ideas which are very similar can be combined, overlapping ones omitted, finally working through until the team can agree, and consensus is reached.

Chairpersons have a number of functions to play. They should open the meeting by explaining the purpose of the meeting, and by making each member aware of the procedures. Furthermore, they can assist the meeting by summing up at various points, such as "I think the meeting is moving in this direction, can we get a consensus on that?" This means that the chairperson steers a fine line between leading (or chairing) the meeting, and standing back and letting members talk.

A supervisor may play the role of facilitator or chairperson, or indeed even recorder. In some meetings, the facilitator's and chairperson's job can be combined. These roles can also be rotated between group members, which is part of the process of trusting employees by letting them take charge.

THE ROLE OF THE SUPERVISOR IN CONSENSUS DECISION-MAKING

Consensus decision-making requires new skills. These include the ability to listen and to be considerate of others on the one hand, and participating and sharing information on the other. The supervisor's role is to foster an atmosphere or team spirit which is conducive to effective decision-making. Consensus decision-making requires a complete new mindset for participation in meetings. The supervisor has to articulate to each and every team member what is required of them and the team. There has to be, finally, a shared vision as to what the team intends to achieve and how.

This is not an insurmountable task, but it does take time and energy, as well as the use of administrative and communicative skills. For example, supervisors must prepare for the meeting (read over the agenda, gather relevant materials such as flip-charts and tape, etc.). During the meeting they have to be assertive, which means stating one's view but not getting angry. The supervisor needs to know when to get involved in meetings and take charge, and when to sit back and let others do the talking. This is the direction supervisory management in general is moving in: it is less about exercising authority, and more about taking responsibility. It is less about being *over* a group of people, and more about being a *part* of a group.

SOME PRACTICAL TIPS ON DECISION-MAKING

As noted, supervisors, when making decisions, should involve others, particularly those who will be affected by the decision. Often supervisors are reluctant to involve employees either because they feel that, as supervisors, they must make the decision themselves, or they think employees are not adequately skilled or willing to help. There is little substance to these claims: employees bring to the workplace an abundance of skills and potential. Therefore, the supervisor should at all times involve employees, and seek help where appropriate. This can result in quicker and more effective decisions, which is what decision-making is all about.

As a supervisor, expect to make bad decisions. In other words, don't let the fear of failure prevent you from making decisions. Making mistakes is perfectly natural. Indeed, there is much truth in the simple assertion that "anyone can make a mistake but only a fool makes one twice". Thus the supervisor has to learn to accept responsibility for decisions that go wrong, but also to learn from those mistakes.

Finally, the supervisor has to understand that decision-making is a continuous process. Therefore, the supervisor has to learn to follow through on decisions, and to implement a process of monitoring and control. Very often, decisions are made but are not implemented, or not implemented in the way planned. There are also times too when inaction is best. Basically, the effective supervisor has to learn to exercise good judgement when it comes to making decisions.

CHAPTER SUMMARY

Decisions are of two types: programmed or non-programmed. In the past, supervisors would primarily have dealt with programmed or routine decisions. Increasingly, as supervisors are called upon to make non-routine decisions, or at least participate in the making of them, new methods of making decisions are called for. Similarly, as supervisors cannot, as was often the case in the past, defer responsibility, an understanding of decision-making is important to doing one's job properly.

Decision-making should be understood as a conscious process of choosing between alternatives. However, decision-making can be aided by a variety of means, including using a logical or steps approach, consensus decision-making or a variety of methods, from SWOT analysis to decision trees. These methods can be used alone or in conjunction with each other, and be supported by computer tools.

Problem-solving and decision-making have to be blended with other considerations, notably the pressure of the job and the resources available. As stated in previous chapters, organisations are attaching greater important to first-line management and increasingly demanding that supervisors, whatever their title, act in a more managerial fashion. Decision-making therefore is a critical managerial activity and it is important that supervisors attach time and importance to it.

References and Further Reading

Bennett, R. (1994) *Personal Effectiveness*, second edition, London: Kogan Page, chapter 7.

Bittle, L.R. & J. Newstrom (1990) *What Every Supervisor Should Know*, New York: McGraw-Hill, chapter 6.

de Bono, E. (1992) *Serious Creativity: Using the Power of Lateral Thinking to Create New Ideas*, London: Fontana.

Drucker, P. (1966) *The Effective Executive*, New York: Harper and Row.

Drucker, P. (1967) "The Effective Decision", *Harvard Business Review*, January-February, pp. 92-98.

European Innovation Programme (1996) *The European Handbook of Management Consultancy*, Dublin: Oak Tree Press.

Hamilton, A. (1997) *Management by Projects: Achieving Success in a Changing World*, Dublin: Oak Tree Press.

Koontz, H., O'Donnell, C. and H. Weirich (1980) *Management*, seventh edition, New York: McGraw-Hill.

Mosley, D., L. Megginson, P. Pietri (1993) *Supervisory Management: The Art of Empowering and Developing People*, third edition, Cincinnati, OH: South-Western, chapter 3.

Simon, H. (1971) "The New Science of Management Decisions", in Welch, L., & R. Cyert (eds.), *Management and Decision-Making*, Harmondsworth: Penguin.

Simon, H. (1979) *Models of Thought*, New Haven, CT: Yale University Press, pp. 10-14.

Part Three

The Management of People

Chapter 12

UNDERSTANDING GROUPS AT WORK

THE OBJECTIVE OF THIS CHAPTER

The defining feature of supervisory management is dealing with people, and with issues as they arise. To execute this responsibility, a supervisor must have an understanding of people first as individuals and then as group members. This is largely because individuals behave very differently in groups.

The supervisor's primary concern with groups is to foster behaviour that is conducive to group cohesiveness. This means being attentive to both group and individual needs and creating an environment which allows each individual employee to achieve their full potential, as individuals and as group members, within the constraints of achieving group tasks. A supervisor, therefore, can gain much by learning about group dynamics — the study of groups — and by watching for ways in which group behaviour can be properly influenced and led in the right direction.

After reading and studying this chapter the reader should have an understanding of:

- Group dynamics
- How to manage groups at work.

An understanding of group dynamics provides the foundation for understanding teamwork, which will be discussed in Chapter 17.

GROUP DYNAMICS

Groups are to be found everywhere. Committees, football teams, a crowd in a pub or at a bus stop are all examples, in one form or another, of groups. However, if one asks whether a committee is more of a group than a queue at a bus stop, the answer is not obvious. To answer this question one must consider the characteristics of groups.

Groups can have some or all of the following main characteristics:

- **Size**: groups have more than one person.
- **Structure**: groups nearly always have some sort of structure, rules or order, which allows them to function and to have cohesiveness. Structure is usually defined in terms of roles, authority and status.
- **Interaction**: group members have to have some form of interaction, or contact, with each other.
- **Interdependence**: group members are usually dependent on each other in order to achieve the group's task(s).
- **Goals**: groups are formed with a goal or goals in mind.
- **Leader**: groups typically, though not always, have a leader who provides direction for the group.
- **Dynamism**: groups are dynamic in the sense of coming into being, growing, decaying and finally dying.

All groups possess one or more of these characteristics. Some groups, being very formal in nature, will possess all of these characteristics. Others, less formal, possess only a few. The crowd at the bus stop is characteristic of an informal group, but is a group nonetheless. It possesses only a few of the above characteristics. A committee, on the other hand, tends to be a formal group and may have all of the above characteristics. It is the fact that these groupings possess a common purpose, have some structure (such as rules) and share norms, which sets them apart from a collection of individuals. As a definition of a group, consider Handy's (1993): "a group is any collection of people who perceive themselves to be a group".

TYPES OF GROUPS

One of the earliest distinctions to be made in group dynamics was between formal and informal groups. Formal groups are groups purposely set up to achieve an objective, whereas informal groups tend to arise spontaneously. Formal groups are also highly structured. For example, a department at work may comprise a group. There is a manager, then a supervisor, followed by various levels of employees. The line of authority is clearly marked and each person has a definite job which is defined in relation to other people's work.

From such formal groupings, informal groups can be developed. Informal groups tend to be based on friendship, arising from the need for a sense of belonging. Leaders emerge more for reasons of personality than position. Informal groups also provide protection and security to individuals, and enhance group members' self-esteem and job satisfaction. Because of the nature of informal groups, membership tends to arise from physical proximity (such as working together) and/or between people who share similar social or professional interests.

A further distinction can be made between primary and secondary groups. Secondary groups are large groupings where members may not know each other. Aer Lingus, for example, may be a secondary group since, while all employees share a common aim, that is, working for the same company, they do not all know each other. Primary groups are specific groups, made up of members who are familiar with each other and interact. They tend to be small. A work group at Aer Lingus, therefore, is a primary group. This chapter is concerned with primary groups.

George Simmel (1902), a famous psychologist, developed a taxonomy of groups based on size. Going from smallest to the largest, there exist, for Simmel, a dyad (two people), a triad (three people), the small group (about four to 20 people), the society (20 to 30 people), and the large group (about 40 plus members). The concern in this section is with small groups, that is, a group a supervisor would manage. This includes both formal and informal groups.

THE FORMING OF GROUPS

Groups are formed for many reasons. One is to improve efficiency. A group of people, by combining their expertise, can usually build a product or provide a service better and more efficiently than one person acting alone. Groups may be formed less for efficiency and more for social reasons. They provide not only important social or affiliation needs, but also help individuals define themselves. An example would be an individual who joins a sports club for social, as much as sporting, reasons and who introduces himself as a member of that club. Informal groups also exist in the work environment. Employees who meet in the canteen for tea form an informal group. Such groups help to create a friendly atmosphere. These types of groupings are as important, if not more important, than formal groups. People working in factories can alleviate much of the boredom of factory life by grouping together, thus making work life more pleasant. When work is pleasant, it tends to be more productive. Hence groups have meaning and benefits for individuals and organisations.

THE STUDY OF GROUPS

The study of groups, or group dynamics, a term coined by Kurt Lewin (1936), is concerned with both the individual as a group member and the group itself as a collection of individuals striving to achieve a common goal. As such, it borrows partly from sociology, the study of society, and partly from psychology, the study of individuals. It is sometimes referred to as social psychology.

Some researchers, notably psychologists, see groups as essentially a set of individuals in a collective setting. Group or social behaviour, to them, is the outcome of individual processes, such as motivation, personality, attitudes, etc. Others take a more sociological or broader approach. Indeed, Emil Durkheim, one of the founding fathers of sociology, maintained that large groups of people act with a single mind, which he called “groupmind”, or a collective consciousness. Though the term groupmind is rarely used today, the idea is true: groups, although a collection of individuals, possess something more than individuals and members tend to act in conformity.

This debate between the social and the individualistic approach is, for our purposes, academic. What the supervisor should be aware of is that behaviour is influenced both by social and personal factors. In understanding group behaviour, it is not simply a matter of looking at individual characteristics, such as motivation or personality, but rather of understanding these characteristics in a group setting. In other words, individuals behave differently in groups. The term "group dynamics" is meant to denote that groups are something more than a collection of individuals, and that it is important to understand the processes that underlie groups. Dynamics means that such processes are in a constant flux.

UNDERSTANDING GROUPS

The following section is an account of group behaviour under these main headings:

- Group Development
- Group Cohesiveness
- Group Effectiveness
- Group Structure
- Group Roles
- Group Status.

Group Development

An American researcher, Bruce Tuckman (1965), argues that groups move through five main stages of development from beginning (forming) to end (adjourning) (see Table 12.1). Tuckman's model suggests that group effectiveness is a slow and sequential development. In other words, a high-performing group does not emerge overnight. This is because it takes time for people to familiarise themselves with each other and to learn what is expected of them in the group. Tuckman calls this familiarity the process of norming. As, over the course of time, these issues are sorted out and conflict is resolved, the group becomes productive (performing). Eventually, the group dissolves, usually after the objective is achieved. There is an important lesson in this for supervisors. They have to be aware that, initially, groups go through a lot of conflict. It is only over time that this conflict is resolved and that, eventually, the group performs to its expected level.

TABLE 12.1: FIVE STAGES OF GROUP DEVELOPMENT

Stage 1 — Forming	This stage is characterised by early interaction, along with much ambiguity as to what the group is and will be. In time, this gives rise to growing interdependence of group members on each other and, finally, attempts to build a group.
Stage 2 — Storming	From early on, groups experience conflict. This conflict is often the result of incompatibility of group members. At this stage, members tend to react to each other with negative comments, often criticising and questioning other members' actions, adding further to the tension within the group.
Stage 3 — Norming	Cohesiveness is built up as bonds begin to form between members. At this stage, the group agrees on norms or standards of behaviour, largely unwritten, which regulate their behaviour towards each other.
Stage 4 — Performing	At this stage the group begins to achieve the job it was set up to do. Conflict is minimal and the group members work closely together to achieve harmony.
Stage 5 — Adjourning	When the task is completely finished, the group is finally dissolved. Sometimes this is planned, other times, spontaneous. If spontaneous, dissolution may come as a surprise to group members.

If there is any criticism of Tuckman's model it is that groups do not ordinarily go through such readily defined stages. Moreover, not all groups die off. Others go through various cycles, ups and downs, without developing smoothly. Still others develop in fits and bursts. That is, the group may revert to an earlier stage or pass through the various stages out of sequence. Tuckman is correct to point out, however, that group development is a process.

Ainger et al. (1995, p. 158) have adopted the ideas of Tuckman into a more workable model (see Table 12.2). Supervisors should be aware that in order to bring a group or team to the final stage of the empowerment level, an organisation has to make a considerable investment in training, as well as decentralise authority so that the group functions with a high degree of autonomy. The idea of autonomous (or self-directed) work teams is returned to in Chapter 17 on teamwork.

TABLE 12.2: GROUP LEVELS

Survival Level	This is characterised by late deliveries; poor quality; long lead-time cycle; poor relationships with customers and/or suppliers; poor teamwork, ownership and initiative; unclear strategy and focus.
Reactive Level	There is some response to priorities such as customers and products; however, there also exist islands of conflicting groups or departments; isolated, conflicting systems and processes; and several strategies.
Directive Level	At this level, strategy is determined; priorities and goals are established; communications are promoted; conflict is brought out into the open; and "hit squads" are created.
Proactive Level	Squads now become teams; people continue to set goals and seek approval for initiatives; integration is becoming the norm; customer and supplier focus is paramount; knowing your customer becomes a culture.
Empowerment Level	We now find shortened chains of command; greater trust and responsibility; the elimination of non-value-added activities; and a secure, proud culture.

Source: Ainger et al. (1995).

Group Cohesiveness

Group cohesiveness refers to the attachment members have to each other and to the group as a whole. Group cohesiveness is an important determinant of how well groups perform. A very cohesive group, for example, will demonstrate strong attachment to group goals and, generally speaking, will be productive. A group which lacks cohesiveness, on the other hand, is less likely to be effective, partly because its members cannot work well together.

Cohesiveness can be defined both from an individual and a group perspective. The former refers to a particular individual's attachment to the group, and the latter refers to the overall attachment of members to the group. Formal groups tend to be more cohesive and work groups still more so. Their proximity and time spent together, along with their common interest in their job, usually, though not always, ensure that work groups develop a strong cohesiveness. Failure to develop such will, of course, hamper a supervisor's efforts to lead and direct a group.

Cohesiveness alone does not ensure effectiveness since group members may be socially cohesive but lack something else. This something else usually comes from individual characteristics. Group effectiveness, as will be explained, depends on the motivation of people to work well within groups, and the rewards, social and monetary, that individuals associate with group membership.

There is an important lesson for supervisors in this. Research shows that members of a cohesive group tend to be more satisfied and content at work. In addition, they work better together, hence are more productive. Another way of putting this is that the group provides security to the individual who, in turn, is motivated to work harder. Therefore, it is imperative that supervisors as part of their managerial responsibility build a cohesive team.

Cole (1993, p. 55) lists the factors which affect the cohesiveness of groups as follows:

- Similarity of work
- Physical proximity in the workplace
- The work-flow system and structure of tasks
- Group size (smaller rather than larger)
- Threats from outside
- The prospect of rewards
- Leadership style of management
- Common social factors (age, race, social status, etc.).

Group Effectiveness

As noted earlier, groups are formed for two broad reasons: to achieve organisational goals and to satisfy people's needs, particularly the need to belong. Effectiveness should be examined along both lines. The organisation's concern with group effectiveness depends on what type of business it is involved in. Manufacturing firms are primarily concerned with maintaining and improving high levels of productivity. Service firms, by contrast, are concerned with the quality of the service provided. There are other goals, such as controlling costs and staying within budget, improving sales, growth, etc., which are important, too, and should not be omitted. Finally, within firms there are departments which provide services, and others which build products. Therefore, group effectiveness is dependent on what the group does and what its aim is. Group effectiveness will be defined here in broad terms as meaning how well a group performs in meeting its objective.

Employees also have an interest in how groups perform. However, their interests are different from organisational ones. These interests include such needs as personal satisfaction, both with the group itself and with other group members, and the opportunity for self-fulfilment and self-definition. This is not to say, however, that employees lack interest in production issues. Indeed, most, if not all, employees do care that firms and, in particular, their department does well. Rather, it is to say that employees are primarily interested in groups from their own perspective.

A group is most effective when the goals of individual members are in congruence with organisational goals. The modern term for this is teamwork or more specifically team spirit. Team spirit refers to the ability of the leader in a group to obtain the commitment of their team to achieving the task. High team spirit will make for a more effective group. Low team spirit makes for a poor group. Team spirit is not entirely an outcome of how well group members interact, but also of the quality of the leadership of that group. As a leader of a group, a supervisor can positively affect the performance of that group.

Group Structure

An important characteristic of groups is that they have structure. Structure refers to the underlying pattern of stable relationships among group members. Without such structure, contained in its rules, standards and norms of behaviour, and roles, the group will soon decay. Structure thus gives a group a sense of protection from the outside, as well as providing solidarity and comfort on the inside.

Tuckman's (1965) model of group development, discussed earlier, used the term "norms" to describe standards. In work, groups develop various rules, procedures and standards of behaviour, some of them unwritten, to regulate their own behaviour. These may include certain standards regarding, say, tea breaks or cleaning up one's work area. These standards are usually in addition to company rules or, alternatively, act as a substitute for, or are contrary to, company policy. Even informal groups have structure. Indeed, such informal groups, over the course of time, have a tendency to become structured or more formal in nature on the basis of the status and power of individuals.

It is preferable that the norms of a work group be compatible with the official rules or company policy. However, this need not always be the case. Often, employees develop their own rules which regulate, in many instances more effectively, the behaviour of the group. For example, employees may have strict rules on who cleans up and does preventative maintenance which actually make for a better work environment and productivity. A supervisor should be concerned with informal rules only to the extent they are counter-productive.

Norms, both written and unwritten, should not be too rigid. A work group needs to change with time. This is certainly the case in today's competitive and global world. For example, employees are retrained and asked to rotate between work stations. Similarly, with new teams in the workplace, often the role of team leader is rotated. In all, this gives rise to the need for flexibility or, in short, less structure. The effective supervisor needs to know when to apply rules, and when not to. This places increasing demands on one's ability to "read" the situation appropriately. The days are almost gone when one could simply follow a rule book.

Group Roles

One person's relationship to another in a group is typically defined in terms of roles. A supervisor, for example, is expected to be a leader, a manager, a motivator, a problem-solver, a decision-maker, etc. All are roles and the competent supervisor can move easily from one role to another.

A distinction is made between task and socio-emotional roles. The former refer to roles which are necessary to achieve a particular task, hence the name. The latter refer to roles which satisfy the emotional needs of a particular group. For example, leaders may be motivators, in part, due to their charisma. Task roles, not surprisingly, are more easily defined. A person at work may be a driver, or a machine operator, who performs that particular task. Socio-emotional roles are much less distinguishable. Within a group someone emerges who, unofficially, is the spokesperson, or the compromiser, or the joker, etc. Both task and socio-emotional roles emerge in groups because, typically, no one person alone can perform all roles. Very often, work has to be delegated, either because the supervisor lacks the technical competence or the time or energy to perform the task. Roles, therefore, are instrumental in helping a group achieve its objectives. Moreover, they help to solidify a group, as well as ensuring that each individual contributes their best.

A supervisor should be aware of the problems that are caused by roles. Among the problems are:

- Role conflict
- Role overload
- Role underload
- Role ambiguity.

Role conflict occurs when roles conflict with each other or overlap. Some people may perform many roles, some of which are in conflict with each other. This is called intra-role conflict. Similarly, two people may play the same role in conflict with each other. This is referred to as inter-role conflict. Role overload and role underload occur either because one's job has too many (overload) or too few (underload) requirements. For example, individuals may be overqualified for a job, with little to challenge them. Alternatively, a person may be in a position of authority, yet lack the capabilities or the time to perform the job satisfactorily. Role ambiguity refers to instances where roles are not clearly defined. It tends to occur most frequently for new positions. By contrast, a role that is well-established usually has come to mean predetermined behaviour.

Group Status

Status differentiation refers to the way in which individuals acquire status or authority in groups. Research shows, for example, that over the course of time some group members are afforded status which stands them apart from others. There are a number of different views on how status is given to groups. Some suggest that external credentials are most important. Others see personal attributes as significant. For example, research clearly shows that groups have a tendency to give leadership to people with the most qualifications (a doctor on a committee tends to chair) or to the person who is the most vocal. For informal groups, power and persuasiveness tend to be the defining characteristics of the person who emerges as the leader or dominant character in the group.

There is much research to suggest that if people wish to gain power and influence over others, they assume behaviour that conveys that message. Similarly, people who expect to be dominated will equally show preference for it. The supervisor has to work towards achieving an egalitarian group which treats all members equally. The supervisor should make sure that new employees are accepted into the group. Similarly, the supervisor should be sure not to be cut off from the group. Such exclusionary tactics may make it difficult for supervisors to influence their employees to higher performance.

CHAPTER SUMMARY

Individuals have personalities which are unique; as the Chinese say, out of ten fingers, nine are different. However, personality is conditioned by a range of social factors and, in particular, by participation in groups. Therefore, people are essentially the product of their personality and of the social groups which they grow up in and belong to. There is much in an individual's behaviour that is common to most people, largely because individuals model their behaviour on norms within the groups they are members of.

Because of this interplay between personality and social factors, a supervisor needs to be aware of the processes at work in a group. With this knowledge, a supervisor can influence, in a positive way, group behaviour. That means removing obstacles and providing incentives that lead to better group performance. Furthermore, they have to channel individual creativity and initiative towards the attainment of group objectives. Finally, the supervisor builds the right atmosphere for good working relationships between all group members in part by giving workers the authority and responsibility necessary to achieve agreed goals.

References and Further Reading

Ainger, A., Kaura R. & R. Ennals (1995) *Executive Guide to Business Success through Human-Centred Systems*, London: Springer.

Bennett, R. (1994) *Personal Effectiveness*, second edition, London: Kogan Page, chapter 6.

Betts, P.W. (1993) *Supervisory Management*, London: Pitman, chapter 5.

Cole, G.A. (1993) *Management: Theory and Practice*, fourth edition, London: DP Publications, p. 55.

Handy, C. (1993) *Understanding Organizations*, fourth edition, London: Penguin, pp. 150-1.

Lewin, K. (1936) *Principles of Topological Psychology*, New York: McGraw-Hill.

Mosley, D., L. Megginson, P. Pietri (1993) *Supervisory Management: The Art of Empowering and Developing People*, third edition, Cincinnati, OH: South-Western, chapter 7.

Simmel, G. (1902) "The Number of Members as Determining the Sociological Form of the Group", *American Journal of Sociology*, 8, 1-46, pp. 158-96.

Tuckman, B.W. (1965) "Development Sequences in Small Groups", *Psychological Bulletin*, 63, p. 387.

Chapter 13

THE SUPERVISOR AS MOTIVATOR

THE OBJECTIVE OF THIS CHAPTER

Motivation refers to the inner drive of people. It is commonly referred to as the "why" of behaviour. That is, it asks the question "why do people act the way they do?" From a work perspective, it is important to know why some people work harder than others; why some people are motivated to do something, and others not; and why one factor, such as pay, functions as a motivator for one person and not for another. These questions are particularly important for supervisors. They are in charge of a group and are responsible for the output of the group. To obtain the maximum out of that group, people's needs, both individual and collective, have to be addressed. Failure to meet these needs will result in dissatisfaction, and, ultimately, low productivity. Figure 13.1 contrasts the characteristics of motivated and a demotivated staff. It goes without saying that the effective supervisor should aim for the former.

The following theories of motivation will also be examined in this chapter:

- Elton Mayo and the Hawthorne Studies
- Abraham Maslow and his needs theory
- Douglas McGregor's Theory X/Theory Y
- Frederick Herzberg and his Motivation–Hygiene Theory.

These approaches, while representing only a fraction of the work that has been conducted on motivation, constitute the main theory in this field. It should be stated that there is no magical solution to motivation. However, the supervisor gains by an awareness of the different approaches, theoretical and practical, to motivation.

FIGURE 13.1: MOTIVATION AND DEMOTIVATION

Characteristics of a highly motivated staff:

- Productivity and work morale is high
- People show enthusiasm for work
- There is co-operation and a willingness to accept greater responsibility
- Change is introduced more easily and with greater success

A demotivated workforce is noted for:

- Unwillingness to co-operate or participate in new programmes
- A careless attitude to the job
- Absenteeism and high turnover
- High number of grievances
- Poor quality/service, and low productivity.

THE NATURE OF WORK

The sociologist Karl Marx argued that work means more than just getting a wage at the end of the week. Indeed, as Maslow (1943), an American psychologist whose work is examined later, was to argue, work provides the mechanism to achieve self-fulfilment or purpose in life. Unlike Maslow though, Marx was adamant that, by fragmenting work, capitalism subverts the ability of people to achieve this self-fulfilment. Instead, the result is alienation or the dehumanisation of work.

Alienation is an important concept for the supervisor to understand. It refers to the loss of the meaning of work that results from the distancing of workers from their output. There is a two-fold process in operation here. Firstly, as noted, work is divided into fairly minor and repetitive tasks. Secondly, the workers must work for someone, under their supervision, thus losing further control. Reference is often made to the assembly line worker who performs a repetitive task, often lasting less than a minute, in some cases no more than a few seconds. Individuals have no "feel" for the final product and often cannot grasp the totality of the manufacturing process. As a result, they become alienated or separated from the process of work. The meaning of work is thus changed: instead of self-fulfilment, boredom, frustration and, worse still, (from an employer's perspective) low productivity is the result. Means and methods of supervision along with an incentive wage system are introduced to ensure that the worker maintains a consistently high level of productivity. The individual receives in return wages but this only partly compensates for the drudgery of work.[1]

Marx faulted capitalism for alienation: the endless search for profit requires business owners to control workers largely by fragmenting work and de-skilling workers. Today, it is believed that it is technology rather than capitalists themselves which causes alienation. The invention of better machines, and better ways of doing things, have pushed concern for the individual further and further into the background. Indeed, in Chapter 16, one will learn about new production methods, such as Just-in-Time production and Total Quality Management, which are designed to make organisations more productive. While they include the potential for improving the lot of the worker, it is also possible that these new work strategies may result in increased demands on people. Thus instead of the cliché, "work smarter, not harder", the reality of modern working life for many appears to be "work smarter, work harder". Ireland, in recent years, has experienced a great number of rationalising programmes which have changed the quality of work life, many would say, for the worse. As noted earlier, in research conducted for this book, many supervisors pointed out that they were under greater pressure from the intensity of work, and wages were less of a motivation to work.

A number of observations can be made about work. First, as Marx correctly pointed out, work has a meaning, but industrialisation has distorted that meaning. Second, the meaning of work for an individual is not entirely job-determined. Rather, a person's life outside work is equally, if not more, important. In this

---

[1]For a full account of the division of labour, see Chapter 3, on Frederick Taylor, and Chapter 16 on world class manufacturing.

way, material rewards can (and do) compensate for the drudgery of work. Thirdly, work is as much a social as an individual activity. Thus, in understanding motivation it is important to consider not just the individuals but also the social context in which they work. Finally, it can be said that the meaning of work for an individual can be any of the following:

- Work that leads to self-fulfilment
- Work that is neither satisfying nor annoying
- Work that is experienced as painful drudgery.

The remainder of this chapter deals with management writings on the subject of motivation. Almost all seem to accept the central Marxist view that work has important implications for people, but that this has been changed, perhaps irreversibly, by industrialisation. However, all theories suggest ways in which work can be improved to make it more meaningful, more enjoyable and therefore more productive. For the supervisor, or student of management, it is important to be aware of these theories. However, it should be clearly understood that there is no consensus on what is the best motivator; rather, a range of factors, some psychological, some social, come to bear on the issue.

THE HAWTHORNE STUDIES

The Hawthorne studies were a set of experiments carried out at the Western Electric Plant in Hawthorne, just west of Chicago, from 1924 to 1936 (see Figure 13.2). The studies themselves were not particularly important. In point of fact, the research was poorly conducted and the proper explanations came long after the research was finished. However, the findings that people like to work in groups rather than alone, and that employees have needs other than wages which have to be addressed, were extremely important. It is for this reason that the Hawthorne studies and the school they gave rise to, the Human Relations School, are so widely quoted.

The studies were initially begun by the company itself. It was assumed that increased lighting would lead to improvements in productivity. The tests found no direct relationship between the two. A select group of employees was singled out, broken into two sub-groups, a control and a test group, and told they formed part of a research group. When lighting was altered, either increased or decreased, for the test group, productivity rose. More strange still was the fact that productivity rose in the control group despite no change in the intensity of the lighting.

The researchers were puzzled. Elton Mayo, an Australian, based at Harvard, was brought in to explain the results. He continued on the research much along the lines the company had been pursuing. Workers, all female, were split into two groups. Alterations in their working conditions were made every few weeks. This included changing rest periods, length of work day, etc. The women were observed by the researchers who constantly sought feedback from them. Productivity consistently rose. The various stages of the research are summarised in Figure 13.2.

Though the research set out to measure the effect of working conditions on productivity, the explanation for productivity improvement had more do to social reasons. When supervised, which is what the researchers were doing, people worked harder. Further, employees became more productive because they felt special. They had been singled out for the experiment and wanted to do a good job. More importantly, the researchers sought feedback from the women, allowing them to have input into the research to the point of choosing their own working conditions as well as allowing them every opportunity to air dissent. The research had unintentionally produced a cohesive work group.

From a research perspective, this behaviour is now called the "Hawthorne effect". It refers to why the research was poorly conducted. That is, if people are aware that they are being studied, and particularly if they have input into the design of the research, they tend to alter their behaviour and thus produce artificial results. From the perspective of motivating people to work, the Hawthorne studies show that human factors are as important as pay and physical conditions. People need to work in groups, feeling part of them and working within them. Moreover, it mattered little whether it was a formal or an informal group, as long as a person belonged to that group. Thus, work or rather levels of productivity are not determined as much by physical characteristics, as Taylor and his followers had argued, as by group dynamics. By default, therefore, the Hawthorne studies, which began as a study of productivity, became years later a study of social relationships at work.

FIGURE 13.2: THE STAGES OF THE HAWTHORNE STUDIES

Company Stage: (1924-1927). Begun by the company itself with the division of a select group of workers into two groups: a test and a control group. Only the latter experienced a change in lighting. Despite such different treatment, productivity increases of similar dimensions were experienced by both groups. Further variations in light brought similar increases in productivity. Baffled by the results, the company called in the Harvard researchers.

Relay Assembly Test Stage: (1927-1929). The Harvard researchers isolated six female workers in the relay assembly section. In consultation with the women, a series of changes in working hours were made (altering rest periods, lunch breaks, etc.). Almost regardless of the specific type of change, productivity rose.

Interview Stage: (1928-1930). In order to ascertain employee attitudes towards working conditions, supervisors conducted a series of interviews with employees. Designed as structured interviews to last about 30 minutes, interviews normally stretched to over an hour and involved much discussion between the interviewer and the interviewee. In all, some 20,000 employees were interviewed.

Bank Wiring Observation Room Stage: (1932). Similar to the second stage, 14 employees, in this case all male, were isolated and observed over a period of six months. No changes were made in their working conditions. The researchers found that the men formed into an informal group that offered a measure of protection against the researchers.

Counselling Stage (1936). Drawing on experiences of the earlier research, this part of the research involving sitting with employees and, in the context of counselling interviews, soliciting their views on working conditions.

The Hawthorne Studies in Perspective

The Hawthorne studies have to be placed alongside Taylor and his principles of Scientific Management (discussed in Chapter 3) to comprehend fully their significance. By Taylor's reasoning, employees were inherently lazy, and had to be paid an incentive rate to ensure high productivity. Worse still, in groups employees loitered. To Taylor, the solution to the latter, which he termed soldiering, was to fragment work and stress close supervision. Taylor thus focused on work, ignoring, for the most part, the employee. The human relations approach was the opposite: a focus on the employee not on the work.

The Hawthorne studies have important implications for the organisation of work in firms. Supervisors and managers need to be aware of social needs and cater for them if employees are to be productive. The view that man is a social animal, and the Human Relations School that held it, has dominated thinking in the management field. A number of different writers, all writing from a similar perspective, argue differently on the subject of motivation. All have focused on the social side of work, playing down the productive element. These various perspectives are examined next.

MASLOW AND HIS HIERARCHY OF NEEDS

According to Maslow (1943), people are motivated by the desire to satisfy needs which when grouped together can be listed in hierarchical form (see Figure 13.3). Furthermore, people tend to satisfy their needs systematically, starting at the bottom with the physiological needs and then moving slowly up the hierarchy as each need is satisfied. People always have needs so that when one need is fulfilled, another takes it place.

Maslow's views can be listed as follows:

- Unless a particular group of needs is satisfied, a person's behaviour will be dominated by it and won't progress to the next set of needs.
- It is possible for a person to move down the hierarchy. Someone at level 3 can revert to level 2 if circumstances change, for example, if their job security is seriously threatened.

- Once a need has been satisfied, it no longer affects behaviour.
- Needs that remain unfilled will dominate a person's behaviour.

FIGURE 13.3: MASLOW'S HIERARCHY OF NEEDS

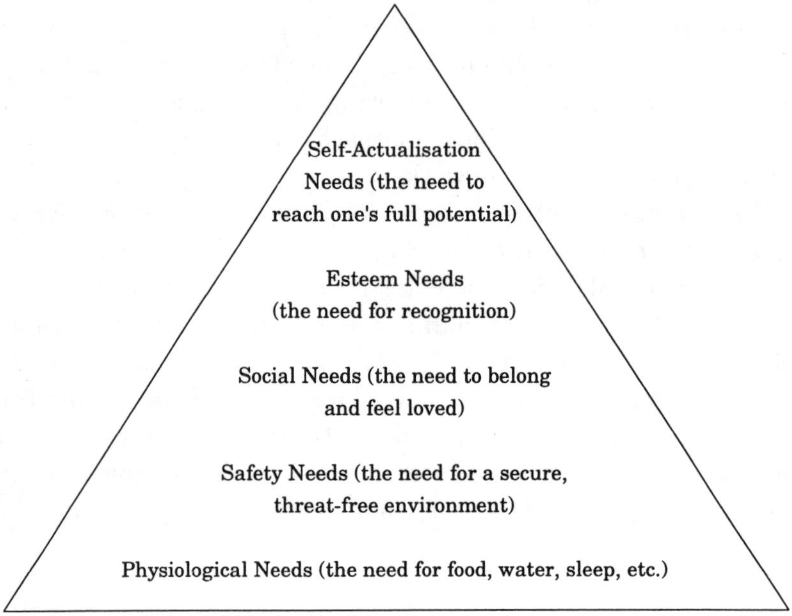

The Usefulness of Maslow's Hierarchical Needs

The Maslow approach, perhaps because of its simplicity and breadth if not also its optimistic view of human behaviour, has been very influential in management. For the supervisor, it points to the particular importance of satisfying basic needs first. Thus, employees' immediate or lower needs are wages, which allow them to provide food and shelter for themselves and their families. Once they are satisfied with their wages, job security becomes important. Once content with wages and job security, personal growth, or self-actualisation in Maslow's terms, takes precedence. Second, Maslow's view indicates that needs are dynamic and individualistic. Research has shown this to be the case. Needs differ according to the individual and will vary from time to time. The supervisor has to be aware of such changes and be responsive to them. Third, to avoid apathy, which finally results when needs are unfulfilled, supervisors must be able to implement the right action at the right time.

Another feature of the Maslow approach is to link each group of needs with a motivator, as follows:

Need	Motivator
Self-actualisation	Personal growth, learning, new skills, the exercise of responsibility
Esteem	Promotion, support, praise, recognition
Social	Friendly co-workers, work groups, sports groups
Safety	Job security, safe working conditions, fair treatment, pension scheme
Physiological	Salary, good working conditions, rest breaks

Despite its popularity, Maslow's notion of hierarchical needs is subject to much criticism. In the first instance, it is too simple to explain a very complex issue. There are many interrelated factors which affect a person's motivation to work, and these factors are difficult to separate. Further, motivators are not always hierarchical and vary from individual to individual, and from situation to situation. Finally, the theory can be difficult to apply to work situations and it lacks scientific evidence.

McGREGOR'S THEORY X AND THEORY Y

In his book *The Human Side of the Enterprise*, Douglas McGregor (1960), also an American, argues that managers have two contrasting views of employees. One he called Theory X, the other, Theory Y (see Figure 13.4). Theory X regards employees as being naturally lazy, poorly motivated to work and requiring discipline and control. It is roughly comparable to the view expressed by Scientific Management, or Taylorism, namely the assumption that the more individuals are paid, the harder they work. It was management's job therefore to motivate employees to work. This is achieved by focusing on the task that needs to be done, rather than the people, and by using a mixture of persuasion, rewarding, and discipline.

FIGURE 13.4: MCGREGOR'S THEORY X/THEORY Y

Assumptions of a Theory X Supervisor	**Assumptions of a Theory Y Supervisor**
1. People have a natural dislike for work and work only because they have to.	1. People want to work and have the potential to take pleasure from it
2. Disliking work, people have to be forced to work	2. To achieve self-fulfilment in life, people need to work
3. Authority is necessary in work because without it people would not work	3. People want responsibility and want to do a good job
4. Money is the primary motivator in work	4. Self-discipline is the most effective form of control.

The second view is more positive. Workers are viewed as wanting to work. Liking work they do not have to be controlled, coerced or disciplined. They will not only accept but also seek responsibility and use skill, ingenuity and hard work to better themselves. Hence, the manager does not necessarily motivate people but creates the conditions which are conducive to higher performance. These are the assumptions of Theory Y. It is closely related to the traditional view that it is only through work that people reach their full potential, or what Maslow refers to as self-actualisation. According to McGregor, Theory Y is a more accurate view of people, though the Theory X view can dominate, particularly in large organisations.

These labels, Theory X and Theory Y, which have become very popular in the US, are generally applied to describe an individual's style of management. As noted, part of the satisfaction derived by employees depend on their relationship with their immediate supervisor. This relationship, in turn, is dependent on the view the supervisor has of people. Does the supervisor have a positive attitude to people, or do they consider subordinates to be lazy and needing supervision? According to McGregor, when managers or supervisors have a Theory X view of people as lazy and unwilling to work, this tends to carry over to the people being supervised or managed. That is, these employees will respond as if they dislike work and thus welcome close supervision. Supervisors who follow the Theory X tend to be coercive and intimidating. They come across as authoritarian figures in the way they give orders and the fact that they rarely allow any input from employees into decision-making. Such a style, McGregor argues, is not conducive to good management as it tends to turn employees away from their work, which they perform grudgingly and well below par. In other words, employees only perform to the level expected of them, which is typically not much.

A Theory Y Supervisor

A Theory Y supervisor is likely to be fair and open, soliciting employees' opinions and views before taking a course of action. This way, employees have the best chance to reach their full potential in work. The end result is likely be a more satisfied and productive workforce. Theory Y does have some disadvantages, however. It places an onus on the supervisor to be open-minded and democratic which demands certain interpersonal skills. Moreover, it is time-consuming, as jobs typically take longer to accomplish. Finally, this view has to be communicated to employees and supervisors must be consistent in their management style.

HERZBERG'S MOTIVATION–HYGIENE THEORY

Thus far, motivation has been examined from the perspective of needs and styles. However, neither specify what factors actually motivate people to work. Another American, Frederick Herzberg (1967), provided a different view of motivation by concentrating on job satisfaction. That is, Herzberg asks, "what aspect of a person's job satisfies them and what aspect dissatisfies?"

To answer this question, Herzberg interviewed 200 engineers and accountants at a variety of firms in the Pittsburgh, Pennsylvania area. They were asked to describe what was satisfactory and what was unsatisfactory about their jobs. From this, Herzberg deduced that certain factors tended to lead to job satisfaction, while others led to dissatisfaction. He then classified the answers into two categories: one he termed motivators or satisfiers, the other, hygiene factors or dissatisfiers. The following are motivators:

- Achievement
- Recognition
- Work itself
- Responsibility
- Advancement
- Growth.

These motivators cause job satisfaction, and are intrinsic to the job. Hygiene factors, that, is those factors which dissatisfy and are extrinsic to the job, are as follows:

- Company policy and administration
- Supervision
- Relationship with supervisor
- Work conditions
- Salary
- Relationships with peers
- Personal life
- Relationship with subordinates
- Status
- Security.

When hygiene factors are taken care of — for example, if salary is adequate— the employee will experience little or no dissatisfaction. However, positive motivation will not result. Thus, while hygiene factors satisfy, in Maslow's terms, the physiological and safety needs, motivators are primarily upper-level needs, such as esteem and self-actualisation. Therefore, in order to motivate someone whose pay is adequate, an organisation has to pay attention to the set of factors Herzberg listed as motivators, namely, achievement, recognition, work etc. The analogy Herzberg makes is to health. Proper food will prevent disease, but not necessarily get one fit. For that, one must exercise. Hygiene factors, therefore, are like healthy food; they prevent dissatisfaction but to motivate one needs something more.

The relationship between the motivators and hygiene factors is complex. Motivators, if present, tend to lead to satisfaction, but if absent do not, necessarily, dissatisfy. Hygiene factors, if present, prevent dissatisfaction but do not, necessarily, result in increased job satisfaction. In short, what satisfies does not necessarily dissatisfy, what dissatisfies does not necessary satisfy. Take pay as an example. It is, according to Herzberg, a hygiene factor. As such, it acts merely to prevent dissatisfaction. Thus, if an individual is paid a sufficient wage, the salary alone will not motivate them. Rather, such an individual requires something else in their job, such as a high likelihood of promotion, or the opportunity for personal growth. If, on the other hand, a person is in low wage employment, pay is likely to cause dissatisfaction. That person is liable to search for another job with better pay.

It can be argued that Taylor was thinking very much in terms of hygiene factors (pay and supervision); similarly Mayo stressed hygiene factors, namely interpersonal relations. Herzberg's approach to motivation is more complex, and thus more realistic. Indeed, Herzberg alludes to the fact that much of what supervisors and managers believed for years motivated people, in reality just alleviated dissatisfaction rather than motivating.

Numerous studies in the US have indicated that often what managers and supervisors believe are motivators, and what employees themselves believe, are completely different. Managers have a tendency to think that pay is a primary motivator. Surveys conducted among employees, however, tend to indicate more qualitative issues, such as fair treatment and a sense of belonging and encouragement, as important to them. This finding has important implications for supervisors. Mosley et al. (1993, p. 236) argue:

What all this means is that employees today expect to be treated fairly by their supervisors. They expect decent working conditions and pay comparable to that of people doing similar work in other firms. They expect company policies to be consistently and equitably applied to all employees. When these expectations are not realised, employees are de-motivated. This condition is usually reflected in inefficiency and a high turnover rate. But fulfilling these expectations does not motivate employees.

Another value of the Herzberg analysis is to classify motivators in terms of intrinsic and extrinsic factors (Figure 13.5). Intrinsic factors relate to things which individuals generally can control themselves. This includes the job itself, and the feelings that an individual has about their job. Factors which lie outside the control of an individual are termed extrinsic factors, and include such factors as the rewards given to the job and the style of management.

FIGURE 13.5: INTRINSIC AND EXTRINSIC MOTIVATORS

Intrinsic Factors	**Extrinsic factors**
Freedom to choose how to do the job	Physical working conditions
Recognition for work well done	Relations with colleagues
Increased responsibility	Relations with the manager
The opportunity to demonstrate personal abilities	Rate of pay
Chances of promotion	Climate of industrial relations
Variety in work	Style of management
Attention to ideas and suggestions for improvements	Hours of work
Praise	Perceived job security

Herzberg's ideas, like McGregor's, have become very popular in management. Also, the results have stood well against research. In fact, Herzberg (1987) himself later interviewed both manual and clerical groups, and produced the same results. Furthermore, he goes beyond Maslow and McGregor and actually lists the factors which satisfy and dissatisfy.

THE SUPERVISOR AND MOTIVATION

Supervisors' concern with motivation is not entirely individual. Rather, they have to create an atmosphere in the work unit which is conducive to getting the job done. Evans (1995, p. 174) makes clear this point:

> Motivation is not a question . . . of "being nice" to your staff; indeed there are time when a firm approach is better. It is a question of creating a total environment at work where employees work willingly to future the organisation's interest because they feel at the same time they are furthering their own interests.

Supervisors therefore do not motivate people, but rather, ideally, create the conditions which are conducive to higher performance. Further, only some of these "conditions" will be under the control of the supervisor. For a start, supervisors don't always have choice in terms of the staff they supervise. Similarly, factors like technology, pay and organisational culture will be determined by the organisation itself, while others, such as individual commitment and values, may be intrinsic to the individual. Supervisors need to be aware of these limits and aim to make their contribution where it is possible to do so. The following section provides some suggestions on how to motivate employees.

Specific Ways of Improving Motivation

Despite much having been written about the subject, there are no simple rules or straightforward solutions to motivating people. Research shows the following though:

- Employee motives vary and over time employees learn new motives
- Different employees respond differently to different stimuli, hence what motivates one person may not another

- Employee motives are influenced by a number of broad factors, including employee personal characteristics (personality, experience, personal ability, etc.), the organisation (e.g. culture and style of management) and the job itself (e.g. degree of task specialisation and social interaction).

With that in mind, some practical tips can be suggested. It is up to supervisors to apply them as they see fit.

The first is to exercise authority cautiously. In principle, supervisors must be given enough authority to be able to perform their jobs adequately. They, in turn, must give their own employees the authority necessary to carry out their jobs. When employees are given both the freedom and the power to do their jobs properly, they typically are motivated to work harder, and are more content in doing so. This is not the case for all employees, however. Some people prefer not to have to make decisions, but rather are content just to perform the task that is assigned to them. This happens for only a minority of people. As noted earlier, it is imperative for supervisors to get to know all of their employees' needs and to be attentive to them.

The second is to increase what is required of the individual in the job. For example, supervisors should encourage, if not mandate, job rotation. This means that individuals, as part of a work group, will be expected to share out work, performing each other's job, preferably on a regular basis. As noted above, employees should have the authority to make decisions on their own, especially routine decisions. This may include decisions about allocating work, what work gets done first, and so on. People are well capable of making decisions which traditionally were the preserve of the supervisor.

Taking the first two points together, the supervisor should attempt to design or redesign the job to give employees more freedom, responsibility and variety in their position. Moreover, a job should test the ability of the holder, offering a challenge and bringing out the best in them. Thus, no matter how rigid a job, there is room for flexibility. Even in assembly lines, supervisors can grant people more freedom and responsibility without losing control. We have seen many examples in recent years, such as flexitime or job sharing, which have given employees, including supervisors, more freedom and responsibility in their jobs. By and large, these initiatives have been welcomed by employees and have been a success in most organisations.

Third, supervisors should encourage participation where possible. Again this follows the idea of general supervision, namely that employees should be kept informed at all times of impending change, and consulted before any such change is made. Little is lost and much is gained when the supervisor invites submissions from employees and is open and encouraging of their ideas. As pointed out, supervisors who are trusting of employees will have that trust reciprocated. Their job will be easier since less time will need to be spent on direct supervision of employees, with more time available for the other, more demanding aspects of one's job.

Fourth, the supervisor should encourage employees to do their best and praise the employee when work is done according to plan. Disciplinary measures, by contrast, should be exercised lightly and only when absolutely necessary. Do not assume that pay is the employee's primary motivator. Employees, by and large, like to know when they are doing a good job and one of the best forms of encouragement is when a supervisor congratulates an employee on a job well done. This is one of the most consistent findings of research in the area of motivation, namely that pay (for most, though not all, people) is a limited motivator and that praise, remarkably inexpensive, is a very important one.

Finally, the employee should have every opportunity to progress. That means making training available and encouraging the employee to avail of any opportunity for advancement. In this day, in particular, there is much pressure on firms to re-skill their employees. A better trained workforce is more suited to the dynamic and competitive business environment of today. Some firms, particularly those in the technical fields, do provide many opportunities, in-house as well as outside the firm, for employees to take courses. Often some form of tuition reimbursement is available. Others, however, provide little in the way of courses or support for education. Regardless of the policy of the organisation, as a supervisor you should encourage employees to further themselves through education. Some employees and managers are of the opinion that employees need only know what is required to do their jobs. This is a false assumption. Rather, people should always strive to better themselves and learn more than what is demanded by a job. Stated in terms of motivation, people should strive for self-fulfilment and to reach their full potential.

Motivating Oneself

Thus far, the supervisor's role in motivating others to work has been examined. Somewhat forgotten in all of this is how the individual supervisor is motivated. As was pointed out in the first chapter, supervisory management is an important management activity yet it is, generally speaking, underrated and ignored. Besides, supervisors are under great pressure to bring about change and to change themselves. Research conducted for this book would indicate that supervisors are working much longer hours, more is demanded of them, and they are finding it difficult to stay abreast of the constant change that is occurring in workplaces today. In interviews some supervisors alluded to the problem of motivating themselves in light of the uncertainly and dynamism of working life in the 1990s.

How then does a supervisor become motivated? First, the supervisor should aim for self-improvement. This can be done in a variety of ways, from taking a course of study, including self-study, or simply trying to be better at one's job. Second, set objectives: this could include long-term objectives, which may have a strong educational bent, and short-term goals. Finally, try to get as much feedback from fellow employees about your style of supervision. There is a new trend in management today called "360-degree appraisal" in which employees appraise their managers (rather than, or in addition to, the other way around). While potentially faddish, such a development indicates the growing expectations of staff, as well the gains that can be made by actively listening to employees. Supervisors, therefore, are well-advised to solicit opinions as to their management style.

CHAPTER SUMMARY

Motivation is about the behaviour of people at work and, as noted earlier, is a complex process. More complex still are the many attempts made to understand and explain what exactly motivates people to work or work harder. The starting point for understanding motivation is the notion that industrialisation has, for some at least, changed the whole meaning of work away from having the potential to be enjoyable and fulfilling to work which appears to be meaningless and painful. It is the negation of work fuelled by technical developments that gave rise to management writings on motivation and the concern that factors — from money to praise — encourage employees to contribute more. Supervisors, these approaches would argue, must be aware of these factors, and take steps to ensure that the factors which are inside their control — such as management style and job design — contribute positively to the employee's sense of satisfaction from work.

References and Further Reading

Bennett, R. (1994) *Managing Activities and Resources*, second edition, London: Kogan Page, chapter 5.

Betts, P.W. (1993) *Supervisory Management*, London: Pitman, chapter 11.

Evans, David (1995) *Supervisory Management*, fourth edition, London: Cassell.

Gunnigle, P. & Flood, P. (1990) *Personnel Management in Ireland: Practice, Trends, Developments*, Dublin: Gill and Macmillan, chapter 5.

Herzberg, F. (1987) "One More Time: How Do You Motivate Employees?", *Harvard Business Review*, September/October.

Herzberg, F., Mausner, B. & Synderman, B. (1967) *The Motivation to Work*, New York: Wiley.

Kelly, G. & R. Armstrong (1991) *20 Training Workshops for Developing Managerial Effectiveness*, Volume 2, Aldershot: Gower.

Maslow, A. (1943) "A Theory of Human Motivation", *Psychological Review*, Vol. 50, no. 4, 1943, pp. 370-396.

McGregor, D. (1960) *The Human Side of Enterprise*, New York: McGraw-Hill.

Mosley, D., L. Megginson, P. Pietri (1993) *Supervisory Management: The Art of Empowering and Developing People*, third edition, Cincinnati, OH: South-Western.

Tiernan, S., Morley, M. & Foley, E. (1996) *Modern Management: Theory and Practice for Irish Students*, Dublin: Gill and Macmillan, chapter 6.

Chapter 14

LEADERSHIP

THE OBJECTIVE OF THIS CHAPTER

Leadership refers to the ability to influence others, their attitudes and their behaviour, towards the achievement of goals. Evans (1995, p. 207) defines it as "the art, skill or process of influencing people to work towards the achievement of group or larger organisational goals".

Leadership implies willingness and co-operation, and is, by definition, a reciprocal process. In other words, leaders lead, people follow. Leadership is not about power. Power refers to the ability of one individual or group to achieve its goals, typically against the wishes of another individual or group. By the same token, leadership is not about controlling people. Control implies coercion and manipulation, in short, power. Leadership is particularly important for supervisors because they are in a position to influence, that is, lead or manage others.

Like motivation, leadership is very much a dynamic process. It goes beyond personality and is closely linked with behaviour. As such, it is influenced by many factors, including the personality of the leader, the behaviour of the group of employees being led or managed, and finally by organisational culture. As with motivation, there is no one way to lead. Rather, much depends on the situation and people concerned. The supervisor benefits from an understanding of the academic writings on leadership and also by attempting to put into practice the insights gained from studying leadership.

After reading and studying this chapter, the reader should have an understanding of:

- What leadership is
- The following theories of leadership: trait, style, action-centred leadership and superleadership.

TYPES OF LEADERS

It is generally accepted that there are various types of leaders including:

- Traditional leaders — leaders by right of birth. Royalty is the most often given example of a traditional leader.
- Charismatic leaders — those who lead by virtue of their charisma, that is, the attractiveness of their personality. Gandhi would be cited an example of a charismatic leader.
- Democratic leaders — those who are elected to their position, such as a politician.
- Situational leaders — those who are leaders by virtue of being in the right place at the right time.
- Appointed leaders — those who take their influence directly from the position they hold.
- Functional leaders — leaders by what they do, rather than by what they are. Managers are said to be functional leaders.

Regardless of the type of leader, leadership implies giving direction to followers. Without direction, there will be uncertainty and a lack of co-ordination.

TRAIT THEORIES

The early or classical management theorists tended to focus on the personal qualities of the leaders or managers. Thus, a good manager was probably an individual (usually male) who was, among other things, intelligent, authoritative, and decisive. These may be seen as innate qualities, that is, traits or attributes individuals are born with, thus giving rise to the false view that leaders were born, not made.

Gender and social class were the two main traits that were confused with good leadership qualities. Men were thought to be better leaders than women; leaders emerged from the upper class, and only by exception from the lower classes. Intelligence similarly was another trait mentioned in this regard: earlier studies indicated that people who were intelligent made good leaders. Finally, the ability to perform a task well, particularly a task which a group sets itself to, was seen as a valuable leadership trait.

The trait approach is subject to much criticism. To begin with, equating leadership with certain personality traits is now considered outdated. More recent research shows no clear correlation between certain traits, such as intelligence, gender, social class, etc., and effective leadership. In fact, there is little agreement as to what, if any, traits are desirable in leadership, or indeed that training can actually improve leadership potential. Furthermore, many of these notions were based on social and sexual biases, and there is no shortage of traits that can be identified with leadership. Finally, leadership involves the ability to motivate more than command and depends as much on followers as the leader.

There is, however, something to be learned from this approach. Leaders who are capable and well-liked do possess certain qualities, among them intelligence, well-roundedness, self-assurance, initiative, etc. Not all of these qualities are innate. Some can be learned and/or improved upon. Table 14.1 compares what are perceived to be positive and negative traits of leaders. The reader should note that such a list is subjective, and leaders have been known to display contradictory traits and vacillate, when the occasion demands, in their style of managing/leading. This list of traits is in no way exhaustive and the reader is welcome to modify it.

The final usefulness of this trait approach is that it recalls the discussion in Chapter 5 of the qualities of a supervisor. Among the qualities often mentioned by senior managers as imperative to the job of supervisory management were decisiveness and a sense of responsibility, self-confidence and a high standard of professional behaviour and accountability.

TABLE 14.1: SOME TRAITS OF LEADERS

Positive Traits	Negative Traits
Intelligent	Authoritative
Able to influence people	Unable to compromise
Likeable	Domineering
Able to empathise with others	Dogmatic
Able to inspire people	Inconsiderate
Well-rounded	Ruthless

STYLE THEORIES

Rather than focus on personal attributes, style theories focus on identifiable behaviour. Styles refer to different approaches (or styles) that managers adopt when managing people. In most cases, theorists proposed extreme positions. McGregor, examined in the previous chapter, is a case in point. The Theory X manager is authoritarian and favours strong disciplinary and control systems; the Theory Y manager, by contrast, appears democratic, open-minded and is sympathetic to employees' needs. Other theorists stress a range of leadership styles.

The following section examines three other style theories, namely:

- Likert's Task and Employee-centred Leadership
- Tannenbaum and Schmidt's Continuum of Leadership Behaviour
- Blake and Mouton's Leadership Grid.

Task and Employee-centred Leadership

Similar to Theory X, task- (or job)-centred leadership[1] is where the supervisor concentrates primarily on completing the job. The job is typically broken down into small elements, and each employee has to perform a set of tasks. The duty of the supervisor is

[1] Rensis Likert coined the terms "job-centred" and "employee-centred". The term task-centred is now favoured over job-centred (see Likert, 1961).

to ensure that each and every employee carries out the task exactly as prescribed. This type of supervision, aside from requiring very close monitoring of staff, may also entail disciplining employees for failing to reach the standard. Rather than being concerned about productivity, an employee-centred supervisor, on the other hand, focuses attention on employees, catering for individual and group needs. The argument is that looking after employees' needs is the best way of ensuring that the department or group reaches its objective.

The terms task- and employee-centred management can be restated in supervisory management terms as close and general supervision. Close supervision is almost a military-style approach to supervision. Orders are given; employees, having little or no input into the decision-making process, have to carry them out, and control measures are rigidly enforced. General supervision entails a more hands-off approach.

Often supervisors don't have the flexibility to impose their own style of management, as factors such as the organisation of work or the culture of the organisation restrict the supervisor's freedom to manage. While this may be so, it cannot be denied that in dealing with people there are usually options. A supervisor should place as much trust as possible in employees, deal with them openly and fairly, and encourage them to use their own initiative. To sum up, an effective supervisor aims to be an employee-centred leader. The terminology — Theory Y, employee-centred, general supervision, and more lately participative and democratic management — is irrelevant. What is more important is that an individual treats people fairly.

CONTINUUM OF LEADERSHIP BEHAVIOUR

Management behaviour, according to two American researchers, Tannenbaum and Schmidt (1973), can be arranged on a continuum with, at one extreme, a supervisor who exercises total authority over employees (by making all decisions personally), and at the other, a supervisor who allows employees considerable freedom (by involving and consulting with them) (see Figure 14.1). The advantage of this approach is that, rather than choosing between two opposing styles — Theory X or Theory Y, task or employee-centred leadership, close or general supervision — a supervisor can choose a point on the continuum which best suits the situation at hand. According to Tannenbaum and Schmidt, the point on the continuum will be affected by consideration of a variety of factors, including the supervisor's personality, the employees who are being supervised, the organisational culture and tradition within the organisation, the task at hand and the pressures of time.

FIGURE 14.1: CONTINUUM OF LEADERSHIP BEHAVIOUR

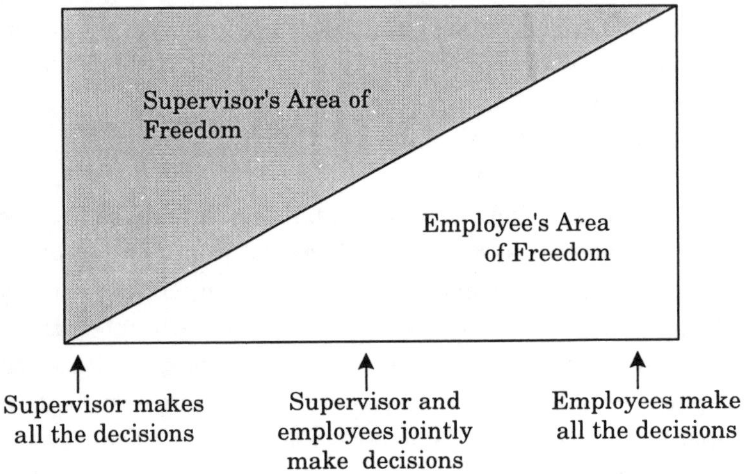

THE LEADERSHIP GRID

Another "style" approach to leadership has been developed by Blake and Mouton (1964), two American academics. Rather than two options (Theory X, Theory Y), or a number of points on a continuum, supervisors are offered a choice of 81 reference points on a 9 x 9 grid (see Figure 14.2). Similar to Likert's view, the grid maps two main factors: concern for people (vertical axis) and concern for production (horizontal axis). Unlike Likert's work, Blake and Mouton designed this approach to be used as a development tool for the training of managers. Using this model supervisors can identify their leadership style on the matrix and, if necessary, improve it. A person's style, i.e. their position on the grid, is learned from a combination of exercises that includes completing a questionnaire and participating in group discussion and practical exercises. The managerial grid is thus a diagnostic tool used in management development courses.

FIGURE 14.2: BLAKE AND MOUTON'S MANAGERIAL GRID

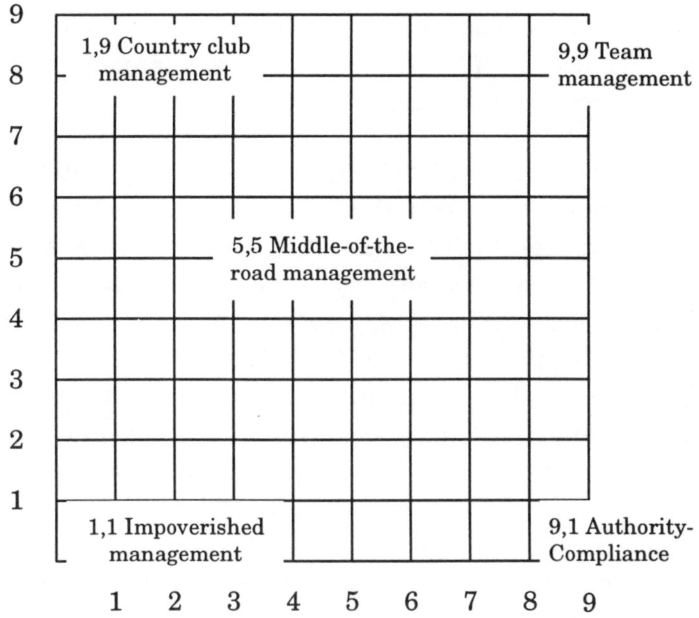

For the sake of clarity, Figure 14.2 shows just 5 (of 81 possible) reference points. These are as follows:

- 1,9 — illustrates a supervisor who shows primary concern for people rather than production. Blake and Mouton term this "country club management" in that these supervisors tend to avoid the pressures of getting the job done by leaving it up to the employees.
- 1,1 — indicates a supervisor who shows little concern for either people or production. Hence the term "impoverished management" because leadership is absent.

- 9,1 — "authority-compliance" indicates a supervisor whose primary concern is production, what Likert terms a job-centred supervisor.
- 5,5 — "middle-of-the-road management" blends both people and task concerns but only to the point of performing adequately.
- 9,9 — "team management" shows the highest concern for both production and people thus allowing the maximum output from a given set of resources.

The advantage of this model lies in it training potential — supervisors who are curious about their management style can opt to use the model. Another benefit of the model is that it highlights the need to balance both people and production (tasks). As was argued in earlier chapters, research shows that supervisors are under greater pressure to get work done. With the increasing educational standards of young people entering the labour market today, it can be argued that people need less supervision. Furthermore, because of broader job responsibilities supervisors often need to spend more time on getting their own work done and less time actually supervising people. Betts (1993, p. 178) argues correctly that "an effective leader finds the right balance between concern for people and concern for production". Achieving that balance is no easy task, but it must be recognised, in the first instance, that there is a need for balance.

FUNCTIONAL OR ACTION-CENTRED LEADERSHIP

John Adair (1979), a Briton, developed the concept of functional or action-centred leadership.[2] He argues that leadership is less a case of personality or style, but more of responding correctly to the situation at hand. Making a distinction between individual, task and group needs, he argues that effective leadership is a product of what is done to meet these different, and sometimes conflicting, needs:

---

[2] See also Chapter 17 on teamwork, a subject which Adair has written about a great deal.

- Task functions: defining the task, making plans, allocating work and resources, ensuring quality and building processes.
- Group maintenance functions: fulfilling group needs, motivating, building a cohesive team, ensuring a sense of belonging, building skills through training.
- Individual maintenance functions: accounting for individual needs, rewarding, praising, training, counselling.

Adair (1988, p. 7) writes:

> Your effectiveness as a leader depends on your ability to influence — and be influenced by — your teams and the individuals who make up those teams, so that all concerned can be involved in carrying out a common task. You have to ensure that the required tasks are completed satisfactorily while at the same time supervising the team so that teamwork and team identity are maintained and developed. At the same time, you must recognise that each person in the team is indeed an individual who has needs, hopes, ideas and so on which must be realised if the individual is going to be effective. If you concentrate too much on achieving the task whatever the cost, then sooner or later your team will start to disintegrate; likewise if you fail to recognise individual needs you will inevitably fail to spot the rotten apple, what means that soon you will have a rotten barrel and, once again, the team will disintegrate.

Adair also argues that, aside from striking a balance between these different needs, the supervisor must also recognise that at times certain needs take overriding concern. Sometimes, the situation demands that the supervisor give preference to task needs, such as the completion of a project. At other times, individual needs are more important and have to be addressed first. This approach therefore adopts what in management is termed the contingency approach, whereby how one handles a task is contingent on the situation at hand.

Despite much popularity, Adair's views are open to criticism. For example, it is often argued that people prefer consistency in a leader's behaviour. This was a point made earlier: an individual who constantly changes style invites criticism. Secondly, action-centred leadership requires that an individual be a good judge of circumstances. Supervisors can, however, misread a situation, and thus make an inappropriate response. What supervisors can learn from action-centred leadership is that they must be flexible and able to treat each situation uniquely. Indeed, most management consultants today maintain that modern managers or supervisors need to be flexible in their approach to situations, and make less use of preconceived ideas about how to lead or motivate employees.

SUPERLEADERSHIP

Manz and Sims (1989) provide an alternative and more modern view on leadership. They argue that leadership styles have developed from the traditional "strong man", where discipline and intimidation were used to control employees, to the modern-day concept of the "superleader" where self-leadership is prominent. The "strong-man" view is associated with the classical or early school of management where, it was argued, disciplinary measures were necessary to control unruly workers. Today, because of a range of factors, employees require much less supervision and control. However, while the ability to self-supervise is evident in most employees, it is management's job to create the environment where self-supervision is the norm rather than the exception. As Manz and Sims argue, the role of the leader today is to lead others into leading themselves. They describe the principles of superleadership as follows:

- An important way to measure your own success is through the success of others.
- What makes you successful at one level can be counterproductive at a higher level.
- The strength of the leader is measured by the ability to facilitate the self-leadership of others, not the ability to bend the will of others to one's own.
- If you want to lead somebody, lead yourself.
- The best of all leaders is the one who helps people so that, eventually, the leader is not needed.

- Give people a fish, and they will be fed for a day; teach them to fish, and they will be fed for a lifetime.

Central to this view is the idea that people can lead themselves. This notion of self-management was first mentioned in Blanchard and Johnson's widely read and aptly titled *The One Minute Manager* (1981). In this book, the authors argued that managers, by and large, spend far too much time managing or supervising people when, in fact, employees were quite capable of managing themselves. Instead, managers need to spend "quality time" (which is one minute a day) encouraging and praising employees and then giving them the freedom to do their own jobs.

CHAPTER SUMMARY

The research on leadership points to three important factors — the quality of the leader, the characteristics of followers, and the nature of the situation — all of which must be blended into action which produces positive results. It is clear that employees work better when their supervisor shows an interest in them, allows them the freedom to develop and is attentive to their needs — this approach is called a concern for people or employee-centred leadership. But leadership is also about getting the job done — concern for production or task-centred leadership. Hence the supervisor has to balance the requirements of the job with a concern for people, recognising that at particular times one can take precedence.

The more recent research on leadership focuses on self-leadership. Leadership in modern terms is thus about setting the right example that allows employees to lead themselves. It is similar to the view of motivation: a supervisor creates the environment which allows employees to excel. The rationale for this is that employees potentially can model their behaviour on a supervisor, altering their behaviour in response to what a supervisor does (or does not do). Supervisors cannot change someone's personality, but they can, through leadership, direct employees' behaviour towards higher performance by setting the correct example. Supervisor should not refrain from demanding high standards in their own behaviour and of those that they manage.

References and Further Reading

Adair, J. (1979) *Action-Centred Leadership*, London: Gower.

Adair, J. (1988) *The Effective Supervisor*, London: The Industrial Society.

Betts, P.W. (1993) *Supervisory Management*, London: Pitman, chapter 13.

Blake, R.E. & J. Mouton (1964) *The Management Grid*, Houston, TX: Gulf Publishing.

Blanchard, K. & S. Johnson (1981) *The One Minute Manager*, CA: Blanchard-Johnson Publishers.

Evans, David (1995) *Supervisory Management, Principles and Practices*, fourth edition, London: Cassell, chapter 8.

Likert, R. (1961) *New Patterns of Management*, New York: McGraw-Hill.

Manz. C. & Henry P. Sims (1989) *Superleadership: Leading Others to Lead Themselves*, New York: Prentice-Hall.

Mosley, D., L. Megginson, P. Pietri (1993) *Supervisory Management: The Art of Empowering and Developing People*, third edition, Cincinnati, OH: South-Western.

Tannenbaum R. & W. Schmidt (1973) "How to Choose a Leadership Pattern", *Harvard Business Review*, 51, May-June, pp. 162-80.

Chapter 15

INTERVIEWING SKILLS

THE OBJECTIVE OF THIS CHAPTER

Many supervisors have to conduct a variety of interviews at work — employment interviews, performance appraisal interviews, counselling interviews, grievance interviews, disciplinary interviews and exit interviews — but they are done fairly infrequently and then usually close together. Yet they demand great skills and time on the part of the interviewer. This includes, prior to the interview, a considerable investment in preparation, and in the interview itself the need for certain interpersonal skills that vary from the ability to listen and understand to the ability to take control of a situation. Central to any interview, however, is the idea that the interviewer make the interviewee feel relaxed by talking with them, not to them or at them. As with communicative skills in general, interview skills can be improved upon and eventually mastered.

This chapter will concentrate on the following types of interviews:

- Employment interviews
- Performance appraisal interviews
- Counselling interviews
- Disciplinary interviews
- Grievance interviews.

Though the basic techniques are common to all interviewing situations, supervisors should be familiar with each type of interview and especially the variations in method between them.

APPROACHES TO INTERVIEWS

There are essentially two approaches to interviews, directive and non-directive. With directive, also called structured, interviews, the interviewer controls the pace of the interview, whereas in the latter, the non-directive or unstructured interview, the discussion is more free-wheeling with the interviewee doing most of the talking.

In a directive interview the interviewer is in full control. Having prepared well, the interviewer usually makes use of a questionnaire which guides the interview along. For example, in a employment interview, the interviewer will typically follow the order in which questions are laid out on the questionnaire, making sure that all questions are asked and keeping notes of the responses.

In the non-directive interview, by contrast, the interviewee is encouraged to talk openly and freely without precondition. However, the interviewer is likely to stimulate the discussion by asking very general and open questions in order to keep the interview fairly focused. Counselling interviews, among others, are often conducted this way. This type of interview, as we will learn later, is often used in dealing with employee problems and concerns.

The next section examines different types of interviewing, beginning first with employment interviews, then performance appraisal interviews, counselling interviews and, finally, ending with disciplinary and grievance interviews.

THE EMPLOYMENT INTERVIEW

Employment interviews are more likely to be conducted, for legal reasons, by the human resource department. Where supervisors have responsibility for employment interviews it tends to be a limited role, where they sit on panels or are consulted at the later stage of the selection process. The latter is common in manufacturing firms, especially where prospective employees are to be assigned to a supervisor's department; the supervisor would be consulted in hiring as well as promotion decisions. The exception to this is for casual employment. For example, in the hospitality sector, which employs more people in the summer period, and in organisations which employ a lot of contract labour, supervisors and department heads would have a primary role to play in recruitment and selection. Responsibility in this case would also extend to performance appraisal interviews, particularly where, say., an employee on contract may be interviewed with a view to full-time recruitment.

The remainder of this section will deal with employment interviews which supervisors conduct either alone or in a group, but where they are in charge. Further, the terms interviewer and supervisor will be used interchangeably.

The Employment Interview in Perspective

The objective of the employment interview is to pick the best person (or who is perceived to be the best person) for the job. This is a very difficult and time-consuming activity that is occasionally fairly speculative. Moreover, the costs of making a mistake are high. The supervisor may have to live with that decision by coping with a poor performer. Furthermore, given the tremendous investment firms make in individuals, the cost of a wrong hire can be great. Finally, the interview is often the first (and sometimes last) impression an individual has of the firm so it is important to portray a positive image. In all, it is important that employment interviews are done properly.

Preparation

Two key elements can be identified in the preparation for an employment interview: the preparation of a job description and/or job specification, and a questionnaire to be used in the interview itself.

A job description is a statement of information about a particular job. It includes information on the key tasks, responsibilities, authority, and purpose of the job: so a delivery person may have to drive a vehicle, sign documents, load material, and supervise an assistant, etc. A job specification lists the criteria or skills necessary to perform the job adequately: a delivery person has to have a driving licence, for example. Job specifications can be based on ability (such as how to drive) or qualifications (must hold a driving licence). Either way, a job specification lists the various skills, ability or knowledge needed to perform a particular job.

A questionnaire allows the interviewer to focus attention on asking appropriate questions as well as giving them more time to listen to and observe the responses of each candidate. The lack of a properly prepared questionnaire, by contrast, often means that the interviewer has to be always thinking about the next question. Further, comparisons are difficult without similar information on each candidate.

The following advice may be useful in preparing a questionnaire.

Firstly, avoid unnecessary duplication. Some firms already have detailed employment application forms, which, along with CVs and letters, provide considerable information on candidates.

Secondly, the interviewer should include in a questionnaire only questions which are relevant to the job. There is a consensus emerging in Ireland that it is better to ask job-related questions and concentrate less on biographical information, particularly personal data. For example, it matters little (for most jobs) whether a person is male or female, married or single, or has children or not. Indeed, some of the questions run foul of the law, particularly regarding sex discrimination.[1]

Thirdly, much can be gained by talking to employees and other supervisors since they may see angles that the interviewer has overlooked. It is also a good idea to consult with the personnel or legal department regarding employment law.

Fourthly, the list of questions should be fairly comprehensive in the sense of providing as much information as necessary to make the right decision. It is generally advisable to have between ten and fifteen questions, some of which should be non-directive. This questionnaire should be typed up and photocopied for all candidates and distributed to all interviewers. Notes can be made on each copy if necessary.

---

[1] This includes the Anti-Discrimination Pay Act, 1974, and the Employment Equality Act, 1977, both of which are summarised in Chapter 19.

Making Sense of Documentation

Both in the preparation and the assessment, interviewers should have in their possession a range of documentation on each candidate. In addition to a job description and a job specification, this can include a completed application form, a curriculum vitae, a covering letter, along with, possibly, letters of recommendation. These are typically circulated by the human resources department, preferably in advance of the interview. This information can be compiled in a dossier on each person, cross-referencing if necessary. In the preparation process, the supervisor can check to see if any information is missing or needs clarification during the interview.

Test results may also be available. Applicants may provide recognised educational and vocational certificates that include both proof of attendance and a final grade. The supervisor should be familiar with the various certificates available, which include not only the junior or leaving certificate but also the various apprenticeship, VEC (Vocational Educational Committee), FÁS, and City and Guilds of London certificates.

The Surroundings

Most employment interviews are conducted on-site. This way, it is less disruptive to the interviewer and the interviewee gets a feel for the organisation. However, it is preferable to use a private office where the potential for interruption is minimised. Telephone calls should be put on hold, so that complete attention can be given to the interview. Similarly, no other employees should be within hearing distance, and the surroundings should be as comfortable as possible. The interviewer, generally speaking, sits opposite the interviewee. Conditions should be such that the interviewee does not feel threatened or under pressure.

Interviewing the Candidate

People can feel apprehensive and tense at the prospect of being interviewed. Therefore, the interviewer should make every effort to reduce this apprehension. This can be achieved in a variety of ways, including greeting the interviewee warmly, offering them tea or coffee, and quickly establishing a first-name basis.

Sometimes interviewers link the initial conversation to the job, such as "how did you find out about the job?" or "do you know someone here?" The purpose of these questions is to give the interviewee time to relax and to ease into questions. Once begun, however, the interviewer should not waste too much time in pleasantries but get down to the business at hand.

Employment-related Information

Perhaps the most important employment-related items have to do with previous jobs. This includes not just the number of organisations an individual has worked in, but also how they performed in those positions, and what sort of training, if any, did the individual receive. One should also ascertain why the candidate wants to work for the organisation, and what sort of a future they might have with it. This entails assessment of how well the individual will get along with existing staff and how receptive they are to supervision. Ask yourself "would I want to supervise this individual?"

As noted, the final part of the interview should be a question-and-answer session, in which the interviewee asks the questions and the interviewer provides the answers. The candidate will want to know various particulars about the job and the organisation. This includes the terms and conditions of employment, including holidays, pensions, overtime, sick pay, and other relevant information. Where possible this information should be provided.

Some interviewers prefer not to discuss this information until a second interview. Others will only discuss this information with candidates who they feel have a chance of being selected. However, the interviewer has to treat all candidates fairly and without prejudice. Therefore, it is imperative to disclose the same information to all candidates.

Questions to be Avoided

As noted earlier, the interviewer should avoid, where possible, personal questions. This is because personal questions have the tendency to unsettle people and may raise issues from a legal and moral perspective. Table 15.1 contains a suggested list of questions to ask, and questions not to ask. It is up the interviewer to decide which are appropriate.

TABLE 15.1 QUESTIONS TO ASK AND QUESTIONS NOT TO ASK

The following questions are to be avoided:

- Are you married?
- Do you plan to get married?
- Do you plan to have children?
- What kind of baby-sitting arrangements do you have?
- What will you do if your children get sick?
- Are you likely to quit if you get married or have children?
- Is your spouse from this area?
- Does your spouse live with you or contribute to your support?
- Is your spouse likely to be transferred?

The following questions can be asked:

- What was your absentee record at your prior place of employment?
- Do you know of any reason (for example, transportation, or any other reason) why you would not be able to get to work on time and on a regular basis?
- Are you available to work overtime? If so, are there any limitations or restrictions on your ability to work overtime (including weekend overtime, if required)?
- We are looking for employees with a commitment to this organisation. Are there any reasons why you might not stay with us?
- What are your career objectives?
- Do you intend to stay in the area?
- Are you willing to relocate to this or any other area?
- Do you foresee any reasons why you would not be able to travel for business reasons?
- Are you willing to work on weekends and evenings?

Making the Decision: Choosing Between Candidates

No two interviews (for the same job) are alike. That is, interviews have a tendency to drift in different directions dependent, not just on the questions asked but, most importantly, on the responses given. This is perfectly natural and if the interviewer, not being experienced in interviewing, finds that a set of interviews were varied, they should not be too concerned. The skill comes in the ability to assess candidates. This requires good judgement on the interviewer's part. To be more precise, assessing a candidate is more than just matching a candidate's skill with the requirements of a job. Rather, one has to compare one candidate's qualifications and potential with another's.

There are some potential pitfalls to selection that are worth noting. Avoid, where possible, making hasty judgements particularly in the early part of the interview. It is well known that interviewers tend to form their opinions early on in the employment interview, in some cases after a few minutes. Similarly, avoid judging a candidate on one or two elements of their qualifications. This is often called the "halo" effect. It happens where interviewers are biased towards an individual just because they have a degree or served an apprenticeship or have worked in the industry before. Rather, judge people on their overall capabilities and talents. Similarly, avoid over-generalisation, that is, assuming that because the candidate behaves in such a way at an interview, they will behave like that all the time. Some people are natural interviewees, being well able to assert themselves, others, perhaps in the majority, are shy and can be intimidated by the whole process. Therefore, judge people on as broad a base as possible.

A decision on the overall candidate should be made after all interviews are conducted. Similarly, no candidate should be informed as to how they have done until all interviews are concluded. Further, communication should be in writing. Generally speaking, the successful candidate is informed first and, when they accept, only then are other candidates informed. Most interviewers prefer to delegate to the human resources department the task of informing candidates given their experience and expertise in this field. Besides, there are certain legal and procedural requirements that have to be followed that an interviewer may not be aware of.

PERFORMANCE APPRAISAL INTERVIEWS

Performance appraisal interviews (or appraisal interviews for short) are conducted to assess how well (or badly) an individual is doing in their job. Such interviews are standard practice in some organisations, particularly in the services sector. The leading Irish banks, for example, regularly conduct them, as do most colleges and universities. They are conducted, not only for compensatory reasons, but also to provide feedback on how well an employee is doing. Such feedback acts as an important incentive for an individual to do the job better. This is especially so for employees of large organisations. The size of the organisation, along with the bureaucracy that goes with it, can give the impression to an individual that they have no part to play in organisational effectiveness. A formal appraisal system helps in bridging the gap between organisational effectiveness and an individual's job.

They also serve another purpose. Employees have the right to know about their job performance, and how it can be improved. Supervisors have an obligation to discuss with their staff how well they are doing in their jobs, and what can be done to improve their performance.

The final advantage to appraisal interviews is that they give individual employees the opportunity to air their views, and thus for organisations, and particularly supervisors, to listen to employees. Employees are often the source of very good suggestions. These won't be voiced unless there is some process in place that provides for regular communication between management and employees.

Supervisors usually conduct appraisal interviews. This is because they know employees best. Typically, they are carried out once a year. Any longer and the information would be outdated and any shorter and they would become routine and less meaningful. These evaluations become part of an employee's personnel file and can play an important role in staffing decisions, particularly relating to promotion and compensation.

Appraisal interviews are similar in some ways to employment interviews. That is, just as the latter makes a comparison (between the requirements of the vacant position and the skills of each candidate), the former also make a comparison, in this case between the performance of employees and their job requirements. However, appraisal interviews attempt to change behaviour, whereas employment interviews try to predict future behaviour.

The Performance Appraisal Form

Supervisors have an obligation to their staff to evaluate them fairly and accurately. Just as in the employment interview this means that the supervisor has to follow a certain process. There are two parts to this process, the completion of a performance appraisal form and an interview. The former will be dealt with first.

Many organisations provide standard forms to aid the process of performance appraisal. They serve two purposes. First, they ensure uniformity by grading all employees on the same factors. Secondly, they aim to limit personal bias on the part of the supervisor. Some of these forms list a series of factors which serve as criteria for measuring the performance of an individual in a job. The following are some of the factors which are most likely to be included in these forms:

- Ability to follow safety requirements
- Ability to show initiative
- Ability to use personal judgement
- Ability to work with customers
- Ability to work with fellow employees
- Absenteeism
- Adaptability to new practices
- Co-operation with management and others
- Degree of supervision required
- Knowledge of the job
- Performance in the job
- Productivity and quality of current work
- Punctuality.

For each of these factors, the supervisor may be provided with a number of choices. It could be a numerical scale, such as from one to five. A score of five, for example, would mean that the employee had scored excellently on a particular factor, such as time-keeping. Other appraisal forms use sentences or short phrases which the supervisor, as the appraiser, is expected to respond to. An example may be: "Would you describe the job holder as good, average, or poor in dealing with customers?" This is important: performance appraisal systems are not a contest in which employees are ranked. Rather, they are designed to help employees better themselves in jobs.

Regardless of the way they are structured, performance appraisal forms are usually easy to complete, particularly for the experienced supervisor. However, there are certain rules or standards which one must abide by. These are similar to the ones mentioned above with respect to employment interviews. For example, one should not allow the rating of one factor to influence excessively the ratings of other factors (the so-called "halo effect" again). There is a natural tendency, if an employee rates well on one factor, particularly an important one, for the supervisor to rate that individual high on all factors. The opposite can occur too. One way to avoid this problem is to rate all employees on a single factor first before starting on the next factor. Teachers and lecturers use the same method in correcting examination papers, namely mark the same question for everyone so as to remove any potential bias carrying over from one question to another.

Secondly, one should behave with the utmost professionalism. This means, as in employment interviews, evaluating people on employment-related issues only. In other words, detach yourself from any personal feelings, and do a professional, if cold job. This means judging people on their job performance, not their personality.

Conducting the Performance Appraisal Interview

Once the appraisal form is completed for everyone, the interviews are begun. Basically, this entails sitting down with the employee and going over the ratings on their appraisal form. As with employment interviews, the supervisor has to conduct this interview in a professional manner. There are also some rules to follow. To begin with, the interview should be held shortly after the appraisal form has been completed. Second, given the confidential nature of the discussion, the interview should be held in an office which is private or at least out of sight and sound of other employees. Third, employees should be given sufficient notice of the meeting to allow them time to prepare.

Once the interview has begun, the supervisor should attempt to put the interviewee at ease by beginning the interview with some friendly conversation. Thereafter the supervisor should state the main purpose of the interview which is to evaluate the employee's performance in objective terms. It should also be pointed out that each employee is going through the same process and that no one has any advantage. Finally, one should bring to the employees' attention the benefits for them of appraisal interviews. These include the opportunity to question any aspect of their job and organisational policy, and to make suggestions if necessary.

The core of the appraisal interview, however, is to agree on evaluations that are listed on each employee's appraisal form. Basically, this means going through the appraisal form with the employee, and agreeing on the rating. The employee should be asked for feedback. The possibility exists, of course, for appraisal interviews to turn into a heated debate. Employees may question a supervisor's judgement and demand a higher rating. If you have done the job properly, and been fair with all employees, then you should stand by your decision. In most appraisal schemes the dissatisfied employee has the right to appeal to the supervisor's boss.

It is essential that the supervisor acknowledge any improvement the employee has made since the last interview. By the same token, one has to point out areas in which the employee has not performed up to scratch, and how these can be improved. The supervisor should also discuss any possible future training or, indeed, promotional opportunities. Finally, the employee and the supervisor should agree on further goals.

Before the appraisal interview draws to a close, the supervisor should make sure that the employee has fully understood what has happened. This can be achieved by asking for feedback. In this case one has to be certain that the employee has fully understood the appraisal system and their role in it.

When the interview is ended, and thus the performance appraisal process concluded, all relevant documents should be filed in the appropriate place. Many organisations allow employees complete access to their file. Thus the supervisor has to make sure that their judgement stands up to scrutiny. As with employment interviews, while judgement is to some extent subjective, the proper process, when followed, allows for objectivity.

COUNSELLING INTERVIEWS

The word "counsel" means to give opinion after deliberation. Hence counselling interviews tend to deal with problems. A supervisor may be the only person, or at least the most accessible one, that employees can turn to when they have problems. It was mentioned in interviews for this book that given the changing demographics of work in Ireland —more two-earner families and lone parents working, along with changing age-profiles for well-established firms — that more problems will surface in work. Hence the greater need for counselling.

How should one conduct a counselling interview? Begin by placing the interviewee at ease. This is more difficult to do because of the emotional aspect of these interviewees. Still, you could begin by saying "I am glad you have come to me", or "I have been looking forward to talking with you", or "my door is always open to employees". These statements are far better than saying "what's your problem?", or "why did you come to me, can't you see someone else?" Thus conversational skills are important.

The skills required for counselling interviews are listening and understanding. Empathy is the key word. It means putting oneself in the shoes of the interviewee. What is the person feeling? How strong do they feel about the issue? One must listen attentively, rarely interrupting and, especially, avoid making any judgements. Sometimes it is enough to nod the head, or smile which simply denotes to the employee that one is listening and that one cares. There may be times when intervention is necessary. This is because employees may mask the problem or deny that a problem exists. In such instances, try using persuasiveness to get at the root of the problem. If one intervenes, remember that the idea of the counselling interview is to encourage the employee to talk, not the supervisor. Thus, keep your comments short. One possibility is to restate what the employee had said earlier in order to get the conversation back on track. Another is to offer advice or make suggestions which force the employee to face up to their problem.

Aside from the ability to listen, understand and empathise, some counselling interviews may also require that a supervisor be able to offer good advice. This turns on the ability of supervisors to make good judgement, which is borne out of skill, experience and training. Be careful, however, with giving advice. In the first instance, the employee may only want to talk and may not be looking for advice. Second, unless one is a trained therapist, it is very difficult to give useful advice. Instead, the supervisor should help the employee identify the problem and, if it is a serious one, possibly refer them to someone inside or outside the organisation who is more qualified to deal with it.

DISCIPLINARY INTERVIEWS

Disciplinary interviews are typically undertaken for either of two reasons: where there is a breach of company procedure, such as excessive absenteeism or tardiness, or where there is insubordination or an employee fails to meet a job standard. The outcome of such a procedure may range from no action to dismissal. Gunnigle et al. (1995, pp. 221-35) have advocated that all grievance and disputes procedures should be formalised in writing as part of a company policy. They argue further that first-line management has a primary role to play in grievance and disciplinary administration in that such issues should be dealt with at supervisory level. Therefore, it is imperative that supervisors familiarise themselves with company policy and legal rights.

The same rules apply for disciplinary interviews as for structured interviews. The interview should be held in a private office when there is peace and quiet. Interviewees should be informed well in advance and told of their rights in this regard, which include legal and/or union representation. The interview should be begun by stating very clearly what the purpose of the meeting is, and time should be afforded to the employee to respond. The employee should be made aware that they are not being singled out for special treatment. Moreover, the transgression should be explained clearly and fully to the employee, and confirmed by asking for feedback. The supervisor should indicate to the employee the reason or reasons for having the rule, and that its breach violated company policy, if not also an industrial relations agreement. Finally, at the close of the interview the supervisor should make sure that the employee has fully understood the nature of the proceedings.

There are some important differences with disciplinary interviews, however. The first relate to the rights which apply to employees by virtue of the common law and, in the case of unionised firms, agreements and/or custom and practice. It is the organisation's duty, not necessarily the union's, to inform employees of their rights in this regard. The legal rights referred to are the principles of natural justice and include the right to representation, the right to a fair heading, that employees be fully informed of company policy and that policy be evenly and fairly applied. These are summarised in Chapter 19.

The second difference with disciplinary interviews is that they demand an assertive stance on the part of the interviewer as well as important preparation. The supervisor should state the issue or issues clearly and unambiguously. They should have all the necessary documentation regarding the discipline. In the case of an employee being disciplined for constantly showing up late, this means a record of the exact days and times the employee was late, as well as company policy on lateness. The employee should be given plenty of time to put forward their side of the story. There may be an angle that has been overlooked, hence the importance of listening and understanding at this point. The interview should ideally conclude on the same note it began, on friendly terms. In some instances, the supervisor may have to take an action, other times that decision can be postponed. What that action is depends on a host of factors, notably the situation and company policy.

Despite the terminology, not all disciplinary interviews involve handing out discipline, such as suspending an employee. Rather, the simple act of sitting down with someone and pointing out very clearly what element of a person's behaviour is unacceptable is often sufficient in itself.

GRIEVANCE INTERVIEWS

A grievance is a formal complaint by an employee that alleges an infringement of their employment rights. It indicates dissatisfaction on the part of the employee which may in some cases include complaints about the style of management. While in principle a grievance is taken by an individual employee, they could be acting for a group of employees, and in unionised firms very often the shop steward takes the case on behalf of the individual. Therefore, any decision taken by a supervisor could have important industrial relations implications. It is important that supervisors be aware of the procedure for handling grievances and consider the full implications or potential implications of any decision taken. As with disciplinary issues, if in doubt, the supervisor can and should consult the personnel department.

Although policies vary from organisation to organisation, and particularly with the size of the organisation, generally speaking, in a unionised company a shop steward will air a grievance to the employee's immediate supervisor, usually in the company of the aggrieved employee. Non-union companies often have a "parallel procedure" that is loosely based on unionised procedures. That procedure also dictates that if the issue cannot be resolved at first-line management level it proceeds to the next level, usually involving the personnel manager, and thereafter third-party referral, such as the Labour Relations Commission, before any form of industrial action can be undertaken. As with disciplinary methods, it is widely accepted that grievances should be dealt with by supervisors in a timely and appropriate manner and must be in accordance with legal principles.

The supervisor should establish the facts of the case, if necessary searching for more information. A decision should be made on the basis of the facts, and any necessary advice sought from the personnel department. The decision of the supervisor should be communicated to the shop steward in timely fashion, outlining in clear terms not just the decision, but also the reasons for it. Finally a complete record should be kept.

Grievance and disciplinary interviews are part of a formal procedure in any organisation which should be in writing, be communicated to and understood by all (management, employees and unions) and be fairly and consistently applied. A central tenet of such procedure is to resolve issues at the appropriate level (usually between a supervisor and an employee), by following agreed procedures, and without recourse to industrial action or third party referral. Such formality does not preclude the supervisor from dealing with issues in an informal manner. Indeed, in conducting research for this book, some supervisors expressed a preference for using the informal approach in order to avoid what they saw as unnecessary "form-filling" and the attention of the union. Despite any perceived benefits of such an approach, it is imperative that the supervisor applies common sense and good judgement to every individual situation, and where appropriate follows agreed procedure. The purpose of such procedure is to establish and maintain sound labour relations and it is widely accepted that procedures, in the case of disciplinary measures, have reduced the incidence of industrial action (Murphy, 1989). The supervisor should also be aware that the purpose of the personnel department is to assist and advise first-line management in the exercise of disciplinary and grievance administration.

CHAPTER SUMMARY

There are two broad approaches to interviewing, the directive and the non-directive interview. Directive implies structure and is most suitable to employment interviews and to a lesser extent performance appraisal interviews. Not every supervisor conducts employment interviews, but the techniques are well worth knowing. This includes preparation, groundwork, using comfortable settings, starting the interview off on a friendly note, taking questions and being able to put the interviewee at ease. Unlike employment interviews, the purpose of the appraisal interview, since the employee is already in the organisation, is to change behaviour not predict it.

A non-directive approach is more suitable to counselling interviews. Here the supervisor offers advice or counsel to employees. Counselling interviews tend, in the main, to deal with employee problems, which can include problems at work and problems outside of work. The ability to conduct counselling interviews effectively depends much on how well a supervisor can listen, sum up a situation and help the employee arrive at their own solution. Unlike employment interviews which have a clear purpose, counselling interviews are far less defined. Indeed, at times the employee may be unsure of what the root of the problem is.

Disciplinary and grievance interviews fall in between the directive and non-directive interview. Basically, disciplinary interviews involve the supervisor explaining clearly, with documentation, when and how the employee infringed rules, and how their behaviour can be improved upon in the future. Grievance interviews allow employees the opportunity to voice their complaints and have, like the disciplinary interview, important industrial relations implications.

References and Further Reading

Bennett, R. (1994) *Managing People*, second edition, London: Kogan Page, chapters 1 to 8.

Gunnigle, P., McMahon, G. & G. Fitzgerald (1995) *Industrial Relations in Ireland: Theory and Practice*, Dublin: Gill & Macmillan.

McClave, Henry J. (1986) *Communication for Business in Ireland*, Dublin: Gill and Macmillan; chapter 11 deals with the employment interview from the perspective of the interviewer and the interviewee.

Mosley, D., L. Megginson, P. Pietri (1993) *Supervisory Management: The Art of Empowering and Developing People*, third edition, Cincinnati, OH: South-Western, chapters 11-14.

Murphy, T. (1989) "The Impact of the Unfair Dismissals Act, 1977, on Workplace Industrial Relations" in *Industrial Relations in Ireland, Contemporary Issues and Developments*, Dublin: Department of Industrial Relations, Faculty of Commerce, University College Dublin, pp. 247-52.

Stanton, N. (1996) *Mastering Communication*, third edition, London: Macmillan, London; chapter 6 is on interviewing, and chapter 7 on being interviewed.

Part Four

The Management of Collective Resources

Chapter 16

TECHNOLOGY AND CHANGE: FROM TAYLORISM TO WORLD CLASS MANUFACTURING

THE OBJECTIVE OF THIS CHAPTER

World class manufacturing (WCM) is the term used to describe a new form of management system which is coming into vogue, particularly among multinational firms. WCM is an American term. The Germans prefer the expression "lean and mean production". Both terms seem to mean the same thing: a new approach to manufacturing that is premised on making people "work smarter not harder". WCM replaces Taylorism as a way of organising the production process. Taylorism, as was noted in Chapter 3, is an individualistic approach to manufacturing. WCM, by contrast, is a holistic approach.

Despite much use of the term, particularly in the media, there is no standard definition of world class manufacturing. Rather, the term functions as a tag to denote a whole range of practices that have been implemented in recent years in response to increased competition and the new focus on quality. These elements can be grouped under the following headings:

- New technology
- New business techniques, such as Just-in-Time production and Total Quality Management
- New forms of work organisation.

This chapter describes these elements and deals with how each affects the role of the supervisor. It begins, however, by explaining the factors that gave rise to world class manufacturing and, in particular, the distinction between price and quality competitiveness.

After reading and studying this chapter the reader should have an understanding of:

- The role of the supervisor in a manufacturing firm and how this is changing
- World class manufacturing
- The importance of quality and new technology to the modern manufacturing plant
- How to deal with change, particularly new technology and new ways of manufacturing.

The chapter is based primarily on research work carried out abroad by the author. This has been written up elsewhere (Harvey, 1993, 1994; Harvey and von Behr, 1994).

WORLD CLASS MANUFACTURING

The term "world class manufacturing" was originally coined in 1986 by Richard Schonberger, an American management consultant. According to him, WCM represented the best response to increased competition for American firms. Schonberger, an academic and business consultant, had really given a name to a process that had begun in the early 1970s. After the oil crises, many American manufacturing firms opted out of manufacturing entirely. Those that stayed in manufacturing either invested in expensive state-of-the-art technology, or shifted operations overseas to low-wage countries. Neither gave the competitive edge necessary to do business in a global environment. The core of the problem was to develop a way of manufacturing that was both cost effective and responsive to demands for high-quality products delivered quickly to the marketplace.

It was only during the mid-1980s that American manufacturers changed their strategy which has, in time, allowed them to regain their prominence. This strategy was based primarily on a reorganisation of production designed largely to make manufacturing more competitive. In time, this strategy became more widely known as world class manufacturing.

American multinational firms, themselves drawing upon Japanese practices, have had an inordinate influence on management practices in Ireland. Partly responsible for this is the wide number of American firms based in Ireland, as well as the publicity afforded to many successful US firms, among them Nike, Apple, Microsoft, Harley Davidson, and many others, which has led other firms to copy them. The author spent many years researching in the US and Germany, and this chapter will draw upon much of that experience, particularly at Harley Davidson.

The importance attached to WCM in Ireland can be gauged from the following clause taken from the Programme for Competitiveness and Work:

> . . . the Government and the social partners recognise the importance of changes in the production process and in skill needs, in work organisation, in working conditions and in industrial relations to realise the potential for growth and job creation arising from new technologies and changes in society. The introduction and implementation of World Class Manufacturing throughout Irish industry will be encouraged and supported.

In the current Partnership 2000 agreement, the notion of innovation, competitiveness and good industrial relations is given further impetus by the commitment to change of the social partners, IBEC and ICTU:

> Partnership is an active relationship based on recognition of a common interest to secure the competitiveness, viability and prosperity of the enterprise. It involves a continuing commitment by employees to improvements in quality and efficiency; and the acceptance by employers of employees as stake holders with rights and interests to be considered in the context of major decisions affecting their employment.
>
> Partnership involves common ownership of the resolution of challenges, involving the direct participation of employees/representatives and an investment in their training, development and working environment.

Partnership 2000 is aspirational. Not all firms implement all the elements of world class manufacturing, nor in the way the literature and management consultants and indeed Partnership 2000 suggest. However, many of these practices, such as Total Quality Management, are becoming widespread not just in manufacturing but in the services sector as well. This trend is likely to be accelerated in the coming years. So if many of these practices, such as Just-in-Time production (defined below) seem alien now, it is only a matter of time before they become standard practice.

PRICE VERSUS QUALITY

An understanding of the major change in the way global firms do business must begin with an appreciation of the difference between competing on price or on quality. Traditionally, firms have competed on the basis of one or the other but not both. For example, Mercedes Benz is a high-quality car. People who buy Mercedes cars pay a high price for them, but expect a quality car for their money. At the other extreme — price competitiveness — are firms that sell products solely on the basis of price. A Lada, for example, is an inexepensive car. It does not compete in the same market as Mercedes or BMW.

This distinction between price and quality gave rise to a further distinction in how the production process, and thus work, was organised. Firms which stress price as a selling feature typically mass produce. Further, they tend to use dedicated equipment, such as an assembly line which is staffed by, relatively speaking, low-skilled employees (this is referred to, academically, as a low-wage, low-skill system). Firms that compete by manufacturing high-quality products use general-purpose computerised machinery, operated by highly paid and highly skilled employees (a high-wage, high-skill system). A familiar argument being made now in the European Union is for firms to shift their emphasis more towards the latter. This is because, with increasing competition from what are termed the newly industrialised countries (NICs), such as Taiwan and South Korea, this competition based on price will intensify. Irish firms, and particularly multinational firms based here, cannot compete successfully on price alone and continue to pay such high wages.

What are the changes firms have to make to compete successfully in the international market? Central among these changes are improving product quality, increasing the range of products sold, and delivering products in more timely fashion to the marketplace. In effect, firms need to customise production, primarily as a matter of competitive survival. This involves a move away from the Tayloristic approach to organising the production process towards what has already been defined as world class manufacturing. Such a change has affected firms the world over, Ireland as much the USA, but particularly affected are firms which operate on a global basis. These firms have been leaders in making a move away from Taylorism.

The type of decision-making that firms make regarding the ideal production process — in reality, the setting of performance criteria and goals by top management — may be broadly referred to as a firm's "manufacturing strategy" since this, theoretically speaking, refers to management's framing of constraints and opportunities that exist in the internal and external environment and how best to respond to them. Strategic decision-making is relevant to the extent that it frames the overall picture, usually by the establishment of performance criteria that new technology and new forms of work organisation must meet, and into which subsequent (and lower-level) managerial action must fit. Supervisors are concerned with these changes at the point of production.

The next section summarises those changes by first outlining the mass production system and the concept of Taylorism upon which mass production is based. There is an important lesson for supervisors in this. As pointed out, they are at the vanguard of this movement towards world class manufacturing since many of these changes take place on the shopfloor and involve drastic changes in employees' jobs. Second, WCM demands much of the supervisor. To begin with, it is often supervisors who must implement and oversee the changes that are taking place. Because WCM is a systems or holistic approach to managing the production process, as distinct from Taylorism which is very individualistic, the supervisor has to be aware of the totality of the production process. This entails understanding the way the production process is organised under Taylorism, and the changes that take place with WCM and, in particular, how the supervisor's job fits into this.

MASS PRODUCTION AND TAYLORISM

Taylorism involves the reduction of tasks into their most basic elements. Unnecessary elements are removed, and the remaining ones are simplified so as to be capable of being carried out with the minimum of effort. Pay systems encourage this process: performance standards are ascertained through a series of systematic work measurements. Once the task is broken down into its most basic elements, a job evaluation study is conducted and the pay for the job determined. Pay is thus linked to production: the higher the productivity of one's labour, the more one is paid.

As little thought is involved in carrying out the task, the possibility for error is significantly reduced, and the job can be performed repetitively with less fear of making a mistake. The more the job is reduced the easier it becomes to substitute mechanical for human labour. Departments, like functions, become specialised with little interaction and little communication. Products are designed, mass-produced and mass-marketed with little thought for, or need of, co-operation between departments and between employees.

Quality concerns are expressed to the extent that by simplifying the process it is assumed that fewer mistakes will result. In this way, quality becomes secondary to quantity, in the same way as skills become secondary to hard work. Inefficiencies do result: quality suffers; inventories, and therefore costs, remain high; parts get lost or stolen as no one takes responsibility for their delivery. However, these inefficiencies are offset by the high profitability of mass production.

Although this system requires considerable indirect labour to oversee it — industrial engineers, supervisors and quality engineers — and is premised on low skills, overall it was successful. It thrived until about the 1970s when certain developments — increasing global competition and shifts in consumer taste — demanded change. As a result, manufacturing firms are moving towards a more flexible form of mass production. As noted, central to the changes occurring is the need to widen product diversity, improve product quality, and increase the speed of delivery of new products to the marketplace. Moreover, this has been done while still being cost-competitive.

These are global changes, and Irish firms have come under considerable pressure to change. Even the public sector is making changes to be more "user-friendly" and customer-oriented. As noted, firms that compete in the international arena, and especially multinational firms, are making the most changes, but indigenous firms are also being forced to adapt to a new way of manufacturing — or go bust.

WORLD CLASS MANUFACTURING: WHAT DOES IT MEAN?

Much is changed with world class manufacturing. In assuming new responsibilities, employees are expected to contribute more, productively and socially, the latter mainly in terms of contributing their knowledge and know-how through participation in team or group work. Skill levels are increased as employees are required to be more motivated, more innovative, and more responsive to change. No less affected are managers, particularly engineers. As authority is decentralised to the shopfloor, employees and managers are expected to co-operate more closely. Engineers, more accustomed to working off the shopfloor, are now expected to work alongside production workers, ironing out problems as they occur. Some firms are rebuilding office facilities on or near the shop floor, thus increasing the interaction between white- and blue-collar staff.

As noted earlier, supervisors are likely to assume the responsibility of implementing these changes. This puts great emphasis on the managerial ability of supervisors. Communicative skills are a must. Similarly, supervisors have to be able to motivate their staff towards organisational performance, in effect channelling any negative energy towards change into support for the new approach. Furthermore, supervisors will require greater conceptual skills, such as the ability to analyse, reason, synthesise, and interpret information so as to be able to make effective decisions. These skills are particularly relevant to problem-solving and decision-making which was dealt with in Chapter 11. Finally, supervisors, as will be argued in the next chapter, will have to develop the skills to lead people in groups or teams.

WCM also gives rise to new forms of organisation that cut across departmental lines and have far less hierarchy than before. Most cited are teams comprising both design and production people. A long-standing criticism of mass production, for instance, has been the separation of functions like production, sales and marketing into separate and discrete entities of the firm. Often products were designed, produced and marketed with little cooperation. Now, with the pressure to introduce new products to the marketplace in shorter time, concurrent engineering is becoming increasingly popular, especially in the highly internationalised automotive industry. Concurrent engineering, also called "simultaneous engineering" or "design for manufacturability", is the integration of the engineering and manufacturing operations into one organic element. The opposite of this is "sequential engineering" where each functional group hands over responsibility to the next group, and so on down the line, with little interaction between groups. As sequential engineering represents the old way of doing business, concurrent engineering is the new approach to designing and manufacturing products.

In world class manufacturing, as job classifications are broadened, flatter pay structures should become the norm. Aside from encouraging employees to learn and use more skills, the compensation system should also accommodate the need for employees to participate in group work. This way, conceivably, the responsibility for quality and delivery can be placed on employees, preferably being internalised in the group. Further, instead of being focused on one's own job, as is typical under the Taylorist logic, employees are encouraged to take a systematic or holistic view, noting where their job fits into the overall process, including the final product, and noting customers' concerns, and how it relates to other employees' jobs. Compensation practices that seem well-suited to world class manufacturing include pay for knowledge and salaried rates. Both encourage the development of a polyvalent (multi-skilled) workforce performing a range of tasks which cut across traditional job lines.

To stay competitive, firms need to adopt all or most of the elements of world class manufacturing. This is certainly the case in Ireland. IBEC, for example, fully endorses WCM as a potentially very rewarding way of organising work. Documents released by SIPTU, Ireland's largest union, indicate that many firms are well into WCM. IBEC is encouraging member firms to adopt these changes, as well as providing guidelines on how to implement them, while SIPTU is providing advice and guidance to its members on how to negotiate change. SIPTU, to its credit, does not advocate a policy of refusal to accept change, but rather encourages members to negotiate the type of change that would enhance employees' skills and increase their job security. Both IBEC and SIPTU, to varying degrees, are of the opinion that WCM, once successfully implemented, can substantially improve the ability of Irish firms to compete successfully on the domestic and international market.

THE ELEMENTS OF WORLD CLASS MANUFACTURING

Thus far, we have examined the broad outlines of world class manufacturing. This section is more specific: it examines in detail the various elements that constitute WCM. As noted earlier, the various elements that make up WCM are:

- New business techniques, such as JIT and TQM
- New computerised technology, notably FMS and cells
- New forms of work organisation, notably multi-skilled, multi-functional work.

Just-in-Time Production

Traditionally, firms have operated what can be termed a Just-in-Case (JIC) approach to stock. In such a system, parts, components and products are stored in warehouses and accessed when needed. Often hundreds, if not thousands, of parts are stored at any one time. A Just-in-Time (JIT) approach, by contrast, requires that no excess stock be carried. Rather, parts are delivered only when they are ready to be used. JIT is therefore defined as supplying the right part(s) at the right time and in the right number.

With the JIC system, a person typically fills out a form requesting parts and supplies from a stock room or warehouse. These parts are then delivered in large number. In a JIT system parts are supplied to the employees as they are needed. These parts are not stored in-house, but rather, are transported by suppliers to the factory as they are needed. Further, in the ideal JIT system, no forms need to be filled out. Rather, stock is barcoded and everything computerised. In one American firm, employees have telephones at their workstations, and simply ring suppliers when parts are needed.

The auto industry in the States has led the world in the adoption of JIT practices. In many cases, suppliers deliver parts right down to the workstation. Some of these plants operate with just one hour's supply of parts. Every hour, new parts are supplied.

Not surprisingly, with such short buffers, JIT can put great stress on employees and supervisors. A blip in the system can cause untold problems. Most American firms, however, carry a week's buffer to protect against these problems. Harley Davidson is not untypical of American firms here. Organising work in cells, that is groups of machinery staffed by one or two employees, these cells carry a whole week's buffer of stock. The company has plans to reduce this to one day. Harley also operates a form of JIT system referred to as Kanban, or what they call MAN (Material as Needed). Kanban systems are elements of JIT where a employee requests a part by using a card system. Harley have found that by supplying materials only when they are needed, they can free up space. Moreover, less materials have gone missing. The final saving Harley have attributed to their MAN system is a smoother flowing production process.

JIT dates back to the late 1960s when the Toyota Motor Company in Japan began experimentation with new forms of production, and General Electric in 1980 was one of the first American companies to switch to a JIT system. There are many Irish companies implementing JIT, mostly foreign multinationals. JIT is an extremely simple method of managing stock, and this simplicity, along with its effectiveness, can explain much of its popularity. However, it is worth noting that in Germany, JIT is humorously referred as Just in (a) Traffic Jam. This is because, given Germany's high population density and heavily congested roads, moving parts by road proved to be counter-productive. In fact, this relates back to the previously mentioned buffer of carrying one week's stock as security against potential problems. Japanese firms, and some American auto firms, however, have been successful in implementing JIT systems in the ideal way.

JIT strives both to simplify the production function and to maximise the elements — capital, labour and machinery — that make up the production process. Its successful implementation, however, depends on the ability of a firm to make far-reaching changes in the organisation of work, especially the need for decentralisation of authority. The changes in work organisation that are necessary are examined in the section headed "cellular manufacturing".

Total Quality Management (TQM)

Quality control, in the factory of old, used to be a case of examining the final product to see if it worked the way it was supposed to work. So, for example, the engine of a car was started: if it worked, it was passed; if it didn't, it was sent for repair. The parts that made up the engine, valves, pistons, etc., were not tested until the engine was fully assembled. Quality control, moreover, was the responsibility of one person or department, and one only. Workers on the production line, therefore, had little interest in quality control. Instead, they focused on assembling as many products or parts as possible since they had an incentive, the piece-rate system, to do so. Finally, the priority in the traditional firm was to keep production costs low in order to achieve greater profitability. Quality was therefore seen as an acceptable cost. That is, the traditional factory operated under the assumption that there would always be faulty parts but as long they were kept to a minimum, the benefits of mass production would more than account for their cost.

The new approach to quality, commonly referred to as Total Quality Control or Total Quality Management, turns on its head the old view of quality control. Unlike the traditional approach which accepts bad parts, and builds quality in when the product is fully completed, the new approach aims for 100 per cent quality, and quality has to be built into the production of parts. Furthermore, rather than having one person or department responsible for quality control, under TQM everyone in the organisation is responsible for quality, and no expense should be spared in building a quality product. Indeed, under TQM, the stress is on continuous improvement and preventative maintenance. Thus, problems, ideally, should be spotted before they arise, and the production process should be constantly improving.

TQM has many advantages. To begin with, there are the savings in scrap and rework. These come about, as we will learn shortly, by making employees responsible for quality. Secondly, a higher-quality product is built. Thirdly, the production process, and particularly the flow of parts from one station to another, can be improved immensely under TQM by removing any glitches caused by faulty parts. Fourthly, the TQM approach is more productive, given that there are fewer faulty parts. Finally, TQM is more attentive to customers' concerns, particularly their need for high-quality products.

The Japanese Gurus

TQM is associated with Japanese businesses, and in particular, with W. Edwards Deming. An American by birth, his ideas were rejected by American businesses as too costly and inappropriate, and he went to Japan to help with the post-war reconstruction. There he found a ready made audience who would listen to his philosophy on improving quality. In various books and articles, Deming argued the need to improve quality and promoted the following 14 principles:

1. The company should publish a mission statement on quality which should be distributed to all employees.
2. Everyone in the organisation, from top management to employees, should be involved in improving quality. Top management, in particular, must demonstrate its commitment to quality.

3. Concentrate on identifying mistakes during the production process rather than after the product is manufactured.
4. Suppliers should be selected on the basis of their ability to supply quality products and not on price, which is secondary.
5. Aim for continuous improvement (or *kaizen* to use the Japanese term).
6. Training should be provided to everyone that needs it, including suppliers.
7. Employees should be encouraged to co-operate by using a participatory style of management.
8. Develop a strong climate of trust between employees and management.
9. Stress teamwork.
10. Get rid of all slogans. Instead, provide the right processes and training for employees to improve quality.
11. Avoid quotas and aim for total quality.
12. Provide complete training to, and the right equipment for, employees.
13. Encourage employees to aim for self-improvement through education.
14. Create a culture which aims for total quality.

Deming, therefore, aims for a long-term, holistic approach to quality. In simple terms, he argues the need for a culture in an organisation dedicated to maintaining high-quality standards. His influence has been phenomenal with nearly all international firms promoting, in one form or another, a quality product. Despite his dislike for slogans, TQM has given rise to numerous catchphrases, including "do it right first time", "build quality into the part", and "quality is job 1".

The Supervisor and Quality

The supervisor's role in quality was first recognised by a Japanese academic, Professor Ishikawa, who, in the early 1960s, promoted the concept of "quality circles". He was involved in training supervisors how to deal with quality. Ishikawa quickly stumbled onto the idea that the best way to maintain high-quality standards was to make a work group, not one individual, responsible for it. As will be argued in Chapter 17, it is the dynamic and participative nature of work groups, which supervisors lead, that allow them to problem-solve effectively. In Ishikawa's view, individual employees should make suggestions and the quality circle — the term coming from employees sitting around in a circle — takes up a study of them. The idea of a circle, it is worth remarking, is that no person sits at the head of a table and dominates proceedings. Rather, each employee is equal and expected to make a contribution. It is the supervisor's job, as leader of the quality circle, to encourage participation.

The concept of quality circles is less popular now, but the idea of a work group taking responsibility for quality is still very much alive, particularly in the notion of teams. Furthermore, as the person responsible for the work group or team, the supervisor plays a pivotal role in quality control. As pointed out, making the employee responsible for the quality of parts they produce is at the core of quality improvements in recent years. However, it is not enough to *tell* a employee that they are now responsible for quality. Rather, the employee has to be *trained*.

In some cases, this involves a completely new mindset, particularly where this is a departure from current practices. Second, it involves making the tools and the authority available to employees. For example, some American firms did away with the idea of a central tool crib where, previously, employees had to request extra tools or parts by signing a slip. Now, with tool cribs located in their workstations, employees are free to take what tools they need. In all, this means placing greater trust in employees. This in turn puts extra responsibilities on supervisors to ensure that employees do not abuse this trust.

As a supervisor, what would your role be in Total Quality Management? First, as noted, you have to take responsibility for seeing that your staff is capable of maintaining high-quality standards. This may entail putting new processes into effect, or seeing to it that employees get extra training. It may also mean that you have to learn more about new quality methods than employees and be there to advise and train them. It may also mean co-ordinating more with middle-level management, especially engineers, who set the initial quality standards in place. Quality is, as Deming noted, not a once-off affair, but rather, a process of continuous improvement that involves everyone in the organisation.

Secondly, Total Quality Management means communicating more. Like quality circles, groups or teams are the vehicle of maintaining high-quality standards. You will have to lead such groups. This author has come across many instances in American firms where teams had to present reports on quality to higher-level management. Indeed, in one firm, everyone in the organisation had to present to management the results of a project undertaken by a group headed by a supervisor. Therefore, communicative skills are important to WCM.

Thirdly, having responsibility for the group, you will have to motivate and lead it towards higher-quality output. This means instilling in each and every member of the work group a pride in their work. In some regards this is not difficult, since most employees already take great pride in their work and do want to build a high-quality product. However, you have to build a culture which stresses quality at all times. In practice, that can be difficult. For example, with preventative maintenance, employees have to take on new tasks, which they may be reluctant to do. The importance of quality, however, has to be communicated to all employees and all employees have to be involved in it. The best way of doing this is to organise your staff in groups, communicating with them constantly, such as through weekly meetings, and showing them the quality products they are producing. Regular communication, along with the proper processes and training, are the keys to high-quality standards.

New Technology

The first element of world class manufacturing examined was new Japanese business techniques, notably JIT and TQM. The second broad element of WCM is new technology. Much of the technology associated with mass production is what is termed "dedicated" machinery. It is dedicated to the extent that it can do only one thing, such as assemble or machine a particular product. A switch to another product often entails a new production line. New computerised technology is significantly different from the non-computerised technology it replaces. Essentially, its flexibility provides the ability to switch from one product to another in real time which, in computer terms, means as close as possible to zero. The following section provides first an overview of computerised technology, and secondly, the implications of this for employees and supervisors. New technology, however, and especially new microelectronics technology, alone is not part of the WCM philosophy. Rather, it is the way technology is used that counts. This, as we will learn next, means having highly-skilled and highly-motivated employees at the controls of computers.

The implementation of computers has been accelerated in recent years by two factors: the fact, firstly, that computer hardware (though not software) has become increasingly cheaper yet more powerful; and secondly, new developments in computerised technology, particularly the ability to convert analogue signals into digitised data which can then be transmitted over telephone lines and reread by a computer. A modem is a case in point. It converts a computer's digital signals into analogue signals in a process referred to as Modulation — the MO in modem. A modem at the other end reconverts the dialogue signals back to digitised ones in the reverse process called demodulation — the DEM in modem.

The technology used in your television is very differently configured from the technology used to run computers. Yet there have been great strides made in recent years linking the two. This is what is termed telecommunications. The latter represents a merging of microelectronic technology and communications systems. Of concern here is this ability of modern technology to "capture", store and manipulate diverse information, and how this process can affect work, principally in the manner of allowing for more operator feedback, greater control, and to a lesser extent, automatic monitoring of work. Mostly it has been used to automate the production process.

Automation

The term "automation" is traditionally understood to refer to the process of mechanisation, or the replacement of manual activity by machines. More lately, though, automation has been used in a rather general sense to denote the junction of computer science and manufacturing, as the computerised control of the production function. There are different forms of automation.

Fixed automation refers to where the sequencing of operations, which are usually kept fairly simple, is largely determined by the equipment configuration. Once in place, the equipment, referred to as dedicated equipment, is very inflexible and return on investment is gained only by high production rates. A transfer (or assembly) line is a case in point.

Programmable automation (PA), the second category of automation, is the process of controlling machine tools by programmable instructions. A classic example is a CNC (computer-numerically-controlled) machine which is, essentially, a conventional machine — such as a lathe or milling machine — which is controlled by a computer. Instructions on how to perform a function are fed into the machine by a tape unit and the operator's job becomes less one of machining and more one of programming. With computerised control the sequencing of events at each machine can easily be changed by reprogramming, something which can be done off the shopfloor. Programmable automation is normally associated with batch production, that is, with the manufacture of small to medium lots and, to a lesser extent, with the metalworking industry. However, other industries, including the brewing and baking industries, are using computer-numerical tools with great effect. Guinness and the leading bakeries all use computerised equipment in the manufacture of their products.

The final category of automation is *flexible automation*. It is really an extension of programmable automation though it has been the subject of much interest in recent years. Essentially, with flexible automation, the aim is to have the production system produce a wide variety of parts with minimum delays for setups and changeovers. A manufacturing system commonly associated with flexible automation is a Flexible Manufacturing System (FMS). It is worth mentioning in detail here, in part because Apple Computers in Cork have FMS and, in part also, because FMS is seen as the so-called factory of the future.

Flexible Manufacturing Systems

Briefly, a flexible manufacturing system (FMS) consists of a number of large machines or cells linked by a materials-handling system, both of which are under the control of a centralised computer. In other words, a FMS is a fully integrated, fully programmable and minimally-manned manufacturing system. Thus, every thing associated with the manufacture of parts and components — the supply of parts and tools, the machining, the movement of stock, etc. — is controlled by a computer.

Having flexibility (or more correctly programmability) in terms of the materials-handling system in the use of multipurpose tools, specifically CNC machinery, and in the manner in which all are controlled centrally, allows a FMS to produce a wide variety of parts at any one time, as well as to make frequent changes in its production run in an economic and timely fashion. In this way, economies of scope as well as scale are realised. Economies of scope are defined as the realisation of a wide variety of product differentiation in an economic and efficient manner. This point was alluded to earlier, namely, that firms have to manufacture a wider range of products to meet different customers' needs.

The objective of FMS is to be able to react quickly to changes in product demand and design, particularly in the routing of materials, adding new parts if need be, and the setting up of machinery for a new production run, all of which can be done automatically (or as near as one can get to automatically) by a computer. The more a factory is automated, the more it comes close to being what is termed an unmanned or "lights out" factory. To date, there are only a few factories of this kind in the world. Indeed, the degree of automation world-wide, save for Japan and Sweden, is very low. This is partly because new technology is extremely expensive and somewhat questionable in its performance. It is prone to breakdown, and does not always deliver as expected. Instead, most firms have implemented a system commonly referred to as *cell* or *cellular manufacturing* which is premised on making equal changes in work organisation and technology. It is sometimes referred to as "Humanware" because the core of the system is designed around people, not machines. Cellular manufacturing is a sort of halfway house between zero and full automation, and has been receiving much attention in Ireland and elsewhere because of its benefits and low cost.

Cellular Manufacturing

Cellular (or cell) manufacturing (CM), in essence, refers to the physical layout of a factory floor where dissimilar machines — e.g., a lathe, a broach and a milling machine — are grouped together into various groups or cells with the aim of fully producing a family of parts. Within each cell, employees, now termed cell operators, are expected to perform many functions (from set up to quality inspection). This broadening of job content is referred to as horizontal job loading (the addition of more tasks) and vertical job loading (the increase in responsibility). As a result, many functions previously the responsibility of indirect labour — like quality assurance and supervision — are shouldered on to cell operators. Therefore, apart from the fact that employees may operate more than one machine in a cell, some working simultaneously, they may also be responsible for more tasks, such as inspections, material handling, quality control and preventive maintenance. This compares to the traditional environment in which an employee performs a single, usually fairly repetitive, task constantly.

Cells are either of two kinds, manned or unmanned (that is, robotics). Manned cells are by far the most common given that robotics technology is far from perfect and requires much investment.

Manned cells fall into two categories: multiple or single operator. A single operator has one employee or cell operator; a multiple operator cell is staffed by more than one employee, giving it the advantage of numerical flexibility, that is, the ability to adjust the number of employees in a cell when demand changes. In multiple operator cells, operators work in groups (typically the cell defines the group). The group is responsible for its own decisions and for the operation of the cell as a whole. Workers ideally rotate through the various positions sharing the workload. In some cases cell operators are expected to meet in a work team which is typically centred around the cell. It may meet on a regular basis, say once a week, or alternatively on an "as needed" basis to discuss production-related issues.

While single operator cells are, by necessity, small (typically no more than three or four machines) multiple operator cells can vary considerably in size. For example, one multiple operator cell may have three employees, and another could have 20 or more. The latter configurations, where plants are laid out in a small number of very large cells, are sometimes referred to as focused plants. That is, each segment of the plant is "focused" towards the complete production of a particular item. A plant is rarely 100 per cent cellularised. Indeed, more common is where a firm implements cells in a piecemeal fashion, while still retaining elements of job shop, particularly for the production of odd parts.

Cell manufacturing is not a technology as such. Rather, it is a change in the way the floor is laid out, from a functional to a cellular layout. In a functional layout, similar machinery is placed in departments: lathes in a lathe department, milling machines in a milling department, etc. With cells, dissimilar machinery is placed in cell-like configurations, each with the aim of being able to machine a part in full. As a result, the machinery that can be used in a CM system is the same general purpose machinery which is common to the job shop. However, because a cell is expected to manufacture a product in full, thus minimising storage and/or transport costs, extra machinery and tooling are often required. Finally, cells are increasingly being implemented in conjunction with JIT and TQM. Not surprisingly, among the benefits cited with cells are improvements in material handling, shorter lead times, quality improvements and better employee utilisation.

Despite the fact that the cell environment changes the way work is carried out in the sense that employees have to do more and use more skills, the same employee is employed with increased training. The latter usually involves teaching a cell operator how to operate all machines in a cell. In some cases this can be fairly simple: for example, a drill operator entering into a cell that also included milling machines would need to be shown how to operate a milling machine. In other cases, training can mean learning new skills, like programming or TQM, or may involve learning group tactics. The latter is necessary because in multiple operator cells employees are expected to rotate positions, thus sharing work, or to rotate between cells. While this demands extra and, in many cases, continuous training, the extra costs should be well offset by improvements in productivity and quality. As a supervisor, you will probably be responsible for ensuring that employees are trained to the right degree.

As noted, the compensation system may change to reflect the new environment. Individual piece-rate compensation systems are considered inappropriate to cell manufacturing. Three reasons can be given: piece-rates promote employee competition, not co-operation; they fail to take into account the diversity of skills necessary to operate different machinery; finally, piece-rates create the potential for uneven work schedules. More suitable are group incentive systems or salaried rates. Indeed, some firms have been experimenting with new profit-sharing systems, such as Gainsharing and Improshare, in order to stress group solutions to problems, and to emphasise the important and continuing contribution that the production employee makes to the success of the firm. Pay for knowledge, where employees are paid extra for the number of extra skills they learn, is another type of compensation which is receiving great interest now. This way, high-skilled employees can be more easily rotated in different jobs as demand for products changes.

The Importance of Choice in New Technology

The technology that is available to firms today is widespread. Moreover, the same technology can be implemented in many different ways. For example, a firm can choose between degrees of automation, from low to high. It can have stand alone conventional machines, or highly integrated, general purpose computerised machinery. Finally, it can choose to have high-skilled or low-skilled employees. Much research is available to suggest that the way technology is implemented depends largely on the choices made by the affected parties — management, unions, supervisors, and employees.

A Briton, John Child (1972), has been a leading writer on technical change and social choice. He focuses on the decision-making process of technical change, on who makes these decisions and at what level, and on how these decisions are influenced and implemented by lower-level management and employees. According to him, management forms into groups — referred to as "dominant coalitions" or "power-holding groups" — to promote technical change. These groups are not formal, readily identifiable gatherings of managers, but rather cut across normal boundaries to incorporate managers from different departments within a firm. Still, no matter how powerful these coalitions can be in terms of making the initial decision to introduce technology, when it comes to its actual implementation, these decisions can be offset and altered through the actions of lower-level management, supervisors and employees. So one focuses on organisational arrangements — among them collective bargaining and work teams — as well as informal avenues like custom and practice in which employees, engineers and supervisors can have influence on the operation of technology.

The Supervisor and New Technology

Supervisors have an important influence on technology. They are the ones responsible for the way technology is introduced. To repeat what was stated above, top management sets the guidelines for the choice of technology, but supervisors influence it at the point of implementation. Further, because technology is rarely introduced all at once, the process extends over many years and presents many opportunities for people to have an input.

Handling technical change is not easy. For a start, there has been a significant amount of new technology introduced into the workplace of late, most of it resulting in job losses. As a supervisor, the introduction of new technology puts you in a difficult position. You may be on very good terms with employees, but you also have a job to do. Do you side with employees, or take the management view that new technology has to be introduced immediately and in the way they planned?

The first thing to do is find out what you can about the new technology, particularly the reasons for its introduction and its consequences for you and your staff. This can help put aside any misconceptions about the technology, especially with respect to job losses. A widely-held view is that new technology results in job losses. In point of fact, that was not the case with technology in the past, partly because firms experienced growth that offset, by far, the potential downside of any new technology. However, events in recent years have put these findings in question. It is not difficult to cite the case of a firm like Guinness, by no means the exception, which once employed over 5,000 employees in St. James's Gate and now employs less than 1,000. Such statistics put supervisors in difficult positions, particularly where employees may develop a negative attitude to new technology. However, unions now accept that new technology, in spite of the loss of some jobs, can help firms stay in business and thus help employees in the long run. Put this way, new technology is necessary for the long-term survival of the firm, and thus the job security of employees. This is a persuasive argument and one which you must communicate to employees.

Secondly, employees should be consulted and informed about these changes. As noted many times in this book, the supervisor who is open and honest with employees is the better supervisor. Therefore, be honest with your staff about the consequences of technical change. Nobody likes losing their job, or seeing a diminution (or what they perceive as a diminution) of their work status. Worst of all is when it is imposed on employees, without their being informed beforehand. Therefore, involve employees as best you can in decisions relating to technology.

Thirdly, you have to ensure that new technology is implemented in a way that is developing, not downgrading, skills. All too often, firms have short-changed the restructuring process by implementing part of the world class manufacturing strategy. This is a valid criticism made by SIPTU and other unions. WCM involves increasing the responsibilities, freedom and power of employees. In principle, employees should be able to organise their own schedules, and make decisions on their own. As a supervisor, you should not be afraid of the movement towards self-supervision. Indeed, if anything, you should encourage it by giving employees freedom in their jobs. In all, you have to learn that co-operation and trust, as well as open communication, are the essence of world class manufacturing.

NEW FORMS OF WORK ORGANISATION

As noted, there are three broad elements to world class manufacturing. The first two — new business techniques and new technology — have been examined. The final element is what could be termed the high performance work organisation.

Work organisation refers to how work is shared out: who does what, and how. Organising — one of the five management functions identified in Chapter 2 — is a primary concern of the supervisor. Aside from organising their own work, supervisors have to organise the work of a group of employees, seeing that the work is carried out according to plan. These plans are set by top management, but very often supervisors have some discretion as to how the actual work is carried out. There is much discussion in Europe at the moment about the need to increase the skills and know-how of employees. A high-skilled workforce serves two main functions. First, it allows firms to be responsive to market changes and thus more competitive, and second, a related point, it allows firms to pay higher wages and still be competitive.

There are numerous terms used to describe this type of work organisation that is favoured by academics and technocrats in the European Union. One is "High Performance Work Organisation" (HPWO), which is the term used here. This is the American term. Another possibility is "teamwork" (the subject of the next chapter). In Germany, it is referred to as "group work". Regardless of terminology, the type of work organisation required by advanced manufacturing firms is a multifunctional, multiskilled workforce. Workers are highly skilled, highly motivated and expected to perform a range of functions (multifunctional).

What is the High Performance Work Organisation?

Unlike Taylorism, which deskills and demeans work, HPWO enlarges and enriches jobs. Continuous learning and employee empowerment are therefore the centrepiece of HPWO. In other words, employees have to learn constantly, and be given the responsibility and freedom to make decisions on their own. Furthermore, employees are expected to co-operate with others rather than seeing their jobs as isolated elements. This co-operation should, ideally, be extended to participation in teams. These teams should include employees, supervisors and engineers, if not also customers. The idea is not just to tap into the potential that employees have, but also to get employees to think about the production process as a whole, and to be attentive to customers' needs.

HPWO is the link between people and technology. It gives employees the power, training and tools to exploit the capabilities of new computerised technology. As such, it is the centrepiece of a world class manufacturing strategy since the potential afforded by the human element is far greater than that of technology.

Flexibility does not come automatically with new technology or new work practices. Rather, systems have to be put in place, extensive training has to be made available to all employees, and a new era of trust and co-operation has to be ushered in between management and employees, and between management and unions. Neither comes easily or overnight. Nevertheless, it is clear that workplaces have to be redesigned to improve the skills of employees. A better-skilled workplace, in turn, will be more effective in responding to the demands of the new global environment. In a HPWO environment, employees will be more skilled, more motivated to work, interact more and produce more.

Table 16.1 compares models of work organisation — the traditional model under mass production, and the high performance work organisation under world class manufacturing.

TABLE 16.1: MODELS OF WORK ORGANISATION

Traditional Work Organisation	High Performance Work Organisation
High division of labour	Low division of labour
Deskilled, single function	Multiskilled, multifunctional
Centralised planning	Decentralised decision-making
Static	Adaptive
Limited and once-off training	Continuous training
Individual-centred	Team-centred

SUPERVISORS AND WORLD CLASS MANUFACTURING: UNDERSTANDING THE PROCESS OF CHANGE

Change, and the ability to cope with it, is fast becoming the hallmark of a competitive firm. Dealing with change can mean trying times, however, for a supervisor. In the first instance, change is most likely to come to the supervisor's job more than any other's. The American, though not the German, experience with world class manufacturing has tended to mean layers of supervisory management being made redundant. In Germany, it is less of a problem because many supervisors are high-skilled employees whose skills can easily be used elsewhere. Further, progressive labour law, and a system of employee representation that is second to none, does much to voice employees' concerns about new technology. In America, by contrast, because supervisors do not generally belong to unions, and because of the employment-at-will doctrine, supervisors have been dismissed with little thought shown for them. Ireland is more likely to follow the German route, redeploying rather than dismissing supervisory staff. A strong attachment to trade unionism, and a reasonably strong system of employees' rights (relative to America at least) limit the managerial prerogative to lay off employees.

The second reason why a supervisor may experience difficulty implementing change is that much of it is occurring in firms at the point of production where supervisors have their primary responsibility. And there is much resistance to change for various reasons. One reason is the preference for the status quo. Indeed, job practices have become so ingrained in people's minds that change is difficult to imagine, never mind implement. As noted, craft employees are often reluctant to agree to multicraft work, fearing a diminution of status. However, to be fair to the unions, one of SIPTU's main criticisms of WCM is that firms cherry-pick what they want from WCM but refuse to implement practices which are favourable to employees. Thus, at the heart of recent industrial disputes in Ireland are entrenchment and a reluctance on either side to grant concessions to the other. Entrenchment and position-taking have no place in a world class manufacturing strategy. Rather, a strong vision of the future is required. Supervisors have to be able to articulate this vision.

Another reason for resistance, alluded to earlier, is that employees often associate new technology with job loss and thus have an automatic resistance to change. This concern may be voiced by unions who refuse to countenance any change if it means job loss, or it can be voiced by individual employees who do their utmost to resist change. Often the end result is strikes or poor performance. Such resistance may frustrate the supervisor who wishes to make change but finds it blocked. This is made worse by the fact that the company may not provide supervisors with the power to make the sort of changes they feel are best or, alternatively, force supervisors to make change against their wishes. Culture therefore is also an important barrier to change, particularly in instances where employees are content with the status quo, and where they do not understand, or have not had communicated properly to them, the reasons for change.

One should be aware that employees rarely resist change just for the sake of it. Rather, employees express very real and genuine concerns about technical change. Put it this way: if you were an employee at Irish Steel or Team Aer Lingus looking at life on the dole would you resist change? Therefore, as a supervisor, you should be considerate of employees' concerns and fears about technical change, and do what you can to allay these fears.

Some factors are quite clearly outside the control of the supervisor. Of late, many Irish firms have introduced change at the organisational level following high-level negotiations between the union and management. The supervisor then gets lumped with making those changes, and meets with reluctant employees. If faced with such a scenario, supervisors should make it a point to explain fully and early on the reasons for the change and its implications for employees. This has to be communicated to all employees, preferably in one meeting. At the end of the day, however, supervisors may have to introduce change to a unwilling workforce. This requires that they be assertive and strong individuals.

CHAPTER SUMMARY

This chapter made clear the point that firms are under increasing pressure to change their marketing and production strategy in response to external developments. The latter include increased competition in the marketplace, especially of a global nature, and the widespread availability (albeit at a cost) of new technology and new forms of work organisation.

These pressures are forcing firms to move away from the rigidity and individualism of Taylorism to the holism of world class manufacturing. WCM involves three broad elements. These are new business techniques, such as Just-in-Time production and Total Quality Management. Secondly, new technology, which ranges from stand-alone computer-numerically-controlled machinery to high-tech systems such as flexible manufacturing systems, or low-tech solutions such as cellular manufacturing. The final element is high performance work organisation (HPWO). HPWO is regarded as the most advanced form of work organisation in the manner in which it balances technology and skill to achieve a highly flexible form of work organisation.

Many Irish firms, spurred on by the success of American multinational firms, are adopting part or all of these changes. Both IBEC and SIPTU have responded favourably to WCM. That said, as was made very clear in the opening paragraphs, not all firms make a smooth transition to WCM, nor implement all the elements of WCM. Much depends, as noted, on the choices made by firms and indeed management, employees and supervisors. Moreover, it could be argued that a good deal of what is now happening in the public sector, rationalisation, is akin to world class manufacturing: offering a better service using fewer employees and new practices and new technology.

Supervisors have an important role to play in managing change to a WCM system (or indeed in rationalisation strategies). Much of the change occurring is at the point of production. Top management make the decisions regarding which technology or systems to buy, but supervisors have to implement it. It was pointed out that developing the skills of employees is an important element of the success of Irish firms in doing business abroad. That is, long-term competitiveness depends on making far-reaching change now. It is not premised simply on new leading-edge technology, but rather the integration and harmonisation of people and technology, and culture and work. The supervisor needs to be able to channel employees' energies away from the negative reaction to change into promoting constructive change. This demands great skill on the part of the supervisor. The effective supervisor is one who, in seeing change as a challenge, is able to manage change, and thus ensure a more competitive future for all.

References and Further Reading

Child, J. (1972) "Organisation Structure, Environment and Performance: The Role of Strategic Choice." *Sociology* (6) (1) (1972): 1-22.

Harvey, N. (1993) "Automation and Restructuring: How Industrial Relations Affects Change in the Wisconsin Metal Working Industry", IFAC Symposium on Automated Systems Based on Human Skill (and Intelligence). Madison, Wisconsin. September 22-25, 1992. London: Pergamon Press.

Harvey, N. (1994) "The Changing Face of Manufacturing: New Compensation Practices in the German and American Metal Working Industries", *Control Engineering Practice*, Vol. 2, No. 4, pp. 697-705.

Harvey, N. and M. von Behr (1994) "Group Work in the American and German Non-Automotive Metal Manufacturing Industry", *International Journal of Human Factors in Manufacturing*, Vol. 4, No. 1, pp. 1-16. 1994.

Keegan, R. & J. Lynch (1995) *World Class Manufacturing ... in an Irish Context*, Dublin: Oak Tree Press.

Mooney, P. (1996) *Developing the High Performance Organisation: Best Practice for Managers*, Dublin: Oak Tree Press.

Peppard, J. & P. Rowland (1995) *The Essence of Business Process Reengineering*, London: Prentice Hall.

Schonberger, R. (1986) *World Class Manufacturing: The Lesson of Simplicity Applied*, New York: The Free Press.

Tiernan, S., Morley, M. & Foley, E. (1996) *Modern Management: Theory and Practice for Irish Students*, Dublin: Gill and Macmillan, chapter 9.

Chapter 17

CHANGES IN THE ORGANISATION OF WORK: THE RISE OF TEAMWORK

THE OBJECTIVE OF THIS CHAPTER

Firms today are moving away from an individualistic approach to work, reorganising into groups or teams employees who previously worked alone. Thus, instead of having employees, say, on an assembly line each performing a limited and routine task, employees are now organised in groups sharing out work duties. This is called "teamwork", analogous in many ways to a sports team. Teams are more than groups, however. They personify groups at their best: team members complement each other and work towards a common objective, hence their productivity is high.

As with world class manufacturing, the leaders in the establishment of teams are manufacturing firms and particularly multinational companies. Teams, however, are not limited to manufacturing firms, or indeed, within manufacturing to production and assembly. All types of businesses, including the services sector, are moving to teams. Similarly, manufacturing firms have set up teams in sales and finance, spurred on by the success of teams on the shopfloor.

The exact nature of teams varies from company to company. Most teams fall into one of three categories: project teams, management teams or work groups. Project teams are those set up for a specific purpose: teams, it is widely accepted, have particular application to complex problems and are extremely effective in managing change. Management teams are groups made up of managers only: a board of directors is in many ways a management team. Finally, work groups are groups of employees working together. The concern of this chapter is with work groups of the sort a supervisor would lead. More to the point, the chapter makes the argument that organisations should aim for semi-autonomous or self-directed (or autonomous) work teams where the role of the supervisor as team leader becomes that of the facilitator of teams.

Not surprising, given the widespread interest in and adoption of teamworking ideals, the social partners, IBEC (1993) and ICTU (1993), have both produced policy documents on teamwork. Despite their obvious differences, both organisations have argued in favour of teamwork for improving both the competitiveness of Irish business, especially in doing business abroad, and the quality of working life for employees. The latter is an obvious concern of ICTU, less so of IBEC. Still IBEC outlined clear advantages of teamwork to employees, which would carry over to increased productivity for the company.

Teams are less well-developed in Ireland and tend to be associated with American and Japanese multinationals. Moreover, they are more likely to be found in what are termed "greenfield sites", that is, where a company sets up a new plant, often without a union[1]. It is expected, however, that, spurred on by American and Japanese firms, Irish firms, both indigenous and multinational ones, will develop more teams. This will be particularly the case for firms in the electronics industry which has great application for teamwork, especially in assembly. The service sector, to a lesser extent, is affected by the movement towards teams. In Britain, for example, the banking sector is moving towards teams in conjunction with a process of enlarging and enriching jobs. Research in Ireland would indicate that the financial sector is re-organising workers into teams along with the implementation of new image processing technology and changes in work practices, such as broader pay bands. It is likely that Irish employees, regardless of their type of employment, will be expected to work more in teams over the coming years.

After reading and studying this chapter the reader should have an understanding of:

---

[1] This argument is also made by John Geary (1995) in regard to the UK.

- Job design
- What teamwork is
- How to set up and run teams

This chapter should be read in conjunction with the previous chapter (on world class manufacturing) since teamwork forms a strong element of modernising firms. Similarly, the reader should consult Chapter 12 which deals with the behaviour of individuals as group members.

JOB DESIGN

Job design refers to the way tasks are broken down into different jobs, and responsibility or work delegated to individual employees. Davis (1966) provides the classic definition:

> The specification of the contents, methods and relationships of jobs in order to satisfy technological and organisational requirements as well as the social and personal requirements of the job holder.

Job design is thus a compromise between the organisation's needs for productivity, efficiency and quality, and the needs of the individual for interesting and challenging work. There is widespread agreement now that jobs should be more satisfying, and that such changes bring positive benefits, not only from a social perspective but also a technical one: workers who are content with their jobs are more productive.

It is generally accepted that there are three main ways to improving job design. These are:

- Job enlargement
- Job enrichment
- Work teams.

Job enlargement, as its name suggests, refers to increasing the number of tasks a job holder has to do: in effect, giving them more work to do. At the very least, job enlargement has the potential to improve task variety while making an employee busy. Job enrichment, on the other hand, refers to increasing the skills and responsibilities of the job holder: in effect, giving employees more interesting and challenging work with, ideally, less repetitive tasks to do. Taken together, job enlargement and job enrichment, in theory at least, have the potential to improve job satisfaction. Firms benefit because of the association between job satisfaction and output. However, aside from productivity increases, reductions in employee absenteeism, lateness, and staff turnover have been recorded; in addition, work morale should improve, and there should be higher commitment on the part of employees. Finally, more enriched work allows for greater trust between managers, trade unions and employees.

Hackman and Oldman (1980) have argued that jobs should be improved along five core dimensions, including:

- Skill variety: refers to the number of skills a job holder has to use.
- Task identity: refers to the degree to which an employee has to undertake a complete task.
- Task significance: refers to the view that employees can perceive the value or significance of their work for others.
- Autonomy: refers to the degree of control an employee has over a job.
- Feedback: refers the degree to which employees are informed as to how well they are doing.

Following Hackman and Oldman, it can be said that jobs can be enlarged and enriched in the following ways:

- By giving employees more tasks to do, with more control over the job
- By giving employees more autonomy to vary the methods, sequence and pace of work
- By having longer work-cycles and less repetition
- By making employees more responsible for their output including product quality and delivery of products

- By allowing employees to complete a product in full thus reducing task specialisation
- By involving individual employees as much as possible in decision-making relating to their work
- By continuously introducing new and more difficult tasks
- By providing as much feedback as possible on employee's work
- By having as much social contact as is reasonably possible (for example, working in teams)
- By having opportunities for self-development.

Job enlargement and job enrichment date back to the 1970s. Indeed they are associated with efforts to remove the boredom and monotony of assembly line work that came about from the social changes of the late 1960s. Today, both have been given renewed emphasis with the movement towards work teams; job redesign is a major element of teams in the sense that, intentionally or unintentionally, jobs are enlarged and enriched with teamwork and there is a strong emphasis on linkages between jobs. The remainder of this chapter deals with teamwork.

WHAT ARE TEAMS?

A leading writer on teams is the Briton, John Adair (1986). He argues that teams, because of the contribution of highly skilled and highly motivated team members, goes far beyond what individuals alone or together in loosely defined groups can achieve. We think of a group as a collection of individuals working towards a common aim. A team is more. Because team members' talents and skills are complementary they can substitute for and rotate with each other. Quoting Babington Smith, Adair (1986, p. 95) defines a team as:

> . . . a group in which the individuals have a common aim and in which the jobs and skills of each member fit in with those of others, as — to take a very mechanical and static analogy — in a jigsaw puzzle pieces fit together without distortion and together produce some overall pattern.

The key to effective teamwork therefore is congruence. It is not enough simply that four people do a job better than one. Adam Smith, for example, first argued that through a process of the division of labour, that is, specialisation, work could be done more productively. Fourteen men making a pin was more productive than one. Smith's view, the logic behind mass production, was that by performing a highly specialised task each employee becomes highly efficient. One downside of this is that employees become so adept at their particular task that replication by another is difficult. Further, the same individual can only do one task highly efficiently. This is not the case with teams. Members are cross-trained and multiskilled. They work, in Adair's terms, in concert, complementing and helping each other.

A team goes beyond the saying that "many hands make light work". A group, for example, may simply be more efficient at doing a job than an individual. For example, two people may cut the grass in less than half the time it takes one person. This is because in combining the strengths of two people, shortcomings can be limited and advantages stressed. In the grass-cutting analogy, one person may be extremely efficient at operating a lawnmower, another at raking. Together, they make a productive group. A team, however, would imply that these two people use the best of their ingenuity, creativity and skills to do the best job possible. This allows them to go further than a group. For example, they can rotate jobs, and one person can substitute for the other in the event of, say, sickness. Consensus and co-operation, along with skill and training, are the essence of teamwork.

There are cases in which individuals do jobs better than teams. Groups, including teams, are slow to reach decisions. Besides, there is no guarantee that a team makes a better decision than a person acting alone. Similarly, not all tasks can be done by a team. Creative tasks, for example, are sometimes best done by individuals. Finally, not all teams are effective for a variety of reasons, including the inability to reach a working consensus. Indeed, group dynamics can often work in such a way as to negate the potential benefits of teamwork. Despite such misgivings about team or group work, the case for teamwork is very strong. In today's business environment, firms need that competitive edge. To build a product that is better, of higher quality, and cheaper than another requires great effort on the part of each employee. It is not surprising that many of the leading-edge firms in Ireland in both the manufacturing and services sectors are setting up teams.

TABLE 17.1: THE BENEFITS OF TEAMWORK

- Increased flexibility
- Higher productivity
- More responsive to customers
- Increased job satisfaction
- Fewer workers needed
- Better climate to work in
- Greater job security
- Greater commitment of employees
- Increased co-operation and reduction in duplication of effort.

THE BENEFITS OF TEAMS

Flexibility is seen as the main benefit of organising employees into teams (see Table 17.1). Ideally, with sufficiently skilled employees, a team should be able to rotate its members around the various tasks assigned to it. By helping each other, team members should be able to reduce any bottlenecks or, if one team member is absent, the others can fill in, thus limiting any disruption to the production process. Aside from increasing productivity, teams allow a firm to respond more quickly to market changes, which is seen today as the hallmark of success in the extremely competitive global environment. Teams do not, however, automatically lead to increased flexibility. Rather, flexibility depends on a variety of other factors and, in particular, on how well team members are trained and equipped.

The quality of the product or service can be much improved with teams and particularly by making each team member individually, and the team collectively, responsible for the output of the group. This compares to the Tayloristic production process where quality was the responsibility of a specialised department or person. Similarly, for service firms, the service can be improved by making teams more attentive to customers' concerns. In the banking sector, for example, employees, working now as part of a team, are responsible for completing a service in full. Prior to this, most employees worked alone, performing highly specialised tasks.

Finally, being more productive, firms can do more with fewer employees. Teams allow a firm to tap into the creativity and potential that employees have. Team members can make suggestions (perhaps even implement them) that save firms thousands of pounds. For example, after implementing teams, a German firm in the US claimed to be operating at 150 per cent productivity with just 75 per cent of labour.

CHANGE IN WORK PRACTICES AND TECHNOLOGY

These benefits are realised, however, only where far-reaching change is made. A consensus has emerged — broadly referred to as the "integration thesis"— which argues that firms have to make significant changes in both work organisation and technology (McDuffie and Kochan, 1988). This integration thesis, also referred to as the "humanware system", came out of the Massachusetts Institute of Technology (MIT) study of Japanese "transplants" in the US (i.e. Japanese auto plants in America). The best performers, the MIT study found, were the plants which made equal changes in both technology and the organisation of work.

Implementing technical change does not mean the most up-to-date computer system, but, at the very least, firms must have the technology which is necessary to make a world class product or to deliver a world class service.

Similarly, with respect to work organisation, firms need to keep abreast, if not ahead of, current changes. Thus, to succeed with teams, investments have to be made in training and in preparing workers for teamwork. In addition, work organisation needs to be changed to stress less rigid hierarchical structures and job categories need to be broadened. Compensation systems need to be modified if quality, rather than quantity, is the desired focus. Teams require decentralised decision-making and flat hierarchies and hence more participative employee relations. Finally, there has to be increased co-operation between engineers and workers and greater interaction between different departments, notably design and manufacture. With these changes, teamwork can be seen as a holistic approach to competitiveness, balancing technological and people changes, which seeks to modernise businesses. Despite this rhetoric, there are many problems with teams. The following section examines "people" issues particularly as raised by trade unions. Table 17.2 summarises the research on employees and teamwork: as can be seen, these are very real issues raised by employees.

EMPLOYEE ISSUES RELATING TO TEAMS

TABLE 17.2: RESEARCH ON EMPLOYEES AND TEAMWORK

Research shows that:

- Firms often take for granted the acceptance of teams by workers, and thus underestimate the need for training and the need to change the culture of an organisation to facilitate teams.
- Highly skilled craft employees are often the least willing to participate in teams, particularly if they have to work alongside less skilled employees, or perform basic operations such as cleaning or preventative maintenance. This they see as a diminution of status.
- Employees may not want to participate in teams, if they perceive it as having to do more work for no extra pay.
- Employees who work in teams may feel that their individual work does not get the respect that it deserves.
- Employees assume firms are primarily concerned with the drive for efficiency, implementing teams and employing contract labour without much thought for long-term employees.
- Industrial relations issues like extra pay and demarcation come to light typically after teams are set up.

Martin Naughton (1994, 1995), Education and Training Officer of SIPTU, argues that teams can provide the following benefits for employees:

- Improved job security
- Improved work atmosphere
- Enhanced job satisfaction
- Increased pay
- Opportunities for self-development.

And the following disadvantages:

- Job loss and unemployment
- Redeployment
- Work intensification
- Loss of pay and privileges
- Loss of status
- Less opportunities.

A number of reasons can explain this sharp contrast between the potential benefits and side-effects of teams. To begin with, as Naughton makes clear, not all firms implement teams the way they should be implemented, that is, with a view to empowering and upskilling employees. Secondly, Naughton points out that not all firms inform or consult with employees or their representatives before implementing teams. In some cases, bad industrial relations is the problem, in other cases, management expresses a strong preference for not dealing with unions. Either way, without the involvement of trade unions, many of the issues noted by Naughton are not addressed. As a result, teams encounter many problems.

In the final part of his articles, Naughton further elaborates on the problems encountered by employees in the move to teamwork:

- Not being able to work in teams
- Not being able to perform the full range of tasks
- Not being able to benefit from training
- Peer pressure and worse group relations

- Work intensification
- Discrimination based on age or sex
- Health and safety issues.

Recent research would concur with Naughton's findings: most workers prefer teamwork, which they see as more enjoyable and as helping their company compete in the international market, but do point out some real problems. Table 17.3 summarises some of the potential pitfalls of teams that were mentioned in interviews with employees of an Irish firm.

TABLE 17.3: PROBLEMS WITH TEAMS

- **Employees**: disruptive employees, employees who are unable to reach standards; employees who are unacceptable to the group; employees who refuse to take individual responsibility and to participate fully in teams; tendency to offload problems rather than take on work; shortage of skilled labour; excessive job rotation and too much change.
- **Inter-team relations**: difficulties communicating with the other teams and especially with teams on different shifts.
- **"Loose" team** ("we don't really have a team"): a team that does not take on the responsibility that goes with teamworking; teamwork is not the culture of the firm.
- **Team leaders**: leaders who do not provide direction; use of excessive authority; not enough contact with team; unable to handle team members; leaders who supervise not facilitate; a facilitator can make a decision and have it questioned by the team; reluctance by facilitator to take on problem.
- **Processes**: meetings which are poorly organised, or not enough or too many meetings; little or no consensus in the group; members who do not or cannot contribute; lack of focus in a team; members work only to their own agenda or interested in own issues; little co-ordination; tension over who does a particular job; lack of communication between shifts; excessive reactive work; accounting for unscheduled work; recurring problems not been attended to; overwork; inability to prioritise in teams; the lack of change and dynamism in a team.

- **Industrial relations**: issues of pay that arise over time (increased basic rate, premium pay, overtime); problems relating to overtime; shop stewards who don't co-operate with teams; wrong pay systems; lack of integration between human resources and industrial relations strategy; inability to deal with industrial relations issues in the team.
- **Technical**: excessive drive for efficiency; tremendous wear and tear on machinery; old machinery; lack of equipment; lack of attention to monitoring and preventative maintenance; lack of training on new machinery.
- **Management**: lack of support of top management; engineers who refuse to co-operate with shop floor employees; lack of co-operation between staff.

Supervisors should be aware of these concerns, not least because they will have to deal with the consequences of them. In conducting research in the US and Germany on cellular manufacturing, I found that organisations set up teams with insufficient planning and, in the case of the US, with complete lack of consultation with trade unions. It was supervisors, newly appointed as team leaders, who had to iron out these problems. No supervisor wishes to be in a situation where they have to deal with reluctant or stressed-out employees, with employees who cannot or refuse to work in teams, or to be faced with, after teams are set up, allegations of discrimination or infringements of health or safety issues. It is important, therefore, that supervisors echo the concerns of employees, and are involved in the decisions that lead to the establishment of teams, rather than only to deal with the consequences. Finally, supervisors have to be aware that teams are also a learning process, and that it is only after teams are set up that people come to terms with them.

Teamwork can thus be portrayed almost as a double-edged sword; there seem to be as many shortcomings associated with teamwork as there are benefits. Indeed, the European Community (Wobbe, 1992) has summarised some of the problems in moving from a Tayloristic or individualistic approach to work to a team-based one. These include:

- Management strategies still adhere predominantly to Tayloristic principles
- Mass production rules are still guiding the perception of engineers and management
- Rigidities in organisational hierarchies, status systems and wage structures hinder developments
- A lack of skilled labour
- A prejudice towards the competence of blue-collar and shop floor work by white-collar employers
- Low level of trust in industrial relations
- A lack of broadly applicable knowledge and experience in teamwork
- A lack of participatory development and change in factories
- Accounting and assessment techniques for management decisions are oriented at mass production principles; they lack modern strategic assessment tools for teamwork
- A lack of management awareness and practice for change.

In a survey of 6,000 firms across the EU, the European Foundation for the Improvement of Living and Working Standards (Sisson, 1996), based in Dublin, found that European firms were much further behind Japanese and American firms in their implementation of new forms of work, including teamwork. In a much publicised research project, researchers at the Massachusetts Institute of Technology (Womack, et al., 1990; see also Monden, 1983) found that Japanese production methods (as epitomised by Toyota) use less material, fewer parts, have shorter production operations, and quicker set ups. At the same time, they have better quality, higher technical specifications, and greater product variety. Taking this argument further, a British industrialist, Clive Morton (1994) argues that much of the success of

Japanese companies is due to teamwork, or rather their ability to build upon consensus in the group.[2]

The view of the EC and the European Foundation is clear: the competitiveness and thus the future of industry in the European Union is dependent on making far-reaching change in existing organisations. These barriers, as outlined above, in time have to be overcome: European firms have to be as competitive as Japanese ones.

TEAM EFFECTIVENESS

A work team has the potential to be as effective as the Irish football team (though not as good at football!). Adair (1986) sees three main factors as important to achieving effectiveness: strong leadership, good team players and the right processes. Achieving this effectiveness is, in large part, a matter of fulfilling certain needs. According to Adair, a team has three basic sets of needs: a task need, a group need and, finally, individual needs. A task need is what the group was set up to do, such as build a product or offer a service. Group needs, on the other hand, refer to the need of people to establish a comfortable working relationship with each other and thus build a cohesive group. Finally, individuals have important needs such as the need for recognition and development. A team is most effective when all three needs are congruent. Table 17.4 lists some of the properties of effective teams: this represents the ideal team.

There are some criticisms of Adair's work. As noted earlier, how well teams perform depends to a large extent on how well they are set up. Research has shown that teams function well when team members are located close together, when the compensation system is individual and performance-related, where members have equal status, and where adequate training is provided both to instil the right norms and to ensure that all team

---

[2] Despite Morton's view, there is some dispute as to how well Japanese firms organise teams. For example, the Japanese refer to a team as *Han*; this is the Japanese word for a small organisational unit which has strong military connotations and little or no autonomy. Some commentators are of the opinion that Japanese teams have very little autonomy and are therefore not the role model for European firms to follow.

members are technically qualified to perform all jobs in the team. Hence how teams are set up may be more important than how they are run.

Secondly, it was pointed out by supervisors that, more and more, the need to get the task done, on time and within budget, was seen as the major priority for them. In other words, as businesses become more comfortable with teams, as the skill level of employees continues to increase, and finally as the trend towards a shrinking workforce continues, the need for supervision becomes less. In interviews with supervisors, some pointed out that the need for supervision would become redundant with teams. As will be argued later, this creates the need for indirect supervision which demands a new type of skill, namely facilitation, on the part of the team leader.

TABLE 17.4: CHARACTERISTICS OF EFFECTIVE TEAMS

- The ability to agree upon goals and objectives and to handle conflict in meaningful way
- The ability to communicate democratically and openly and usually by consensus
- Members have clear idea of their roles and work assignments (functional and team) and what the purpose of the team is
- Good relations with other teams and regularly communicate with others
- Have informal processes and a climate of trust
- The ability to share responsibility, often rotating jobs and even the leadership of the team
- The ability to be self-critical and forward-looking
- Members listen to and care for each other.

TEAM LEADERSHIP

Leadership is vital to any team. Even autonomous teams, despite their name, have some form of leadership, whether it be a rotating leadership, or a facilitator who is responsible for other teams too. Belbin (1981, p. 50) asks a relevant question:

> Is the best leader the one who is most acceptable to the group, with the personal behaviour and image that most fits what people look for in a leader? Or is the best leader the one most likely, during the tenure of the office, to enable the team to reach its goals? If a choice is to be made between these types of leader, then from a management standpoint there is only one option: the effective leader has to be chosen.

The question of who becomes leader of a team is more difficult today. Certainly, in the past, the natural choice for leader was the supervisor: indeed supervisors came into their role in large part because of the need to manage larger groups of workers; common sense dictated that the senior operative be made the supervisor. Today, for a variety of reasons that include decline in union strength and increasing competition in the marketplace, companies may well select who they believe is the best person to be the leader, often using psychometric tests to ascertain who are the best people to work in and to lead teams.

No team that I studied in the US or in Germany was completely autonomous. Generally, firms appointed team leaders from the existing workforce, typically the supervisor. This recognises that supervisors are in the best position to provide team leadership. In conducting research in Ireland I found that organisations with teams, and particularly those in the financial sector, were making do with far fewer people. With the move to teams, selected employees are offered early retirement, and the extra demands have to be met by a smaller workforce. In such scenarios, supervisors are often given responsibility for a greater number of employees. They become a leader, not necessarily of one team, but often of many teams. Usually the job title changes, from supervisor to facilitator. Responsibilities also change: instead of being in charge of a group of employees performing a single function, the team leader is now responsible for multi-skilled, multi-functional teams. Hence the need for a broader range of technical skills.

The Role of the Team Leader

A leader is one who directs a group towards the accomplishment of a goal or task in the same way as a conductor directs an orchestra, that is, by channelling the energy of its members in a constructive and cohesive way. The role of the team leader, therefore, is to combine the skills, abilities and commitment of all members and direct them towards a common purpose. This will necessitate that the leader, at least initially, makes sure that the team is properly staffed and trained, that they have the tools and the support necessary to do their job and that the right processes and norms conducive to overall team effectiveness are in place. It requires also that team leaders get employees to think in holistic terms, and to be concerned about the customers', rather than their own, concerns, and that co-operation is the norm rather than the exception. The team leader is also the spokesperson for the group, meeting with other teams and with management. Finally, the team leader has to be conscious of the fact that dynamism is an important trait of an effective team: change has to be a feature of all teams, such as the rotation of jobs between and within teams.

The Supervisor as Team Leader

Adair (1986, p. 116) makes a pertinent point:

> . . . effective leadership is founded upon respect and trust, not fear and submission. Respect and trust help to inspire whole-hearted commitment in a team; fear and submission merely produce compliance.

When a team is first set up, the priority for the team leader should be providing direction for the team, and helping to build group norms. Direction should be provided, as Adair notes, on the basis of trust, not authority.

Over the course of time, as the team matures and it becomes more comfortable with managing itself, the team leader should become distanced from the team. Indirect supervision may well be the appropriate term for this development. The team leader should delegate as much as possible to the team, and in encouraging participation and involvement, work towards the goal of self-supervision. A team leader should be available when needed by the team, for example when there is a problem they cannot resolve, but otherwise must allow team members the freedom to supervise themselves. Table 17.5 provides guidelines for facilitators on how to ensure the team takes responsibility for itself.

TABLE 17.5: GUIDELINES FOR FACILITATORS

- Delegate as much responsibility as possible to the team.
- Provide feedback to each team member. Support employees who make mistakes.
- Encourage team members to rotate jobs. Provide extra training if necessary.
- Demonstrate how each member's role contributes to overall team performance.
- Rotate leadership of team. Give ownership of the team to the team.
- Actively involve team members in decision-making.
- Value the contribution of each team member.
- Show interest in team members. Be approachable and understandable. Keep team members informed.

There are certain instances in which team leaders have to take responsibility. One issue which is coming increasingly to the fore is that of dealing with workers who cannot, for one reason or another, reach the standard of the team. Unfortunately, there is no simple solution to this problem. If faced with such a problem, the team leader should work with the individual and the team to find a solution which is in the best interests of all. Certainly increased training can help to solve the problem, although, at the end of the day, the team leader may have to take decisive action by removing the individual from the team. Team leaders have to be conscious in such instances of the need to balance their responsibilities towards individual team members and towards the team as a whole. When conflict arises, facilitators may have to revert back to their supervisory role.

TEAM MEMBERS

Teams can be of two kinds: composed of employees who are similar in skills, or employees with very different skills. The latter complement each other, whereas the former can more easily substitute for each other. It can be argued that it is better to have teams with employees of similar and high skills, since then jobs can be rotated and employees can cover for each other. However, this is not always possible due to the specialisation which is necessary for some tasks: members of an orchestra or a football team are, generally speaking, highly specialised. In Germany, on account of the highly customised nature of the metalworking industry, the norm is to have high-skilled employees in the team; while capable of doing each other's jobs, employees are highly specialised and work on set jobs. In the USA, in comparison, most teams have employees with different skill levels. Rotation is more difficult, but the team as a whole can perform a wide range of tasks. Ideally, teams should have enough skilled employees to make sure that the task can be done, and enough cross-trained employees to enable some rotation to occur. Finally it should be noted that there is still a role for functional specialisation in organisations: teams therefore should not be taken to the extreme.

Selection of Team Members

A team member performs both a functional role (such as production operative) as well as one that contributes to team maintenance (team role). In addition, members should not be limited to any one particular job, but rather rotated through the various positions or jobs in a team and indeed in some cases between teams (in assembly teams, very often, rotation is compulsory given the repetitive nature of the job; in other cases rotation may be mandated by the team leader or undertaken by the team itself). Who then is the best person to select for a team?

There are broadly three main categories to be considered when recruiting and selecting staff. Apart from legal requirements, these categories include the qualification of the person for the job, the fit of the individual to the team, and the potential of the individual to add value to and grow within the team.

It is often argued that social skills should be given priority since attitudes are harder to change than skills: this is called the "hire for attitude and train for skill" approach. Adair (1986, p. 128), for example, emphasises the importance of careful selection of team members, and notes that skills include the ability to work as a team member and the possession of "desirable personal attributes" such as willingness to listen, flexibility of outlook, and the capacity to give and accept trust. Table 17.6 lists a variety of skills needed for teamwork.

However, for many organisations the reality may be that there is an industrial relations agreement that requires seniority to be used for selecting team members, or else that employees whose jobs are being organised into teams be given the first opportunity for inclusion. Finally, in instances where the entire department, or indeed firm, is being reorganised into teams, the issue of selection is redundant. More crucial in these instances is that sufficient training be conducted, and that individuals "buy in" to the process.

With regard to psychometric tests, Neumann et al. (1995, p. 231) have argued:

> . . . managers typically pick the "best" operators for pilot or early phase team development. It is also not uncommon for organisations to ease out or move to other jobs those individuals who do not seem to fit the teamwork ethos. The assessment of "fit" is made sometimes via psychometric tests or periods of probation. Sometimes, whole categories of people are assumed to be unsuitable — assumptions which do not stand up to research. For example, older people can be prepared to work in teams as readily as younger people.

My own research would bear out this point: there are many problems with teams, not least of which is the question of "fit". However, as organisations move further and further in teams, team selection becomes a non-issue since almost everyone has to work in a team.[3] However, organisations have to learn to live with the

---

[3] My research on cell manufacturing would indicate that a manufacturing plant cannot be 100 per cent cellularised. However, I have come across an Irish firm which organised every employee, from the security staff to the managing director, in teams.

early problems, recognising that team members bring their own individual strengths and weaknesses to a team which complement and cancel each other out. As Neumann et al. point out:

> Within a team, individuals still have strengths and weaknesses, good days and bad days. Working well as a group allows one person's strengths to compensate for another person's weakness.

Teams are about teams, therefore, not individuals. The aim is to develop the culture of the team which improves every team member's performance; this is true to the old saying, a rising tide lifts all ships.

TRAINING FOR TEAMS

It is accepted now that there are two types of learning which can occur in organisations: adaptive and generative learning. Organisations ordinarily perform adaptive or single-loop learning and deal with situations as they arise. Training — a degree, an apprenticeship, etc. — is often undertaken once in a lifetime and skills improved upon through a mixture of experience, trial and error and on-the-job training.

Generative or double-loop learning, on the other hand, demands new ways of looking at the organisation by challenging commonly-held assumptions, norms and goals. This view has given rise to the concept of the learning organisation. A learning organisation is one which is dedicated to constant improvement or learning. Employees for their part are expected to pursue life-long learning opportunities, constantly returning to the classroom for "top-up" knowledge.

The learning organisation has particularly relevance to teamwork. Teams demand much of people: members are expected to work closely together, and to rotate within and between teams. To achieve this, team members need a common language, an appreciation of each other's contribution, a strong sense of their roles and responsibilities, and a better understanding of the whole process (see Table 17.6). They need, in addition, proper facilitation which demands a broad range of skills of the part of what was the supervisor, but is now the team leader. The team leader should provide the very minimum training necessary for skills: there should also be a focus on technical training as well as (but certainly not limited to) training in social processes. Finally, the team leader should encourage, if not mandate, members to take the training.

TABLE 17.6: SKILLS FOR TEAMWORK

- Empathise
- Listen actively
- Be creative and innovative
- Act independently
- Problem-solve
- Criticise
- Give feedback
- Manage conflict
- Make judgements
- Relate to others
- Take responsibility
- Show initiative.

TOWARDS AUTONOMOUS WORK TEAMS

John Geary (1996, p. 20) makes a pertinent point:

> Another important dimension to team working is whether employees are entrusted to manage their team's boundaries, that is, the election of team leaders, the freedom to decide who is permitted to join the team and its life span and the discretion to manage relations with other teams or other members of the organisation.

He suggests that in organisations where the concern for productivity and concern for people is balanced teams have been most successful. He notes the German experience with teams, which is that:

- Group leaders are elected by members

- Participation is voluntary
- Members are free to discuss their own subject for discussion
- There is a special importance attached to certain "social" or quality of working life aspects like the inclusion and integration of older and handicapped employees into the work group.

The evidence is clear: teams work best when implemented properly. When teams do not work out well, it is widely believed that management, not workers, is the problem.

To summarise, teams require:

- Team members who are committed, energetic and willing to work in teams
- Team leaders who can facilitate, encourage and develop teams
- Organisations that involve and consult with employees
- Organisational structures that have flat hierarchies, broad pay systems, participative industrial (or employee) relations, skill-enhancing job design and strong inter-departmental co-operation.

CHAPTER SUMMARY

The organisation of employees into teams has become increasingly popular in firms the world over. In Ireland alone, a number of leading-edge firms, such as Bord na Móna (see Wall, 1994, pp. 35-37), Galtee (see O'Brien, 1994, p. 38) and Aughinish Alumina have implemented teams of one kind or another. There is some variation in teams from the service to the manufacturing sector, and within manufacturing, between discrete-item manufacturing and firms in the continuous-process industry. Despite such variation, teams share one central tenet: teamwork (when properly implemented) encourages employees to go beyond the concerns of their immediate jobs and to understand and participate in the broader concerns of the organisation, including the customer.

Teams are becoming increasingly common, particularly among American and Japanese multinational firms. These firms have to move along with and to some extent ahead of current changes in manufacturing: the need to stay competitive through the adoption of current best practice. The latter includes not just teamwork but a host of ancillary activities that support and encourage widespread change. These activities include human resource management, investment in training, changes in work practices (as detailed in the last chapter on world class manufacturing) and new systems for conducting industrial relations (the subject of the next chapter).

Teams, however, are only effective when tasks, individual and group needs are congruent. This puts pressure on the supervisor, as team leader, to ensure that teams are set up properly with the right mix of social and technical skills, and that once formed, team processes are such that they increase group cohesiveness. This is no easy task. However, the future of European businesses depends on making far-reaching change effectively, and supervisors have a pivotal role to play in this.

References and Further Reading

Adair, J. (1986) *Effective Teambuilding*, Aldershot: Gower.

Belbin, R.M. (1981) *Management Teams: Why they Succeed or Fail*, London: Heinemann.

Bennett, R. (1994) *Personal Effectiveness*, second edition, London: Kogan Page, chapter 6.

Davis, L. (1966) "The Design of the Job", *Industrial Relations*, 6, pp. 21-45.

Evans, David (1995) *Supervisory Management, Principles and Practices*, fourth edition, London: Cassell, chapter 32.

Geary, John (1995) "Working Practices: The Structure of Work", in Edwards, P.K., (ed.) *Industrial Relations: Theory and Practice in Britain*, Oxford: Basil Blackwell.

Hackman, J. & G. Oldman (1980) *Work Redesign*, Reading, MA: Addison-Wesley.

Irish Business and Employers Confederation (1993) "Teams in Action", summarised in *A Joint Approach to Direct Participation: Ireland*, Dublin: European Foundation for Improvement of Living and Working Conditions Working Paper No. WP/95/01/EN, 1995.

Irish Congress of Trade Unions (1993) "New Forms of Work Organisation: Options for Unions", summarised in *A Joint Approach to Direct Participation: Ireland*, Dublin: European Foundation for Improvement of Living and Working Conditions Working Paper No. WP/95/01/EN, 1995.

Keegan, R. & J. Lynch (1995) *World Class Manufacturing ... in an Irish Context*, Dublin: Oak Tree Press, pp. 101-110.

McDuffie, J.P. & T. Kochan (1988) "Human Resources, Technology, and Economic Performance: Evidence from the Automobile Industry", Industrial Relations Research Association, Allied Science Social Sciences Meeting, New York.

Monden, Y. (1983) *Toyota Production System*. Atlanta, GA: Industrial Engineering and Management Press.

Mooney, P. (1995) *Developing the High Performance Organisation: Best Practice for Managers*, Dublin: Oak Tree Press, chapter 7.

Morton, C. (1994) *Becoming World Class*, London: Macmillan.

Mosley, D., L. Megginson, P. Pietri (1993) *Supervisory Management: The Art of Empowering and Developing People*, third edition, Cincinnati, OH: South-Western, chapter 10.

Naughton, M. (1994) "A Case Study for the Joint International Project on New Forms of Work Organisation", International Metal Employees Federation and the European Metal Employees Federation, June, Dublin. Available directly from the author.

Naughton, M. (1995) "The Implications of Teamwork on Industrial Relations", A Presentation to the ICM Conference on Creating, Leading and Motivating High Performance Teams, 24-25th. January, 1995, Dublin.

Neumann, J., Holti, R. & H. Standing (1995) *Change Everything At Once!: The Tavistock Institute's Guide to Developing Teamwork in Manufacturing*, Oxford: Management Books 2000.

O'Brien, S. (1994) "Autonomous Working at Galtee Food Dairygold", *European Participation Monitor*, European Foundation for Improvement of Living and Working Conditions, Issue No. 9.

Sisson, K. (1996) "The Nature and Extent of Direct Participation in Europe: Preliminary Results from the EPOC Workplace Survey", in N. Harvey (ed.) Proceedings of the Workplace Partnership for Competitiveness, EU Irish Presidency/European Foundation Conference, Dublin, pp. 26-34.

Wall, T. (1994) "Union Involvement in Teamworking in Ireland", *European Participation Monitor*, European Foundation for Improvement of Living and Working Conditions, Issue No. 9.

Wobbe, W. (1992) "What are Anthropocentric Production Systems? Why Are They A Strategic Issue for Europe?", Brussels: Commission of the European Communities, FAST Report EUR 13968 EN.

Womack, J.P., Jones, D.T. & D. Roos (1990) *The Machine that Changed the World*, New York: Macmillan.

Chapter 18

INDUSTRIAL RELATIONS AND THE SUPERVISOR

THE OBJECTIVE OF THIS CHAPTER

The term industrial relations refers to the governance of the relations between employees and management. By common usage, however, the term has come to mean relations between unions and management. In that regard, industrial relations deals with issues like collective bargaining, strikes, mediation, and consultation, that is, issues which unions deal with. Non-union firms also deal with industrial relations. Indeed, some non-union firms have staff associations or other forms of employee involvement which, while not affording employees the right to bargain collectively, do provide some form of collective representation for employees. However, this chapter deals mainly with trade unions and mentions non-union firms only to the extent to which certain management practices, notably human resource management, have been a force of change to the union sector. Because the state has taken a more prominent role in industrial relations in recent years, attention will be focused on the role of government, first as an employer, and second in the way various state bodies, such as the Labour Relations Commission and the Labour Court, are staffed and managed.

Industrial relations has been the subject of much change and considerable discussion in recent years. No single explanation can account for this change. Rather, a series of events — most clearly the rise in competition and the advent of new management practices — have forced a hardening of management attitudes in dealing with unions, often referred to as the "new realism" in industrial relations. At the workplace level the adoption of human resource management practices is leading a trend towards the individualisation of the employment relationship and potentially giving rise to an increase in non-unionism. There is the perception, although not supported by research findings, that trade unions have less acceptance in society. At national level there is the emergence of a new way of conducting industrial relations, as epitomised by the new partnership agreement (Partnership 2000), that fuels the view that trade unions have important roles to play in society. Regardless of these contradictions, these developments at national and workplace level have important implications for supervisors. Supervisors have to be concerned with the procedural aspects of industrial relations, such as grievances and disputes handling, and how these can affect the day-to-day management of people.

After reading this chapter the reader should have an understanding of:

- What industrial relations is
- What unions and employer organisations do
- What collective bargaining, industrial conflict and employee participation are
- The procedural aspect of industrial relations and how this affects the work supervisors do.

THE STUDY OF INDUSTRIAL RELATIONS

The study of industrial relations derives from the fact that both employees and management have different goals, yet a strong mutuality of interest in the survival of the firm. Management, for example, is often concerned with growth and profits. Employees have more immediate goals: job security and wage increases. Hence the need for some mechanism for voicing and reconciling these differences. It can also be argued that unions have different goals from the very members they represent, such as survival and growth. Similarly, officials of a union may be guided by self-interest rather than, say, their members' interests.

Despite these differences, and the potential they create for conflict, unions and management have managed to have a lasting and working relationship. Indeed, one of the hallmarks of industrial society is that conflict between management and workers is seen as normal, inevitable and resolvable. Partly responsible for the latter has been the establishment of structures and elaborate mechanisms to deal with the potential for conflict. In other words procedures have allowed us to contain and control conflict. This is what Alan Fox (1974), a British sociologist, has termed "procedural consensus", that is, a consensus or truce that is borne out of adherence to agreed procedures.

The resolution of conflict is dependent upon establishing procedures and institutions which achieve consensus through negotiated compromise. In Ireland, the establishment first of the Labour Court in 1946, and later, the Labour Relations Commission in 1990, has laid the groundwork for the settlement of disputes. In addition to this, the work by the social partners, IBEC (Irish Business and Employers Confederation) and ICTU (Irish Congress of Trade Unions), has developed a consensus at national level that is conducive to maintaining what is euphemistically termed "good industrial relations". That said, strikes do occur, and the relationships between some employers and unions is poor. Overall, however, it can be said with justification that procedures established over the years have helped to contain conflict and make it manageable. It is these procedures which concern supervisors.

THE SUPERVISOR AND INDUSTRIAL RELATIONS PROCEDURES

Typically, the person responsible for industrial relations in a large organisation is either called the personnel manager, the industrial relations manager, or more recently, the human resources manager. This is particularly the case for large organisations, where size alone necessitates a separate department for dealing with personnel/human resources and industrial relations issues. Moreover, large organisations are more likely to be unionised. In small organisations, the owner or management may deal directly with personnel issues. Industrial relations in small firms tends to be less formal and more personal.

Personnel managers deal with a range of issues more commonly referred to as manpower issues, such as the recruitment, compensation, training and development, and promotion of employees. Some of the issues will be negotiated with the unions, others not. Where the power and influence of the unions is strong, more issues tend to be subject to negotiation. Where unions are weak, far less so. Rather, management exercises what is called managerial prerogative, that is, makes unilateral decisions with little or no input from unions. This is somewhat the case for multinational companies in Ireland who often limit the sphere of influence of unions.

The way industrial relations is practised in firms is subject to certain customs and practices, as well as procedures or rules, for carrying out certain operations, notably discipline. Also, management, particularly the personnel/human resources department, may itself have objectives when dealing with unions. A supervisor should know these practices and procedures as well as company objectives. Research shows that responsibility for the conduct of industrial relations policy is ordinarily shared between the personnel/human resources department and line management and that has remained relatively unchanged in recent years.[1] These studies also indicate that, given the strategic focus of human resource management, personnel and industrial relations issues are viewed by senior management as having greater importance in organisations, and that, as a result line management is being afforded more responsibilities in the personnel/human resources area.

A supervisor also needs to have a knowledge of industrial relations and, in particular, the law regulating industrial relations. The latter is dealt with in the next chapter. The former, by contrast, is built upon through a working knowledge of how to deal with people and unions. Because a supervisor is one who is generally promoted from the ranks of employees, they may already have a good knowledge of how unions work (being a current or

---

[1] A European wide study is reported in Gunnigle et al. (1993, p. 31). Research in Ireland is reported in Foley and Gunnigle (1995, pp. 155-8).

former member). However, many organisations, particularly in the public sector, have changed the way they practise industrial relations. Therefore, the supervisor must stay abreast of such changes.

Grievance and disputes procedures, dealt with in detail in Chapter 15 on interviewing, normally dictate that initial compliance or action is handled by an employee's immediate supervisor. It is imperative, therefore, that supervisors know what their responsibilities and obligations are in this regard. A working knowledge of company policy, as well as a willingness to consult with the personnel or human resource department, is the basic requirement of supervisory work.

THE INDUSTRIAL RELATIONS SYSTEM IN IRELAND

The Irish industrial relations system has traditionally been characterised as follows:

- Voluntaristic ideals
- Similarity to Britain
- Adversarial nature
- Openness to change.

Voluntarism means, quite simply, that the parties are free to regulate their own affairs, mainly through collective bargaining, without interference from the state. The state plays a mediating role, largely by setting statutory law and through the staffing of various industrial relations institutions, notably the Labour Court and the Labour Relations Commission. This voluntarism ideal has changed in recent times. Since the early 1970s the state has adopted a more interventionist role in industrial relations. Furthermore, the government's role as employer, and the burgeoning public sector pay bill, has necessitated increasing involvement in industrial relations matters, such as the setting of pay norms (or guidelines) for the private sector to follow.

The second characteristic that the Irish industrial relations system is noted for is its similarity to Britain's. This concept of voluntarism, for example, is a direct import from the UK. The influence of Britain is also reflected in the manner in which unions are organised in Ireland, namely, the division between craft, white-collar and general unions. The first Irish unions were in fact set up by British unions, and became known in time as British-Based Unions or BBUs. As Irish unions were formed, at the beginning of this century, this quickly gave rise to friction between the BBUs and Irish unions. The dispute was not settled until the forming of the Irish Congress of Trade Unions in 1958. That said, Irish and British unions, particularly ICTU and the Trades Union Congress (TUC) in Britain, maintain very close relations. However, the two systems of industrial relations are starting to diverge in many ways. In particular, the growing involvement of Irish trade unions in centralised wage bargaining has drawn them apart from their British counterparts. By contrast, unions in Britain have found themselves very much excluded from government policy formation in recent years.

A third, and indeed changing, characteristic of the Irish industrial relations system is its adversarial nature. Adversarialism, very simply, refers to the idea of different or varying interests between employers and unions, a "them versus us" attitude as it is commonly put. Collective bargaining therefore tends to be antagonistic. Also, unlike much of European industrial relations which has had a long history of employee input into firm decision-making (co-determination), Irish industrial relations is particularly noted for a strong pluralist and adversarial outlook. In many ways, with the development of partnership and a new consensus at national level, Irish industrial relations is becoming less adversarial. Partnership is credited with playing a leading part in the development in recent years of a robust economy — the so-called "Celtic tiger" — and there is a strong attachment to continuing along that path and particularly to developing partnership at the workplace level.[2]

That brings us to the final characteristic of Irish industrial relations, namely, the openness to external influence. The Irish industrial relations system, as it sheds its attachment to Britain, is coming greatly under the influence of European integration,

---

[2] See for instance the argument put forward by Eithne Fitzgerald, TD (1996, pp 10-12), and then Minister of State for Labour Affairs.

and also, to a lesser extent, the influence of multinational companies, American and Japanese ones in particular.

A number of EU directives have had a direct impact on Irish industrial relations. For example, a recent directive dealt with European-wide works councils. Companies which have operations employing more than 150 people in more than one European Union country are required to set up a works council. In addition, the new working-time directive, dealing with among other things the number of hours an employee is permitted to work before overtime comes into effect, will have important implications for employers and employees in Ireland. In all, the influence of Europe is considerable and will continue to be so in the coming years.

Similarly, American and Japanese multinationals are bringing to Ireland a host of new business and management techniques, such as Just-in-Time Production, Statistical Process Control and Human Resource Management which are being adopted by indigenous firms. Many of these multinational companies are setting up non-union operations thereby contributing, along with falling employment levels in manufacturing, to a decline in the rate of unionisation.

Together these influences are changing the face of Irish industrial relations from largely an accommodating approach to unions to a more hardened and professional approach. It is fashioning a system which, while rooted culturally in an old British-style unionism, is strongly centralised and very open to external developments. It should be noted that despite the movement in the EU towards a single Europe, there is still considerable diversity in European industrial relations, hence a European system of industrial relations is unlikely to emerge (see Gunnigle, et al., 1993, p. 32). Indeed, as Bill Roche (1995, p. 1) of UCD has commented, the opposite is more likely occurring:

> Little more than a decade ago the future course of Irish industrial relations seemed predictable enough. The "adversarial model", based on ongoing and heavily bargained compromise between unions and management, appeared secure. Now in the mid-1900s the adversarial model is under considerable pressure and we are witnessing the

> most important series of changes in the conduct of employee relations for at least fifty years. The development of industrial relations can be portrayed as moving from convergence of practices during the period up to the 1970s across regions, sectors, occupations, and plants of differing national origins, towards divergence and fragmentation during the 1980s and 1990s.

The Irish industrial relations system is unique in Europe because of the recent focus on partnership at the national level. But there is no guarantee that partnership will continue, any more than there is agreement as to what model of industrial relations will emerge in the new millennium. The following section discusses one possible direction for the Irish industrial relations, namely, the increase in non-unionism.

CHANGE IN INDUSTRIAL RELATIONS: THE RISE IN NON-UNIONISM

Paul Mooney (1993, p. 20-34), formerly with Trinity College and now a management consultant, has presented an interesting, if somewhat contentious, perspective on Irish industrial relations. He argues that the following major changes have occurred in Irish industrial relations in recent years:

- The development of a non-union sector
- The increased use of part-time and contract labour
- A weakening of trade union power and decline in strike rates.

These changes are similar, he argues, to those happening in British and American industrial relations, and are caused by three major factors:

- Changes in the economic environment
- Developments at political level
- The emergence of what he sees as a high commitment model of work relationships which has significantly altered the way in which collective bargaining has been conducted.

Changes in the economic environment — recessions and increased competition — have led to decline in the strength of trade unions and increasing demands from employers for labour market flexibility. Political changes include increased hostility to trade unions and the recent tendency in Ireland to blame trade unions, rightly or wrongly, for a range of economic problems, notably high unemployment. Finally, the high commitment model of work relationships represents for Mooney a move away from adversarialism to a greater participation of employees and/or their representatives in the business affairs of a company. It manifests itself in the development of teamwork or employee involvement in firms, the individualisation of the employment relationship, and potentially the growth of non-unionism.

Mooney presents the view that there is a new model of industrial relations emerging which is more individualistic and more flexible. It is what employers want, and unions have little choice but to respond favourably. This would include removing what are seen as restrictive practices and placing further limits on industrial action. Because these trends are driven by the marketplace, the failure of unions to respond positively may encourage firms to avoid unions. Hence the real possibility exists for non-unionism to grow in Ireland, particularly given the influence of American multinationals. In many ways, Mooney's view is correct. A serious difficulty facing unions today is the rise in anti-union attitudes among employers, and particularly multinational companies. Research shows that most new multinational companies establishing operations in Ireland are non-unionised.

It is questionable whether non-unionism will continue to increase significantly. Mooney presupposes that the American and to a lesser extent British influence will be dominant and this will lead to further decline in trade union members. Union density — the percentage of the workforce that are union members — is about 55 per cent and declining; it peaked around 1980, at 57 per cent, and has declined since then (Roche, 1997, p. 50). Much of this decline can be explained by the shifts in the structure of employment, away from manufacturing towards services, as well as the rise in unemployment and high emigration in the 1980s, and the increased casualisation of the labour market in Ireland.

Research conducted by the University of Limerick would seem to contradict Mooney's argument. In their study of workplace practices in 1,500 Irish firms, Gunnigle et al (1994) found that 56 per cent of employees were unionised and that 79 per cent of organisations recognised a trade union. They concluded that there is much continuity in industrial relations, and where new management practices have been introduced they have been in addition to the existing collective bargaining structures rather than instead of them. Human resource management, they argued, does not impede the development of unions in the workplace, and non-unionism was, rather, a reflection of traditional anti-union attitudes. Roche (1996, p. 20) makes a similar point: the research evidence does not, as yet, indicate a relationship between new management practices, such as HRM, and the rise of non-unionism.

Ireland clearly has, by comparative standards, a high rate of union density. Irish people, it may be said, have a strong attachment to unions, and feel that unions have an important part to play in Irish economic, social and political life.[3] That is likely to remain so for the foreseeable future. Mooney's view does point to an area in which union themselves have admitted problems, namely, union recognition. There is currently no legal provision, as there is in the US for instance, which mandates that an employer recognise a union. Hence, Irish employers can refuse to deal with unions. New multinational companies setting up in Ireland are less likely to recognise trade unions and there is a trend towards the increasing individualisation of the employment relationship (Gunnigle, 1996, pp. 24-40). Also, the growth in new management techniques, and a more hardened attitude on the part of employers, particularly from the Irish government, has changed the way industrial relations is conducted. This has important implications for those who deal with unions on a daily basis, such as supervisors.

---

[3] This view is borne out by recent research at UL. Gunnigle et al. note: "In a European context, Irish trade unions appear to be relatively strong at establishment level in terms of recognition, density and influence" (Gunnigle et al., 1997, p. 13).

THE PARTIES TO INDUSTRIAL RELATIONS

There are three main parties to industrial relations, namely employers and their representatives (management), employees and their representatives (unions), and the government. An American, John Dunlop (1958), portrayed this best in his notion of an industrial relations system. He argued that together employers and unions agree on a set of rules and these are in turn influenced by other factors, notably budgetary controls, technology, and the performance of the economy. The actors, the external environment, and an ideology or value system which binds all this together constitute what Dunlop called an "industrial relations system". The central feature of an industrial relations system was the establishment of rules which govern the workplace. Rules can be written or unwritten. Written rules are to be found in collective agreements. Unwritten rules are referred to as custom and practice. Rules establish order in the workplace. Industrial relations in Dunlop's view is about order not conflict.

The notion that there are just three parties to industrial relations is coming under greater scrutiny. There are many others on the periphery of industrial relations who have an effect on how employee relations are conducted. A case in point are the civil servants who staff the Labour Court and the Labour Relations Commission. A second example are those who participated in the negotiations that led to the recent Partnership 2000 Agreement which replaced the old PCW (Programme for Competitiveness and Work).[4] Finally, the public are, in many ways, a party to industrial relations. A strike in a pivotal industry, such as banking or transport, can have a major effect on the public. The lesson to be

[4] Although the primary partners to the agreement are IBEC, ICTU and the government, some 19 organisations made submissions to the talks. These included, in addition to the above-mentioned, Construction Industry Federation, Irish Farmers Association, Irish Creamery Milk Suppliers Association, Irish Co-operative Organisation Society Ltd., Macra na Feirme, Irish National Organisation of the Unemployed, Congress Centres for the Unemployed, The Community Platform (made up of a variety of organisations), Conference of Religious in Ireland, National Women's Council of Ireland, National Youth Council of Ireland, Society of Saint Vincent de Paul, Protestant Aid, Small Firms Association, Irish Exporters Association, Irish Tourist Industry Confederation, and Chamber of Commerce of Ireland.

taken from Dunlop is that there are many groups and many factors which come to influence the primary parties in industrial relations, and that rules, while central to the understanding of how industrial relations function, are subject to change.

WHAT ARE TRADE UNIONS?

Trade unions are organisations of employees, dedicated to protecting and advancing their members' interests. The constitution of Ireland guarantees the right of employees to form unions, and to join (or not join) a union of their choosing. The Trade Union Acts of 1941 and 1975, and the Industrial Relations Act of 1990, are the main acts regulating unions in Ireland. In particular, the 1941 and 1975 Acts regulate the manner in which unions can gain licences to negotiate of behalf of their members. Generally, a union has to deposit between £20,000 and £60,000 with the High Court and have at least 1,000 members in the 18-month period immediately preceding the application. Such Acts were formulated in response to the multiplicity of unions in Ireland, and are designed to limit the number of unions being formed. The 1990 Act is a more comprehensive act and covers, among other things, union rationalisation, restrictions on picketing and balloting, and injunctions.

Why People Join Unions

People join and indeed form unions for a variety of reasons. These reasons vary from country to country and have changed over the years. In certain European countries, notably Italy and France, unions are very political in nature, whereas in Ireland, as in Britain and the US, unions have focused more on economic than political goals. As noted earlier, the earliest unions focused initially on getting better wages and improved job security. It is not difficult to see why. At the time unions were formed, workers were undercut by cheaper, unskilled labour, as well as the substitution of mechanical for labour power. In Ireland, as in Europe in general, employees migrating from the rural areas were willing to work for lower wages. In the US, it was emigrants, Irish people among them, who flocked to the new factories being set up on the

East Coast, often undercutting the wages of existing employees and thus threatening their jobs.

The natural response to this threat was to form unions. By banding together, employees learned to protect themselves. In unity there is strength, runs the union motto. Another is: an injury to one is an injury to all. Thus, by organising themselves into groups or unions, employees protected themselves against discriminatory and unilateral action by the employer. Unions, as a result, have focused on standardised policies: treat each and every employee the same. This often runs counter to managerial ideals of treating employees as individuals, rewarding the most productive employees with extra pay and promotion, etc. This difference of opinion is the source of much conflict in industrial relations. Managers prefer to exercise managerial prerogative, that is, make decisions unilaterally, whereas unions act as a restraint on their actions. There are those, such as the Marxist Richard Hyman (1975), who see conflict as the essence of industrial relations.

The reasons people join unions today have changed. There is a considerable body of research from the US which argues that workers make conscious decisions to join or not join a union. That is, workers add up the pros and cons of belonging to a union. On the plus side, workers may ascertain that belonging to a union will result in higher wages, which is usually the case. Against this, there is the cost of subscriptions, or union dues to use the American expression. Workers may surmise that the potential gains to be made from joining a union (the increased wages) offset any negative costs (subscriptions), and thus join. By contrast, some workers may come to the conclusion that are they are better off without a union. While there is much truth in this "instrumental" approach, and indeed it may explain why many workers in Ireland now refuse to join trade unions, it does not account for the fact that many workers, Irish or American, do not always have a choice of joining or not joining a union. Many organisations are now non-union, while others operate some form of closed shop. It is worth noting that there are two forms of closed shop, a pre-entry and a post-entry. A pre-entry closed shop means one must be a member of a union before taking up employment in a particular place. Such agreements, which are of dubious legal value, are common in the construction industry. A post-entry closed shop, sometimes referred to as a union shop, requires that a new employee joins a particular union after starting employment. This often gives rise to what is referred to as "wall-to-wall" unionism where every worker in a particular grade belongs to a union.

Subscriptions vary from union to union. The typical "sub" is about 1 per cent of wages. Many unions have check-off agreements (i.e. deduction-at-source arrangements) with subscriptions deducted automatically from an employee's wage.

Types of Unions

There are, broadly speaking, three types of unions. First, *craft unions*, catering for high-skilled or craft employees. These are typically employees who have served an apprenticeship and often membership is restricted to one skill or occupation. Second, *general unions* which, regardless of skill or occupation, organise all employees in a country. There are no prerequisites for joining a general union. Third, *white-collar unions,* which cater for office and professional employees. These are more likely to be found in the service industry. An example of the latter is the Manufacturing, Science and Finance union (MSF), or the Association of Secondary Teachers of Ireland (ASTI). The Technical, Engineering and Electrical Trades Union (TEEU) is on the other hand a craft union, as is the Irish Print Union (IPU). SIPTU (Services, Industrial, Professional and Technical Union) is a general union, and with nearly 200,000 members is the country's largest union.

There are 56 trade unions which operate in the Republic of Ireland with a total membership of approximately 520,000, which is about 48 per cent of the workforce. For the sake of comparison, there are 17 industrial unions in Germany, or roughly one union per industry. IG Metall, the metal employees union, represents employees in the metalworking industry only. With over 2 million members, it is the largest free trade union in the world, and also one of the strongest.

Irish unions tend to fall into either of two categories: very large or very small. SIPTU, for example, represents nearly one-half of all unionised employees in Ireland. At the other extreme, however, are a number of small unions, numbering less than 200 members in all. Being small they do not always have the financial resources necessary to represent their members sufficiently. Others represent members too well, often to the detriment of the public at large. Multiplicity has also given rise to problems of inter-union disputes. This is where two unions become engaged in a dispute, often involving the employer or employers.

In recent years there have been movements towards amalgamation and mergers. This is made possible by two Acts passed by the government to encourage such developments. One, the 1975 Trade Union Act, made it increasingly difficult to start a new union. This was in part the response to an International Labour Organisation (ILO) study conducted by Johannes Schregle which recommended a reduction in the number of Irish unions. The other, the 1990 Industrial Relations Act, encourages unions to merge by means of financial incentives to cover costs. The recent merging of the largest two unions in the country, the Irish, Transport and General Employees Union (ITGWU) and the Federated Workers Union of Ireland (FWUI) into SIPTU, was the culmination of this strategy. More mergers are expected to take place in the coming years, particularly among small unions.

Unions themselves are well aware of the need for rationalisation. Large, and better-financed, unions will be better able to deal with multinational companies. Unions thus need to be organised strongly in their own country, and to be linked to other unions abroad. Irish unions have always had strong links with British unions. Lately, they have been reaching out to European ones. Despite the trends towards globalisation, international unions are the exception rather than the norm. The best examples are in North America, where many unions have branches in the US and Canada. Some unions operate in both Ireland and Britain, with the National Union of Journalists (NUJ) being a good example.

Services Provided by Unions to Members

Trade unions provide a range of services or functions (see Table 18.1). The representative function is the most widely known. Unions may represent employees collectively as well as individually.

Individually, they represent workers by airing their grievances with management. Collectively, they negotiate on behalf of workers as well as representing them politically. Trade unions, mainly through the Irish Congress of Trade Unions (ICTU), belong to numerous state agencies, committees and boards, including the Labour Court, Labour Relations Commission, Employment Appeals Tribunal, and the Employer-Labour Conference (which negotiates the national wage agreements). On the international front, ICTU is affiliated to the European Trade Union Confederation (ETUC) which is representative of labour movements in Europe, particularly in dealings with the EU Commission, and to the International Confederation of Free Trade Unions (ICFTU) which represents labour movements internationally. In addition to these bodies, ICTU participates in the work of the International Labour Organization (ILO) and the Organisation for Economic Co-operation and Development (OECD). Finally, trade unions provide an important political or social role by representing not just members' views, but also those others who lack an important voice, such as the unemployed and the poor.

TABLE 18.1: SERVICES PROVIDED BY TRADE UNIONS

- Negotiating higher wages (including higher basic rates, minimum and overtime rates, etc.)
- Voluntary redundancies, retirement packages and better pensions
- Better treatment for workers
- Equal opportunity
- Defend workers threatened with discipline
- Better procedures
- Facilities (canteen, sports, etc.)
- Safety and health
- Better working environment
- Ergonomics (less stressful work)
- Job creation
- Redundancy protection
- Recall, layoff rights

- Disputes procedures
- Resolving disputes
- Airing workers' dissent.

Unions provide other services which are less well known. By being a member of certain unions, one can avail of various concessions, among them cheaper car insurance, the opportunity to become a member of their own credit union, or discounted rates for the VHI. Other unions, admittedly the larger ones, offer scholarships for third-level education to offspring of their members. Trends towards seeing unions as "service organisations" is very much influenced by American developments. Increasingly, American unions, faced by declining membership, are providing a wider range of benefits in order to attract members. In the Irish case, it may be said that trade unions are simply responding to new demands from workers.

How Trade Unions are Organised in Ireland

Irish unions operate primarily at three levels: the shopfloor, the branch level and the national level. Most people's association with unions, notwithstanding the publicity surrounding major strikes, is at the shopfloor or workplace level. There shop stewards coordinate all activities of a union (see Table 18.2). These include organising meetings, recruiting members and dealing with the management on a regular basis. A member goes to the shop steward who takes up the issue (however, this does not preclude the member from going direct to the branch secretary or to a supervisor or manager). Failure to resolve the issue at that stage may result in further steps, such as the involvement of the branch official and a hearing at either the Labour Relations Commission or the Labour Court.

The 1993 Code of Practice[5] requires that shop stewards be given reasonable time off for union duties and be afforded certain facilities. These facilities include:

[5] The proper title is "Duties and Responsibilities of Employee Representatives and the Protection and Facilities to be afforded them by their Employers", Department of Enterprise and Employment, 1993.

- The ability to collect union subscriptions
- Having a full-time shop steward
- Communication facilities, such as notice boards
- Time off for meetings.

The shop steward is thus the direct link between the members of the union and the union itself, and, despite being a voluntary official, is regarded as by far the most important official in a union. It is for this reason that unions offer training courses for shop stewards. SIPTU, for example, runs week-long training courses all over the country. A shop steward could receive, in all, a full month's training over a span of one year. This includes discussion of labour law, collective bargaining, health and safety issues, etc. Other unions offer similar courses. Generally speaking, employers will release staff for these courses.

The shop steward's work will vary considerably from organisation to organisation, and within organisations, particularly with different categories of employees, notably white- and blue-collar. In large and diverse organisations, a section committee may be formed. It takes its name from the fact that the shop stewards on that committee will represent particular categories or sections of employees. Some organisations will have committees of unions, such as the Group of Unions in the ESB.

TABLE 18.2: WHAT SHOP STEWARDS DO

- Recruit new members
- Collect money for the union
- Hold meetings and finding out the members' view
- Deal with complaints from workers and advise them of their rights
- See that union policies are carried out where possible
- Make sure that agreements are kept
- Pass on information to members
- Meet management when minor problems need to be sorted out.

Source: McNamara et al., 1994, p. 77.

Branch Level

The branch level co-ordinates all activities for the branch which, typically, is geographically defined. There is both a branch committee and usually a full-time branch official. Branch meetings are generally attended by shop stewards, although in most unions members are free to attend branch meetings. These meetings, usually on a monthly basis, make it easier for the branch secretary to serve their members and for members to have input into union decision-making. Aside from deciding branch policy, the branch committee will elect delegates to the Annual Delegate Conference. The officials of the branch committee, save for the branch secretary, are normally part-time. A branch can be divided into sections to facilitate organisation.

National Level

Most unions have a national executive which looks after the affairs of a union as a whole. Typically, a national executive will comprise a full-time President and General Secretary along with voluntary officials, usually shop stewards. At the Delegate Conference, held either on an annual or biennial basis, motions are passed and officers are elected. Delegates are sent to such conferences as representative of their branches.

Many unions are affiliated to the Irish Congress of Trade Unions, and to trades councils. The latter are groupings of unions on a regional basis, of which there are 37 in the whole of Ireland, north and south. The most well-known trades council is the Dublin Trades Councils which has had a long and checkered history.

Table 18.3 demonstrates how SIPTU, Ireland's largest union, is organised. As can be seen, because of its size, SIPTU organises along regional lines.

TABLE 18.3: HOW SIPTU IS ORGANISED

Regions	There are eight regions in all (Dublin private sector, Dublin public sector, South East, South West, Midlands, West, Northern Counties, Northern Ireland).
National Executive Council (NEC)	The NEC is made up of 31 council members, five elected trustees, and three national executive officers (President, Vice-President and General Secretary).
Branches	There are 135 branches throughout the country. Most have a full-time branch secretary and the remainder have honorary elected branch secretaries. They are supported by full-time assistant branch secretaries and full-time administrative staff. NEC makes the appointment of branch staff. Posts are generally advertised internally, and branch secretaries normally come up through the ranks. Branch committee meetings are held monthly, and confined to elected members of the branch committee.
Annual Delegate Conference	Held biennially. Typically, for every 500 members, a branch sends one delegate to the annual convention. Motions are proposed, and accepted or defeated.
Annual General Meetings	Branch and sections hold AGMs to conduct local business and elect branch and section committees.

Irish Congress of Trade Unions

The Irish Congress of Trade Unions (ICTU) is the umbrella body of nearly all unions in the whole of Ireland. It was originally formed in 1894, as the Irish Trades Union Congress (or the Irish TUC), because it was felt that the British TUC was not devoting enough attention to Ireland. Because of disagreement relating to the nationalist question, a breakaway organisation, Congress of Industrial Organisations (CIO), was formed in 1923 mainly comprising Dublin-based unions. The ITUC became the ICTU in 1958 after much discussion. ICTU celebrated its centenary in 1994 with much fanfare on the streets of Dublin.

Today, ICTU represents 51 out of a total of 56 unions in Ireland, or roughly 95 per cent of all unionised employees. Those unions which are not affiliated tend to be, with some exceptions, very small. The main exception is the NBRU (National Bus and Railworkers Union).

Unions freely affiliate to Congress, and despite this affiliation are very independent. Indeed, Congress relies greatly on the goodwill of its members to abide by its policy. The ICTU is therefore a relatively weak organisation, both in financial and administrative terms. Large unions, such as SIPTU or IMPACT (Irish Municipal, Public and Civil Trade Union, with 25,000 members the second largest union in Ireland) are much stronger. However, ICTU has a high political profile at the national level. For example, it nominates the union side to many government bodies, including the National Social and Economic Council, the government think-tank.

Aside from its political role, ICTU performs a number of important trade union administrative functions, notably the regulation of disputes between unions, and the sanctioning of "all out" and "particular" pickets. Disputes between unions, though infrequent, are disruptive. Furthermore, they are more likely to occur in firms with more than one union and typically are related to incidences where one union poaches employees from another. At their worst, these disputes can lead to strikes, despite the fact that the employer is not involved. ICTU intervenes, at the request of either union, and conducts an inquiry by the appropriately named Disputes Committee. Its recommendation is binding on its affiliates. Failure by a member union to comply may lead to suspension and possibly expulsion. The Demarcation Tribunal deals with, as its name suggest, demarcation issues, that is, where one member union is perceived as encroaching on another union's territory. ICTU investigates at the request of members, issues a recommendation which is binding and non-compliance can lead to suspension and eventual expulsion.

An "all-out" or a "particular" picket are two forms of strikes sanctioned by Congress by its Industrial Relations Committee. A particular picket, also called a "one-union" picket, restricts a strike to one union. However, an all-out picket occurs when one member union wants other unions to respect its picket. The union in question must meet with the other unions involved and the Industrial Relations Committee before an all-out picket is sanctioned. Once that sanction is achieved, which is done in a matter of days, strike notice is served on the employer. Striking employees are allowed to carry banners with the words "all-out strike". This indicates to other unionised employees not to pass the picket. In general, most union members will respect such a picket and refuse to enter. This sanctity of the picket line has always been a feature of Irish industrial relations.

EMPLOYER ORGANISATIONS

In just the same way as employees are organised into unions, so too are employers. Indeed, the largest and most powerful employers' organisation in the country, the Irish Business and Employers Confederation (IBEC), was once known as Federated Unions of Employers (FUE), and is licensed under the same act as trade unions are (IBEC was formed in 1993 after a merger between the Federation of Irish Employers and the Confederation of Irish Industry). However, as employers are made up of organisations, rather than individuals, they are, as a rule, far more diverse than trade unions.

IBEC represents over 4,000 employers in Ireland. Members pay an annual fee based on the size of the organisation. IBEC in return provides a whole ranges of services, including education, training, advice, and support. It represents members in the Labour Court and the Labour Relations Commission and is the main representative of employers in negotiating national wage agreements with the government and the unions, as well as nominating members to a variety of national bodies. IBEC provides a forum for the discussion and promotion of interests which affect employers in Ireland and represents members' views to the government. IBEC is particularly committed to free enterprise and seeks laws and government support which is conducive to this.

Finally, IBEC is affiliated to a number of international organisations including the ILO (International Labour Organisation) and UNICE (the Union of Industry and Employer Confederations in Europe).

IBEC is not the only employer organisation, nor the only type of employer organisation in Ireland. There are other employer organisations, notably the Construction Industry Federation (CIF), which acts as a lobbying group for construction firms. Their brief is not entirely industrial relations, but rather the maintenance of laws and government practice which favour a particular industry. The CIF is thus a trade association, as is the Society of the Irish Motor Industry (SIMI). Trade associations, while registered with the Registrar of Friendly Societies, are not required to hold a negotiating licence, as are employer organisations under the Trade Union Acts.

Another employer organisations is the Irish Small and Medium Enterprises Association (ISME) which recently broke away from IBEC to represent small firms. Its view is that IBEC is too representative of large firms, although IBEC has a sister organisation, the Small Firms Association (SFA) which oversees small firms.

Supervisors should be aware that normally all contact with employers organisations such as IBEC are through the personnel manager, and that employer organisations usually become involved in industrial relations matters when they cannot be resolved at the first level.

THE ROLE OF THE STATE IN INDUSTRIAL RELATIONS

The state intervenes in industrial relations in three ways:

- Its role as employer (public sector labour relations)
- Its constitutional role (as a legislator)
- In the setting up and staffing of industrial relations institutions.

Employment law is dealt with in the next chapter. The state's role as employer is dealt with later in this chapter under the heading

Public Sector Labour Relations. The next section deals with industrial relations institutions, namely the Labour Court, the Labour Relations Commission, and the Employment Appeals Tribunal.

Labour Relations Commission

The Industrial Relations Act, 1990, following the recommendations of the Commission of Industrial Relations, established the Labour Relations Commission (LRC). It is comprised of an equal number of union, employer and government representatives, plus two independent representatives.

The purpose of the LRC is to promote good industrial relations. According to Kieran Mulvey, now chairman of the LRC, the Commission has the following broad functions:

- Provide a conciliation service
- Provide an industrial relations advisory service
- Prepare codes of practices
- Offer guidance on code of practices
- Appoint equality officers
- Provide a Rights Commissioner's service
- Provide an equality service
- Conduct research in industrial relations
- Review and monitor developments in the area of industrial relations.

The LRC is staffed by three types of civil servants: Rights Commissioners, Industrial Relations Officers, and Equality Officers. Industrial Relations Officers (IRO) are responsible for the conciliation service. In the event of a dispute between an employer and a union, say over manning levels, the IRO would convene a conciliation conference, typically in a neutral venue near the firm. The IRO's brief is to try to settle the dispute by conciliation, that is, by getting the parties themselves to agree on a settlement. The IRO does not arbitrate, but does suggest possible settlements. The parties, failing to achieve a settlement, can proceed with the issue to the Labour Court for a full hearing.

IROs hear collective grievances, that is, disputes between a union and an employer. Rights Commissioners, on the other hand, deal largely with individual grievances arising from the Industrial Relations Acts, 1969 and 1990. They may, however, hear collective grievances which are not connected with pay, hours of work and annual holidays. In addition to this, Rights Commissioners hear claims under the following Acts:

- Unfair Dismissals Acts, 1977 and 1993
- Maternity Protection Act, 1994
- Organisation of Working Time Act, 1997
- Payment of Wages Act, 1991
- Adoptive Leave Act, 1995.

As with IROs, Rights Commissioners hear cases only at the consent of the parties, at venues convenient to the parties, and their meetings are held in private and are very informal. If either party objects, the issue is referred to either the Labour Court or the Employment Appeals Tribunal (EAT). The Rights Commissioner issues a recommendation after investigating a dispute. This recommendation is not binding, and parties can appeal to the Labour Court or the EAT, depending on the legislation under which the case is heard. The Labour Court's recommendation is binding.

Equality Officers deal with cases under the following acts:

- Anti-Discrimination Pay Act, 1974
- Employment Equality Act, 1977.

Equality Officers, therefore, deal with cases where there is an alleged infringement of employment equality or pay discrimination. A trade union or the Employment Equality Agency may take the case on behalf of an individual or group of people. In investigating the dispute, the Equality Officers will hear submissions from both parties, and may even visit the workplace in question, before issuing a recommendation. Appeals are to the Labour Court. The Labour Court's recommendation is binding, and enforceable in civil courts. Appeals to the High Court can only be made on a point of law.

Codes of practice are essentially documents voluntarily agreed by the employers and trade unions, and sanctioned by the government. They lay out certain practices or procedures which the parties should follow. For example, the Code of Practice on Disputes Procedures sets out guidelines for resolving disputes without recourse to striking. In effect, the code of practice encourages parties to a potential dispute to make use of various third-party remedies, notably the Labour Relations Commission and the Labour Court, and to accept their recommendations before taking action on the issue. The code is particularly aimed at essential services, and where action by any party would cause considerable disruption to the public.

The final function of the LRC is to provide an industrial relations advisory service. This is particularly aimed at management and unions in firms with recurring industrial relations problems and where recourse to a third-party independent service has the potential to benefit such parties.

Labour Court

The Labour Court was set up in 1946 by then Taoiseach Seán Lemass with the purpose of regulating industrial relations. Until recently, it heard disputes of both interests and rights. The former refer largely to disputes over money issues, while the latter entail an infringement of a collective or individual right. With the establishment of the Labour Relations Commission under the 1990 Industrial Relations Act, the Labour Court now has jurisdiction for disputes of interest as well as functioning as a court of last resort. These typically are collective issues. For example, the Labour Court may hear a dispute between, say, the NBRU and Dublin Bus over a claim by the former for extra wages or a difference of opinion over manning levels (such as was the case recently, over one-person-operated buses). A dispute between the two over, say, a dismissal would be handled initially by the LRC.

As noted, unless a dispute is referred directly to the Labour Court, the Labour Relations Commission hears it first. A recommendation is then issued. Thereafter, either party can appeal and have the issue referred to the Labour Court. The Labour Court investigates and issues a recommendation, which is binding on the parties. It is customary practice for both the union and employers to agree to abide by the Labour Court's recommendation. However, this does not prevent either party from appealing the Labour Court's decision to the Circuit Court.

The Labour Court has, in exceptional circumstances, heard cases directly. This is where the Minister of Labour (now Enterprise, Trade and Employment), under Section 20 of the Industrial Relations Act of 1969, requests the Labour Court to become involved. This has occurred where strikes have threatened the public interest.

The Labour Court hears cases in private, with each party submitting a brief to the court and stating its claim before the court. Generally the employer, if a member, will be represented by an IBEC representative, and the union by its full-time branch official. The court may question each party. Within a short time the Court will issue a recommendation. Unless the parties agree beforehand to be bound by the decision, the recommendation is not legally binding. However, where a Recommendation of the Rights Commissioner is appealed by either party to the Labour Court under the 1969 Act, the decision of the court is binding.

Like the LRC, the Labour Court is made up of representatives from the various parties, and staffed by civil servants. It has four divisions, each consisting of an independent chairperson, one employer and one union representative. The current chairperson of the court is Evelyn Owens. These appointments are made by the Minister for Enterprise, Trade and Employment.

Employment Appeals Tribunals

The EAT is made up of an independent chairperson, either a solicitor or a barrister, twelve vice-chairpersons all of whom are either solicitors or barristers, and 34 others made up equally of trade union and employer representatives. When sitting, the EAT consists of the chairperson, or vice chairperson, and one union and one employer representative. The latter is nominated by IBEC, and the former by ICTU. Meetings are held throughout Ireland.

The EAT, because of its legal role, functions very differently from either the Labour Court or the Labour Relations Commission. That is, while the latter functions in the first instance to achieve a conciliatory settlement between the parties, the EAT adjudicates over issues. Most issues are of an individual nature, such as a person claiming they were unfairly dismissed or treated unfairly because of their sex. The EAT is more formal than either the LRC or the Labour Court, but far less formal than a court of law. However, the EAT has the power to subpoena witnesses and witnesses give evidence on oath. Its determination is issued in writing and is legally binding on the parties. It may be appealed to the Circuit and High Courts.

Public Sector Labour Relations

The state employs nearly one-third of all employees in the country. The ESB, the largest state organisation, at one point employed close to 11,000 employees (this will be reduced to about 9,000 under the current Cost and Competitiveness Review). A particular concern for recent Irish governments is the burgeoning public sector pay bill.

Many state employees, notably the Gardaí and the Army, cannot strike. As a result, they have a different mechanism, referred to as the Conciliation and Arbitration Scheme (CAS). It works as follows: civil servants through their union submit a claim which is then heard by a committee, jointly agreed upon by the unions and the government. They issue a report which is binding on the parties. The CAS deals with claims on many issues, mainly, however, on pay and working hours, but is limited to collective grievances. It is does not handle individual grievances. The CAS includes both conciliation, the first step, and arbitration, the final one. Most issues are resolved at the conciliation stage. An arbitration consists of a legal chairperson, with one representative each from the unions and management. Their report is sent to the Minister of Finance and the relevant Minister. The parties have one month either to accept the award or to submit it for further consideration to the government. The cabinet can either accept or submit it to the Dáil for a vote, an action which is highly unlikely.

There are, therefore, for industrial relations purposes, two types of employees in the civil service: those who are covered by the Conciliation and Arbitration Scheme and those who are allowed to take a claim to the Labour Court. There are also different types of CAS for different employees. An Post and Telecom are unusual in that they have a separate CAS. There is also the Local Government Staff Negotiations Board which oversees industrial relations in the health authorities and local government, and whose representatives occupy the management roles on the CAS.

It is commonly argued that all employees should be allowed to strike. Some see it as a democratic right, while others are of the opinion that the arbitrator's award often favours the employees. This is because, aware that they cannot strike, and thus having no fear of losing wages, employees submit extravagant claims. Research carried out in America does suggest that compulsory arbitration favours employees. Regardless of one's opinion, the CAS is here to stay, and the Gardaí and the Army, among others, are not likely in the near future to be able to strike. There are however moves afoot that will enable the representative bodies of the Gardaí to become members of ICTU.

The civil service is coming under increasing pressure to change, and in particular to break its system of pay linkages in the civil service, as well as to make it more competitive. Trade unions, by and large, accept the need for change. However, they argue it is important to understand the social function that the civil service plays and to account for new technology and change in a socially justifiable way. They accept the argument that the public sector needs to be made more efficient, rather than privatised. Regardless of what the unions say, the civil service has gone through considerable change in work practices, many of which have involved job losses. That is likely to continue in the coming years.

COLLECTIVE BARGAINING

Collective bargaining refers to the system whereby employees and management regulate and jointly determine their own affairs. Collective bargaining is thus a method for resolving conflict and for making rules which regulate and control the behaviour of the parties in industrial relations.

Collective bargaining results in collective agreements. Such agreements provide order in industrial relations by requiring that parties adhere to a given set of procedures in dealing with each other. There are typically two parts to an agreement: the substantive part and the procedural part. The former deals with such issues as wages, holidays, leave, etc. The latter defines the procedures which both parties have agreed to follow. One aspect of this is likely to cover handling disputes. For example, most collective agreements stipulate that the parties agree to resolve differences collectively without recourse to industrial action and to accept the decision of the Labour Relations Commission and the Labour Court. There have been in Ireland some unique developments in terms of regulating disputes. For example, RTE recently established the Industrial Relations Tribunal. Made up of a management and a trade union representative (nominated by the RTE Trade Union Group) with an independent chairperson, the Tribunal is an attempt to resolve industrial relations matters internally rather than by recourse to a third party.

In previous years, collective bargaining was relatively simple and mostly concerned with wages and other terms of employment such as holiday and sick leave. Lately, however, collective bargaining has become more complex, not entirely because of the recent stress of bargaining at national level, but rather because of recent changes, notably the increasing use of new computerised technology in the workplace as well as agreements on rationalisation plans that create new issues like early retirement. Reform of the tax system and job-creation mechanisms were top of the agenda in recent negotiations for national wage agreements. The involvement of organisations representing farmers and the unemployed served only to highlight the growing importance in social, political and economic terms of centralised bargaining.

The emphasis in recent years on centralised, or national, bargaining has given rise to a strong demarcation of bargaining. Thus, bargaining takes place on a national level, but is supplemented by local bargaining. The emphasis on local bargaining has primarily been on productivity or on removing anomalies. This takes place between shop stewards and management. However, not all firms engage in local bargaining.

Centralised Bargaining In Ireland[6]

Urged on by the seriousness of the maintenance craftsmen dispute in 1969, the government established the Employer-Labour Conference (ELC) in 1970 with 21 representatives from the employers and the unions, and an independent chairperson. Five of the employers' representatives were civil servants, in other words representatives of the government as employer. The terms of reference were broad — it was, in theory, to provide "a forum for the discussion and review of developments and problems in money incomes, prices and industrial relations". In practice most of its efforts were to be spent on the negotiating of centralised wage agreements.

The following agreements were negotiated:

- Nine national wage agreements/national understandings between the years 1970-82
- Programme for National Recovery (PNR), 1987-1990
- Programme for Economic and Social Progress (PESP), 1990-93
- Programme for Competitiveness and Work (PCW), 1994-1997
- Partnership 2000 for Inclusion, Employment and Competitiveness (1997-2000).

In terms of content, each agreement has two sections, one dealing with pay (the substantive part), the other, non-pay items (the procedural part). The substantive part consists of two parts, one dealing with the award itself, the other with its timing. There were attempts to move towards equalisation of pay, and to remove anomaly pay through the provision of absolute rather than percentage increases. The National Wage Agreements (NWAs) also included both a "below the norm" (BLN) clause permitting an employer not to pay the agreement if they claimed, and subsequently proved, inability to pay, and an "above the norm" (ABN)

---

[6] For further information on centralised bargaining in Ireland, see Hardiman (1988; 1994, pp. 147-58).

clauses which allowed for the instances in which a union could secure a higher wage increase in return for, say, an increase in productivity. Any dispute regarding the NWAs was referred to the Adjudication Committee and, since it had only conciliatory powers, thereafter to the Labour Court whose ruling was then expected to be binding.

The non-pay issues were a little more complex. With time they became more prominent. The 1979 and 1980 National Understandings were much concerned with social and economic policy. They included, for example, employee tax rebates and improved social welfare, government assurances on job creation, employee participation and maternity leave, and, finally, an employer-labour commitment to improving industrial relations. This has been carried through in the latest agreements, the PNR, PESP, the PCW and finally Partnership 2000.

There are several arguments both for and against centralised bargaining. It can be claimed that centralised wage agreements allow a government more easily to attain its twin economic goals of full employment and price stability (low inflation). Unions equally have much to gain, notably by ensuring that all employees achieve an equitable wage rise. Finally, centralised wage bargaining allows individual employers to plan ahead.

There are also disadvantages to centralised wage bargaining, mostly relating to the size of the award. The NWAs in particular, were noted for giving double-digit increases, while unions, particularly in the leading industries and the public sector, were able to increase pay levels further still through local bargaining. One consequence of this, much alluded to by the government in recent years, was the huge increase in the public sector pay bill. However, the PNR was regarded as very successful in curbing inflation and in creating jobs (though little denting the unemployment figures). As noted earlier, the consensus or partnership at national level between IBEC and ICTU is seen to have added greatly to the strong performance of the Irish economy.

INDUSTRIAL CONFLICT

Conflict may be latent or manifest, legitimate or functional and very often reconciled or mediated through some process. Conflict can be further categorised as individual or collective. Individual forms of conflict refer to action taken by individual employees, such as absenteeism or tardiness or sabotaging work. Employees go sick, reduce their productivity, show up late, etc., in order to express dissatisfaction. Moreover, the number of man-days lost to strikes in Ireland is far less than those lost to absenteeism. Collective forms of conflict refer to action by a group of employees and/or the union. These include:

- Go-slows
- Work-to-rule
- Refusal to co-operate
- Strikes.

Official strikes refer to strikes that have been sanctioned by the union. Unofficial or wildcat strikes are ones for which there is no ICTU sanction. They are typically called on the spot without union consultation and, unless given union approval, are resolved quickly. As noted, the fact that there is increasing acceptance of and reliance on third-party mediation and on written agreements has tended to reduce the number of unofficial strikes. Finally, the 1990 Act has greatly limited trade union liability for unofficial strikes.

The Industrial Relations Act 1990 is now the primary act dealing with strikes. Only a bona fide trade union — a trade union which holds a licence — is protected, and protected only to the extent that the action is in contemplation or furtherance of a trade dispute. The latter is broadly defined to include "go-slows", work-to-rules, and overtime bans. In general, the Act protects employees who picket an employer's place of business, though not their home. The Act requires that a union hold a secret ballot of its members prior to striking, and that, further, the trade union takes steps to ensure that each member is given a reasonable chance to vote without interference. An employer can apply to the courts for an injunction if a union or group of workers take an "unofficial action", that is, where no ballot has been held or if a ballot has not been properly conducted.

A striking employee may receive strike pay which is almost always less than a weekly wage. Strike pay depends much on the state of a union's funds, and on the number of employees involved in a dispute and their contribution to the union. Strike pay may be augmented in various ways, through supplementary welfare allowance, given to dependants, and unemployment benefits which may be paid to employees laid off as a result of a strike. Laid off means that the employee has been issued a P45 and is no longer employed. Not all strikes result in layoff, however. As a result, strikes can cause great hardship for employees, and indeed employers. Hence the call for more regulation, such as compulsory mediation and arbitration.

EMPLOYEE PARTICIPATION AND THE WORKER DIRECTOR SYSTEM IN IRELAND

Employee participation refers to the system of giving employees an input into the decision-making process in companies. The reason is very simple: participation increases commitment, as well as allowing management to tap into the potential offered by employees. In Ireland, employee participation has tended to take the form of worker directors. On the European continent, employee participation is far broader, encompassing the works councils system and board level representation (co-determination). Between the two extremes, the limiting case of Ireland and the broader European focus, lies a multitude of schemes designed to increase employee commitment. These include suggestion boxes, employee involvement, quality circles, work teams and staff associations. Collective bargaining is also a form of employee participation.

There are worker directors in seven semi-state bodies. This was in accordance with the Worker Participation (State Enterprises) Act, 1977, and revised in 1991. In addition to this, a 1988 Act extended further employee participation. All employees vote in the elections, including management. Worker directors are elected every three years, and sit as full directors on the board of directors. They are paid their salary due to their position in the firm, not as directors. However, they receive a stipend for being a director, and are allowed to claim expenses.

The general consensus is that the worker director system, though very limited in scope, has been a success. Worker directors play an important part in mediating and resolving individual and collective disputes. They act as an important communicator between employees and management, and between the union(s) and management. Indeed, often in disputes between unions and the semi-state bodies, a worker director will be the go-between. The fact that the Act has been revised in recent years is an indication, in part, of the success of the system. If there is criticism, it is that the system is not representative enough. Only public sector bodies have worker directors.

CHAPTER SUMMARY

Industrial relations is primarily concerned with the regulation of the relationship between a union (or unions) and an employer (or employers). Traditionally, the Irish industrial relations system has been adversarial and voluntaristic in nature. However, much has happened in recent years to change the very nature of the system. The increasing globalisation of the world's economy, along with the rise of supra-national bodies such as the EU, has opened up Irish industrial relations to external influences. One outcome of these developments has been the consolidation of centralised wage bargaining into a new national consensus referred to as "social partnership". Despite the hype about partnership, it should be understood that many organisations are adopting a more hardened attitude towards trade unions. The adoption of new management practices, notably human resource management, has introduced a new professionalism in dealing with unions and there is a trend towards the individualisation of the employment relationship which runs counter to the collectivist tradition of unions and management engaged in joint negotiations.

Supervisors deal with a variety of issues which have a bearing on industrial relations, including training, safety and health, compensation practices, grievance and disciplinary handling, etc. These issues are being affected by recent changes, including the adoption of new management practices and new ways of conducting industrial relations. It is particularly important to be aware of company procedures and contractual obligations, industrial relations agreements and custom and practice, and how, if at all, these are changing. As pointed out, knowledge of people and situations, along with experience and common sense, can help supervisors deal with industrial relations issues. If in doubt as to what the rules or regulations are, the supervisor should consult with the personnel department. The supervisor should attempt to build a strong working relationship with the shop steward based on mutual trust and respect.

References and Further Reading

Dunlop, J. (1958) *Industrial Relations Systems*, Carbondale, IL: Southern Illinois University Press.

Fitzgerald, Eithne (1996) "Workplace Partnership: The Key to Managing Change", in Harvey, N., (ed.) Proceedings of the Workplace Partnership for Competitiveness, EU Irish Presidency/European Foundation Conference, Dublin.

Foley K. & P. Gunnigle (1995) "The Personnel Function: Change or Continuity", in Turner, T., & M. Morley, with J. MacMahon, K. Foley & P. Gunnigle, *Industrial Relations and the New Order: Case Studies in Conflict & Cooperation*, Dublin: Oak Tree Press.

Fox, A. (1974) *Beyond Contract: Work, Power and Trust Relations*. London: Faber and Faber.

Gunnigle, P. (1996) "Collectivism and the Management of Industrial Relations in Greenfield Sites", *Human Resource Management Journal*, Vol. 5, No. 3.

Gunnigle, P., Flood, P., Morley, M. & T. Turner (1994) *Continuity and Change in Irish Employee Relations*, Dublin: Oak Tree Press.

Gunnigle, P., McMahon, G. & G. Fitzgerald (1995) *Industrial Relations in Ireland: Theory and Practice*, Dublin: Gill & Macmillan.

Gunnigle, P., Morley, M. & C. Brewster (1993) "Changing Patterns in Industrial Relations: Differentiation and Convergence", in *European Participation Monitor*, European Foundation for Improvement of Living and Working Conditions, Issue No. 7.

Gunnigle P., Morley M., N. Clifford & T. Turner (1997) *Human Resource Management in Irish Organisations: Practice in Perspective*, Dublin: Oak Tree Press.

Hardiman, N. (1988) *Pay, Politics and Economic Performance in Ireland, 1970-1987*, Oxford: Clarendon Press

Hardiman, N. (1994) "Pay Bargaining: Confrontation and Consensus", in Nevin, D. (ed.), *Trade Union Century*, Dublin: Mercier Press in association with the Irish Congress of Trade Unions and Radio Telefis Éireann.

Hyman, R. (1975) *Industrial Relations: A Marxist Introduction*, London: Macmillan.

McNamara, G., K. Williams & D. West (1994) *Understanding Trade Unions: Yesterday and Today*, Dublin: ELO Publications in association with the Irish Congress of Trade Unions.

Mooney P. (1993) "Changing Patterns in Irish Industrial Relations", *Irish Industrial Relations Review*, May 1993.

Mulvey, K. (undated) "The Labour Relations Commission — One Year On", unpublished paper, The Labour Relations Commission, Dublin.

Murphy, T. & W.K. Roche (ed.), (1997) *Irish Industrial Relations in Practice*, second edition, Dublin: Oak Tree Press.

Nevin, D. (ed.) (1994) *Trade Union Century*, Dublin: Mercier Press in association with the Irish Congress of Trade Unions and Radio Telefis Éireann.

Roche, W.K. (1995) "The New Competitive Order and Employee Relations in Ireland: Challenges and Prospects", summary of Address to IBEC Annual Employee Conference, "Human Resources in the Global Market", November 16th.

Roche, W.K. (1996) "Trade Unions and Industrial Relations", Working Paper IR-HRM No. 2, Centre for Employment Relations and Organisational Performance, University College Dublin.

Roche, W.K. (1997) "The Trend of Unionisation" in T. Murphy and W.K. Roche (eds.) *Irish Industrial Relations in Practice*, second edition, Dublin: Oak Tree Press.

SIPTU (1994) Guide for Union Representatives, National Executive Council of SIPTU, Dublin.

Turner, T. & M. Morley, with J. MacMahon, K. Foley & P. Gunnigle (1995) *Industrial Relations and the New Order: Case Studies in Conflict & Co-operation*, Dublin: Oak Tree Press.

Chapter 19

EMPLOYMENT LAW

Adrian F. Twomey

THE OBJECTIVE OF THIS CHAPTER

This chapter briefly outlines the basic principles of Irish employment law. The principles in question have changed quite dramatically over the last thirty years due, in large part, to a considerable degree of legislative activism in the area since the establishment of the Department of Labour in 1966.[1] Despite the abolition of that Department in 1993, the pace of reform of employment law has been maintained by virtue of the combined efforts of the Departments of Enterprise, Trade and Employment and Equality and Law Reform. This period of legislative activism has resulted in the introduction of a statutory "floor" of basic employment rights. For that reason, this chapter pays particularly close attention to the primary pieces of employment legislation enacted by the Oireachtas since the Department of Labour began to make its mark with the introduction of the Redundancy Payments Act in 1967.

After reading and studying this chapter, the reader should have a basic understanding of:

- The legal qualities of the employer/employee relationship

---

[1] While the State was served by two Ministers for Labour (Countess Markievicz and Joseph McGrath) between 1919 and 1922, the Ministry of Labour was amalgamated with the Ministry of Industry and Commerce in September, 1922. The Department of Labour was not established until 1966. It was amalgamated with the Department of Industry and Commerce in 1993 to form the Department of Enterprise, Trade and Employment.

- The legal rights and duties attaching to both parties to the relationship
- The content of the main Irish labour legislation
- The ways in which an employment relationship may be legally terminated.

THE CONTRACT OF EMPLOYMENT

The relationship between a master (or employer) and their servant (or employee) derives legal status by virtue of the fact that it is based on contract. Although many employers and employees quite innocently believe that they are not parties to any contracts because they have signed no written agreements,[2] the general rule which should be remembered in such circumstances is that if one is in paid employment, then one almost always has an employment contract of some sort.

Employment contracts, like most other contracts, need not necessarily be entered into in writing.[3] In fact, in most instances, at least part of the contract will be agreed verbally between the parties, while a substantial proportion of many employment contracts is agreed verbally with no written evidence of the contract's terms being created by the parties. The ambit of the employment contract is not, however, limited simply to those terms and conditions which are expressly agreed by the employer and the employee. Employment contracts will also contain terms implied into them by law in the manner outlined below.

Contracts *of* Service and Contracts *for* Services

There are essentially two kinds of contracts under which one may "employ" a worker: "contracts *of* service", under which PAYE workers are employed, and "contracts *for* services", under which one employs independent contractors. It is important for employ-

[2]As Meenan (1994. p. 16) observes, "[f]requently employees state that they 'have no contract'. What they are really saying is that they 'have no *written* contract'."

[3]For an excellent introduction to contract law see Friel (1995).

ers to be able to determine whether they are employing an individual under a contract of service or under a contract for services for three main reasons:

- Persons employed under contracts of service are protected by a range of statutory provisions such as those discussed later in this chapter. In contrast, the rights of an independent contractor are generated almost exclusively by the express terms contained in the contract. So, for example, an individual who is employed under a contract of service can accumulate entitlements under the Minimum Notice and Terms of Employment Act, 1973, or the Redundancy Payments Acts, 1967 to 1979, whereas an individual who is employed under a contract for services cannot.
- Employer can be held legally liable on foot of tortious acts[4] committed by their employees, whereas they are usually not responsible for those committed by independent contractors.[5]
- Persons employed under contracts of service pay tax on a PAYE basis, whereas independent contractors pay tax on a self-assessment basis.

Employment contracts can be extremely complex. For that reason, the courts have found it difficult to define and distinguish between contracts of service and contracts for services. The courts have, however, formulated a number of tests for distinguishing between them. The three main tests, which are outlined below, are the control test, the integration test and the mixed test.

The Control Test

The traditional English method of identifying a contract of employment was to consider the degree of control which the employer had over the employee. As Whincup (1980, p. 6) explains:

---

[4]A tort is a legal wrong on foot of which the victim will usually be able to sue for damages. So, for example, an employer might be sued under the tort of negligence if his employee's careless driving resulted in a car crash or under the torts of assault and battery if his employee physically attacked a client.

[5]See, generally, McMahon and Binchy (1990, p. 748).

> [t]he basic proposition is quite straightforward — the more control A exercises over B's work, the more likely A is to be the employer and B his employee.

According to Drake (1981, p. 6), the control test essentially involves asking four questions about the contract in question:

- Can the "employer" tell the worker *what* to do?
- Can the "employer" tell the worker *how* to do it?
- Can the "employer" tell the worker *when* to do it?
- Can the "employer" tell the worker *where* to do it?

If the answer to all four questions is "yes" then the test suggests that the contract is one *of* service. If not, then the worker should be classed as an independent contractor.

Despite the simplicity and ease of use of the control test, it has, for some years, been regarded as unreliable. For that reason, the courts have attempted to develop a number of more sophisticated tests in order to better analyse the contractual status of more complex modern employment relationships.[6]

The Integration Test

The second standard test is the integration test which was developed in England by Lord Justice Denning in the early 1960s. As Denning himself explained, in *Bank voor Handel en Scheepvaart N.V. v. Slatford*:[7]

> the test of being [an employee] does not rest nowadays on a submission to orders. It depends on whether the person is part and parcel of the organisation.

---

[6]As Drake (1981, p. 6) observes, the control test ". . . has become increasingly unreliable in modern society as the sole determinant of the employer-employee relationship. The growing complexity of modern industrial society with its attendant specialisation, the increasingly impersonal nature of the employment relationship with the employer (usually a corporate employer) more interested in results than modalities and the decline of 'management by fear' are amongst the factors which have highlighted the deficiencies of control as an exclusive test."

[7][1953] 1 Q.B. 279.

In other words, the application of the integration test involves assessing whether the worker is integrated into the business or is merely an accessory to it.

The integration test is rarely used by judges nowadays because of the inherent difficulty in applying it. It has, however, been used on a number of occasions by Ms. Justice Carroll of the Irish High Court. In the case of *re Sunday Tribune Ltd.*,[8] for example, Carroll J. was required to determine the status of the contracts of a number of the newspaper's journalists. One of the journalists in question had written a column for 50 of the 52 weeks in the previous year. She had also taken part in editorial conferences and had received holiday pay. Carroll J. held that the journalist in question was "an integral part of the business" and was, therefore, employed under a contract of service.

The Mixed Test

The third and final test is the mixed test,[9] which essentially involves the consideration by the court of all relevant factors. The mixed test is generally regarded as having originated in the English case of *Readymixed Concrete (SE) Ltd. v. Minister of Pensions and Social Security.*[10] In that case, Mr. Justice McKenna stated that a contract of service exists if the following conditions are satisfied:

- The worker agrees that, in return for a wage or other remuneration, he will provide his own work and skill in the performance of some service for his employer
- The worker agrees, expressly or impliedly, that in the performance of that service he will be subject to the employer's control, and
- The other provisions of the contract are consistent with its being a contract of service.

---

[8] [1984] I.R. 505.

[9] Also referred to as the "multiple factors" test.

[10] [1968] 2 Q.B. 497.

The mixed test, therefore, demands that one look not only at the degree of control exercisable by the employer, but also at all other relevant factors.[11] According to Mr. Justice Barron of the Irish High Court, the following questions are among those which should be asked by a court applying the mixed test:

- Is the worker in business on his own account?
- Does he provide his own equipment?
- Can he employ his own assistants?
- What degree of financial risk does he himself take?
- Is he a member of a trade union?
- To what degree is he responsible for investing and managing resources?
- What opportunity does he have to make a profit?[12]

In recent years, the courts have primarily tended to employ the mixed test when assessing employment contracts because of its inherent flexibility. Both the control and integration tests have, however, been applied in cases over the last few years and, for that reason, should not be ignored.

Common Law Duties of Employers[13]

As has already been explained, employment contracts invariably contain terms which have been expressly agreed, either verbally or in writing, by the employer and employee. Such express terms will, for example, usually include terms relating to the employee's rate of pay, hours of work and annual leave entitlements. All contracts of service will, however, also contain a wide range of what are referred to as "implied terms". Such terms are implied into contracts by the law, on foot of common law rules, legislative provisions and collective bargaining agreements.

---

[11] No single factor, however, is always decisive.

[12] *McDermott v. Loy*, Unreported, High Court, 29 July, 1982.

[13] See, generally, Fennell and Lynch (1993, pp. 128-142); Wedderburn (1986, p. 172); Wayne (1980, pp. 29-34); von Prondzynski and McCarthy (1989, pp. 45-48); and Carr and Kay (1994, pp. 55-79).

So, for example, the common law requires that employers maintain their employees in employment for a reasonable period once they have hired them. Similarly, employers are obliged to pay employees their agreed wages. In most cases, however, they are not necessarily obliged to provide them with work.[14] As Mr. Justice Asquith explained, in *Collier v. Sunday Reference Publishing Co. Ltd.*:[15] "[p]rovided I pay my cook her wages regularly she cannot complain if I choose to take any or all of my meals out."

The third main duty imposed on employers by the common law is the duty to treat employees with trust and confidence. As Carr and Kay (1994, p. 75) explain, English courts and tribunals have, in recent years:

> developed a wide and somewhat indefinite mutual obligation upon each party to a contract of employment to treat the other with trust and confidence.

So, in *Courtaulds Northern Textiles Ltd. v. Andrew*,[16] for example, the English Employment Appeals Tribunal stated that:

> there is an implied term in a contract of employment that employers will not, without reasonable and proper cause, conduct themselves in a manner calculated or likely to destroy or seriously damage the relationship of trust and confidence between the parties (Carr and Kay, 1994, p. 78).

The fourth main duty imposed on employers by the common law is, according to Carr and Kay (p. 78) "an obligation to indemnify . . . employees in respect of any expenses incurred in performing their duties. . . ."

---

[14]There are, however, two specific exceptions to this general rule. The first of those exceptions is where the employee is paid on a commission or piece-rate basis and so needs work in order to earn a living (see, for example, *Turner v. Goldsmith*, [1891] 1 Q.B. 544). The second exception is where the employee is highly skilled and needs to work in order to maintain a particular skill or expertise (see, for example, *Herbert Clayton and Jack Waller Ltd. v. Oliver*, [1930] A.C. 209; and *Langston v. AUEW*, [1973] 2 All E.R. 430).

[15][1940] 2 K.B. 647.

[16][1979] I.R.L.R. 84.

Finally, employers are obliged to inform employees of any steps which they need to take in order to benefit from rights or entitlements which have not been negotiated directly with them.[17] In *Scally v. Southern Health and Social Services Board*,[18] for example, the claimants were four doctors who were employed by the Northern Ireland Health and Social Services Boards. Under Regulations made in 1974 such employees were given the right to purchase "added years" of pension entitlements on highly advantageous terms. That right could, however, only be exercised within a limited time period.[19] In such circumstances, the House of Lords held that there was an implied obligation on the employer to bring the term of the contract to the employee's attention. The Court added, however, that such a duty to inform would only be imposed on employers where:

- The terms of the contract of employment have not been negotiated with the individual employee but result from negotiation with a representative body or are otherwise incorporated by reference
- A particular term of the contract makes available to the employee a valuable right contingent upon action being taken by him to avail himself of its benefit, and
- The employee cannot, in all the circumstances, reasonably be expected to be aware of the term unless it is drawn to his attention.

As well as the commonly implied terms discussed above there are a number of other rights and duties which are regularly imposed on the parties by the courts. Among the duties in question are the duties on employers to take reasonable care for the safety of their employees and to take reasonable care in preparing references. Both of these duties are discussed later in this chapter.

---

[17]See *Scally v. Southern Health & Social Services Board*, [1992] 1 A.C. 294. See also "Employment Contracts may be Wider than Thought", (1992) 10 *IR Data Bank* 7 (July).

[18]*Op. cit.*

[19]Up to February, 1976 by workers already employed, and within twelve months after recruitment for new staff after that date.

Common Law Duties of Employees

In the same way that the common law imposes duties on employers via terms implied in the employment contract, it also imposes duties on employees. The main duties in question are discussed below.

Firstly, an employee is impliedly obliged:

> to present himself at work, in accordance with the contract of [service], and to work at the direction of the employer in return for the implied obligation of the employer to pay wages as agreed (Carr and Kay, 1994, p. 56).

An employee who fails to turn up for work is, therefore, acting in breach of contract. Similarly, employees who are only willing to perform a proportion of their work will usually be deemed to be acting in breach of their employment contract.[20]

Secondly, employees are under a duty to obey their employer's lawful orders provided that the orders in question are within the scope of the contract of employment.[21] A failure to comply with such orders constitutes a breach of the contract of employment and will, in most circumstances, justify dismissal.[22] Employees may, however, refuse to obey an order which is apparently within the scope of their employment where:

- The employer orders employees to do something which would constitute a criminal offence,[23] or
- The order involves exceptional danger for which the employees are not given extra payment.[24]

---

[20]See *Miles v. Wakefield Metropolitan District Council*, [1987] 1 All E.R. 1089; *Wiluszynski v. London Borough of Tower Hamlets*, [1989] I.R.L.R. 259; and *Ticehurst and Thompson v. British Telecommunications plc*, [1992] I.R.L.R. 219. For a discussion of the principles underlying these and related cases, see Twomey, (1993, p. 131).

[21]In *Price v. Mouat*, (1862) 11 C.B. 508, for example, a lace-salesman was ordered to "card" (pack) lace. He refused to do so and was dismissed without notice. The dismissal was held to have been wrongful because the order was not one which was within the scope of the contract.

[22]See, for example, *Waters v. Kentredder Ireland Ltd.*, UD 3/1977.

[23]A contract which revolves around the performance of unlawful activities is void for illegality. See further Friel (1995, pp. 245-260).

Thirdly, employees are obliged to use reasonable skill and care in the performance of their duties. Therefore, if employees are negligent in the performance of their work, they may be regarded as being in breach of contract.[25] This is particularly true if there has been a pattern of negligent conduct by that employee or if the single act of negligence is particularly serious. In *Lister v. Romford Ice and Cold Storage Co. Ltd.*,[26] for example, a lorry driver carelessly reversed his lorry and injured a fellow employee. The employers paid damages to the injured man but successfully claimed an indemnity from the lorry driver on the grounds that he was in breach of his duty to use reasonable skill and care in the performance of his duties.

As a logical extension of the last-mentioned duty, employees are also under an implied contractual obligation to take reasonable care of their employers' property. Employees who negligently lose or damage their employer's property are obliged to indemnify their employer for the loss sustained.

Finally, employees are impliedly obliged to act in good faith (Carr and Kay, 1994, pp. 63-64). This last duty is usually regarded as comprising four distinct sub-categories:

- The duty not to make a secret profit
- The duty to disclose relevant information to the employer
- The duty not to act to the detriment of the employer, and

---

[24]In *Robson v. Sykes*, [1938] 2 All E.R. 612, for example, a merchant seaman was ordered to sail on a ship which was to call at Spanish ports. He refused on the grounds that serious danger was involved on account of the Civil War. He was dismissed for his refusal but he claimed that the dismissal was wrongful. His action succeeded because, while the order was *prima facie* within the scope of the contract, it involved unreasonable danger to the employee.

[25]Even where there is no negligence on the part of the employee, mere incompetence in and of itself may constitute a breach of the contract of employment, particularly if the employee has professed an ability to do the work in question.

[26][1957] A.C. 555.

- The duty not to disclose confidential information.[27]

Terms Implied by Collective Bargaining Agreements

Fennell and Lynch (1993) state that in Ireland, as in the UK, collective bargaining agreements are not legally enforceable. It is, however, generally accepted that where persons commence working in an establishment in which a collective agreement regulates some or all of the terms and conditions of employees in their category, the courts will readily imply the agreement's terms into their employment contracts. Similarly, the terms of a collective agreement are legally enforceable where the agreement is one which is registered with the Labour Court in line with Section 25 of the Industrial Relations Act, 1946.

The international trend, however, is to support the automatic incorporation of the terms of collective bargaining agreements into the individual employee's contract of employment. In such a context it is worth noting that in *O'Rourke v. Talbot (Ireland) Ltd.*[28] the High Court reserved the discretion to deem a collective bargaining agreement to be binding where the parties intended the agreement to be binding and its terms are clear.

Terms Implied by Legislation

As has already been pointed out, contracts of service are affected by a broad range of statutory provisions which imply into them a considerable number of largely protective terms, often referred to colloquially as "workers' rights". These protective terms cover

---

[27]See *Bent's Brewery v. Hogan*, [1945] 2 All E.R. 570; *Faccenda Chicken Ltd. v. Fowler*, [1986] I.C.R. 297. Perhaps the clearest definition of what constitutes confidential information is that elaborated by Megarry V.C. in *Thomas Marshall Ltd. v. Guinle*, [1979] 1 Ch. 227, at 248: "First, that the information must be information the release of which the owner believes would be injurious to him or of advantage to his rivals or others. Second, the owner must believe the information is confidential or secret. Third, the owner's belief under these headings must be reasonable. Fourth, the information must be judged in the light of usage and practices in the particular industry concerned." For a detailed discussion of the employee's duty not to disclose confidential information, see Lavery (1996, pp. 145-184).

[28][1984] I.L.R.M. 587.

such matters as holiday and maternity rights, minimum notice, dismissals and employment equality. The various statutes in question are discussed in detail below.

SAFETY, HEALTH AND WELFARE IN THE WORKPLACE[29]

As the leading Irish textbook on the law of torts explains:

> The law was slow to impose liability in negligence on employers in relation to injuries sustained by their employees. The *laissez-faire* philosophy, which prevailed during the earlier part of the last century, was reflected in judicial attitudes to work related injuries: industry was admittedly dangerous but was clearly regarded as being socially beneficial in the long run; the employee could look after his own interests, and if he chose to accept dangerous employment for an appropriate payment, he should not impose on his employer the obligation to compensate him when things went wrong. In the latter part of the nineteenth century, this philosophy was tempered somewhat, and since the turn of the century the process of dismantling this judicial mechanism has been rapid and radical (McMahon and Binchy, 1990, p. 314).

The resulting duty of care which has been imposed on employers by the courts is essentially comprised of four main elements:

- To provide a safe place of work
- To provide proper plant and equipment
- To provide a safe system of work
- To provide competent staff.

Safe Place of Work

Employers must ensure that a reasonably safe place of work is provided and maintained for the benefit of the employee. They must also supply a safe means of access to and egress from the place of work. The extent to which an employer must protect an

---

[29] See also Chapter 20.

employee from injury on premises not under the employer's control is, however, somewhat less certain. Obviously, there have to be limits to the employer's duty in this regard. As Lord Justice Pearce has observed in the English Court of Appeal:

> if a master sends his plumber to mend a leak in a respectable private house, no one could hold him liable for not visiting the house himself to see if the carpet in the hall creates a trap.[30]

It seems that no hard and fast rules have been articulated on this matter, and that the courts have generally been content to regard it as a question of fact.

Proper Plant and Equipment

The employer has a duty to take:

> reasonable care to provide proper appliances and to maintain them in a proper condition, and so to carry on his operations as not to subject those employed by him to unnecessary risk.[31]

So, for example, in *Deegan v. Langan*[32] the Supreme Court imposed liability on an employer who supplied his employee, a carpenter, with nails which the employer knew were apt to shatter when struck by a hammer.

Safe System of Work

As Mr. Justice McLoughlin explained in *Kinsella v. Hammond Lane Industries Ltd.*:[33]

> [i]f an accident causes injury to a workman and the accident results from a risk of an unsafe system of work, against which the employer should have [taken], but did

---

[30]*Wilson v. Tyneside Window Cleaning Co.*, [1958] 2 Q.B. 110, 121.

[31]*Per* Budd J. in *Burke v. John Paul & Co. Ltd.*, [1967] I.R. 277, 281; quoting from Lord Herschell in *Smith v. Baker & Sons*, [1891] A.C. 325, 362.

[32][1966] I.R. 373.

[33][1958] 96 I.L.T.R. 1.

not take, reasonable precautions to guard, then the employer is liable for damages.

Competent Fellow Employees

Finally, employers owe their employees a duty of care to select competent workmates for them. Before employers will be liable for having failed to provide competent staff it must be shown that they had reason to be aware of their incompetence. This may be proved by specific evidence of knowledge of their incapacity; but it can also be established by proof of a negligent system of "no questions asked" hiring. Moreover, where employers discover that employees are incompetent some time after they have hired them, and then continue to employ them on work which the employer now appreciates is beyond their capacity, they do so at their peril.

The Safety Health and Welfare at Work Act, 1989

Workplace health and safety is not, however, regulated exclusively by the common law. Rather, a substantial role in protecting workers is played by legislation in the form of the Safety, Health and Welfare at Work Act, 1989. That Act imposes duties on both employers and employees in relation to ensuring safety, health and welfare at work (see Chapter 20 for a detailed description of the Act).

EMPLOYMENT EQUALITY LEGISLATION[34]

Irish employment equality law has made remarkable strides since Ireland's accession to the European Economic Community in 1973.[35] In the following four years the Oireachtas passed two landmark pieces of legislation which significantly improved the

---

[34]See, generally, Curtin (1989).

[35]In his foreword to Curtin (1989) Judge T.F. O'Higgins of the European Court of Justice noted that "Ireland's decision to join the European Communities . . . led . . . to profound changes in the law affecting the employer/employee relationship and in particular to the giving to workers of rights of equality in pay and conditions of employment which previously would never have been thought attainable." At xv.

legal position of women workers.[36] The first of those statutes, the Anti-Discrimination (Pay) Act, 1974, as its title suggests, was intended to tackle the problem of gender-based discrimination in relation to pay. While the struggle for equal pay has not yet been successfully concluded, the passing of the 1974 Act was a significant development. As Curtin points out (p. 112):

> The entry into force of the Anti-Discrimination (Pay) Act, 1974, combined with the refusal by the European Commission to permit any derogation by the Irish Government from its European Community obligations, heralded, to borrow James Connolly's terminology, the beginning of the end of the "martyrdom" of Irish women workers.

The second legislative landmark referred to above was the Employment Equality Act, 1977, which made it unlawful to discriminate between individuals on grounds of sex or marital status in relation to conditions of employment other than those concerning remuneration. While the 1977 Act was aimed primarily at eliminating discrimination by employers, it also made unlawful discrimination in activities which are related to employment, such as discrimination by organisations providing training courses, trade unions or employment agencies, as well as prohibiting the display or publication of discriminatory advertisements.

Some further progress was made during Mervyn Taylor's stewardship of the Department of Equality and Law Reform, with the enactment of the Maternity Protection Act, 1994[37] and the Adoptive Leave Act, 1995. All of these statutes are discussed below.

The Anti-Discrimination (Pay) Act, 1974

The primary purpose of the Anti-Discrimination (Pay) Act, 1974, is to imply into contracts of employment a term conferring on the

---

[36]The definitive work on Irish employment equality law, which deals comprehensively with both pieces of legislation, is Curtin's seminal *Irish Employment Equality Law* (1989). Despite the fact that it is almost ten years since its publication, those who are interested in learning more about the Acts in question need go no further than Professor Curtin's book.

[37]Which repealed and effectively updated the Maternity Protection Act, 1981.

employee an entitlement to the same rate of remuneration as that paid to an employee of the opposite gender for "like work". The Act does not cover other terms and conditions of employment. In order to establish one's entitlement to claim under the Act, one must be able to prove that:

- One is "employed under a contract of service or apprenticeship or a contract personally to execute any work or labour".[38]
- There is an identifiable person of the opposite gender (usually referred to as the "male comparator") doing a comparable job with whom one can be compared. A comparison with some hypothetical worker does not suffice.
- One is employed in the same place as the comparator.[39]
- One is doing "like work" to that of the comparator.

The term "like work" may be defined as meaning the same work,[40] similar work[41] or work of equal value.[42] Section 3(a) of the Act applies where the actual work performed by the claimant and the conditions under which it is performed are the same as those applying to the comparator. If there is a difference of practical importance between the parties' jobs or conditions the employer can legitimately pay different rates of remuneration. The equality officer or court hearing the case will, however, closely scrutinise any misleading "labelling" of a job which may constitute an attempt on the part of the employer to disguise the payment of different rates for the same work.

---

[38]Section 1(1).

[39]Paying employees different rates of remuneration because of legitimate regional variations in wage determination procedures is permissible. Nevertheless, where rates are negotiated and determined centrally for a nationwide employer with no regional or geographic variations, Equality Officers have allowed comparisons to be made between colleagues in different branch offices.

[40]Section 3(a).

[41]Section 3(b).

[42]Section 3(c).

Section 3(b) covers those situations where the work performed by the claimant is of a broadly similar nature to that performed by the comparator. It follows that differences which occur only infrequently or which are of small importance in relation to the work as a whole will not result in a claim failing under section 3(b). Section 3(b) is not merely a narrow extension of section 3(a). Rather, it permits frequent differences between the jobs being compared, so long as those differences are of little importance in relation to the work as a whole.

The formulation of section 3(c) focuses attention on the content of the job rather than on the value of the employee's work to the employer. Its purpose is to allow jobs which are radically different in content to be the basis of an equal pay claim if it can be demonstrated that the work performed by the claimant and the comparator are equally demanding. The basic premise behind this sub-paragraph is that women should be able to substantiate a claim for equal pay by showing that their jobs and those of their male colleagues are of equal value in terms of the demands made on them with regard to the sex-neutral factors legislatively elaborated, i.e. the amount of skill, physical or mental effort and responsibility and the quality of working conditions. So, in *Waterford Glass Ltd. v. I.T.G.W.U.*,[43] for example, the Equality Officer found that the degree of skill, dexterity and concentration required of female workers balanced out against the "high level" of physical strength and endurance expected of male general workers.

Claims under the Act are heard by Equality Officers, who, having heard submissions from both parties, issue recommendations. Appeals from an Equality Officer's recommendation are heard by the Labour Court. The Court's determination in such a case may, in turn, be appealed to the High Court on a point of law.

The Employment Equality Act, 1977

The Employment Equality Act, 1977, makes it unlawful to discriminate between individuals on grounds of sex or marital status

---

[43]EP 15/1977.

in relation to conditions of employment other than those concerning remuneration.[44] Section 2 of the Act specifically deems four types of discrimination to be unlawful. The four types of discrimination in question are:

- Direct discrimination on grounds of sex, which arises where a person is treated less favourably than someone of the opposite gender because of their sex. In *Bradley v. Eastern Health Board*,[45] for example, the male claimant telephoned the defendants to apply for a position as a laundry worker and was informed that the position wasn't suitable for men. The Health Board was found to have directly discriminated against the claimant.
- Indirect discrimination on grounds of sex, which arises where, for example, a woman is required to comply with a requirement which is not essential for the job, and where the proportion of men who are able to comply with the requirement is substantially greater.[46]
- Direct discrimination on grounds of marital status, which arises where a person is treated less favourably than another person of the same sex but of a different marital status.
- Indirect discrimination on grounds of marital status, which arises where, for example, a married woman is required to comply with a specific requirement which is not essential for the job and the proportion of single women able to comply with the requirement is substantially greater (or vice versa). In the case of the *Eastern Health Board v. Local Government and Public Service Union*,[47] for example, the Health Board fixed an upper age limit of 27 for applicants for a position as a clerk/typist. A 42-year-old applicant won her case against the

---

[44]An employer affording special treatment to a woman for reasons relating to pregnancy or childbirth (such as giving her lighter work or time off during working hours) is not be deemed to constitute discrimination within the meaning of the 1977 Act.

[45]EE 2/81.

[46]For example, a minimum height for an office job.

[47]DEE 3/81.

Board on the basis that the age limit constituted indirect discrimination against married women. The necessity to be under 27 years of age was, she successfully argued, a non-essential requirement which a far greater proportion of unmarried people could meet.

Section 3 of the Act deems it unlawful for an employer to discriminate on grounds of sex or marital status:

- In the arrangements he makes for recruitment (including the criteria he applies in selecting staff, interview procedures or the instructions he gives to an employment agency)
- In the terms on which he offers the job
- By refusing or deliberately omitting to offer a person the job in question
- In the provision of training, on or off the job
- In regrading or the classification of jobs
- In work counselling
- In the provision of work experience
- In the opportunities he affords his employees for promotion
- In dismissals or disciplinary measures, or in any other disadvantages to which employees may be subjected (including redundancies, lay offs and short-time working), or
- By issuing discriminatory rules or instructions to employees.

The relationship between sections 2 and 3 of the Act was considered by the Supreme Court in the relatively recent case of *Nathan v. Bailey Gibson, the Irish Print Union and the Minister for Labour.*[48] According to Chief Justice Hamilton:

> The obligations imposed on an employer by virtue of section 3 of the Act are not in any way limited by the provisions of section 2 of the Act. This section provides that for the pur-

[48](1996) 7 E.L.R. 114. For a discussion of the case, see Cathy Maguire, "*Nathan v. Bailey Gibson*: Curing Past Injustices?", (1996) *I.L.T. (n.s.)* 232.

> poses of the Act, discrimination shall be taken to occur in the cases set forth at (a), (b) and (c) of the section. The cases referred to therein are clearly cases of direct discrimination and cannot be regarded as an exhaustive description of direct discrimination and do not cover cases of indirect discrimination.
>
> Cases of indirect discrimination are clearly prohibited by the [Equal Treatment] Directive [1976] and section 3(1) and (2) of the Act cannot be interpreted as containing no prohibition against indirect discrimination but must be interpreted as prohibiting cases of both direct and indirect discrimination.[49]

Job advertisements are specifically dealt with by section 8 of the Act, which provides that it is unlawful to advertise jobs in such a way that the advertisement could reasonably be interpreted as intending to discriminate. Advertisements containing job descriptions such as "waiter", "salesgirl" or "postman", which have traditionally been associated with a particular gender will be deemed to discriminate, unless they contain an indication that the job is open to both men and women.

Claims under the Act are heard by Equality Officers, who, having heard submissions from both parties, issue recommendations. Appeals from an Equality Officer's recommendation are heard by the Labour Court. The Court's determination in such a case may, in turn, be appealed to the High Court on a point of law.

Sexual Harassment[50]

While sexual harassment in the workplace is not expressly outlawed by statute it has consistently been held to constitute an infringement of the Employment Equality Act, 1977. In the first Irish case, *A Garage Proprietor v. A Worker*,[51] a 15-year-old female garage/shop assistant resigned after six months in her job, claiming that she had been subjected to continual sexual harass-

---

[49] At 127-128.

[50] See, generally, Harvey and Twomey (1995).

[51] EEO 2/85; ECD 85/1.

ment by her employer. She was awarded £1,000 compensation by the Labour Court which held that freedom from sexual harassment is a condition of employment which an employee of either sex is entitled to expect. The failure of an employer to ensure compliance with that condition of employment constitutes discrimination under the 1977 Act.

As employers are legally liable for the acts of their employees done in the course of their employment it has generally been considered that employers can be successfully sued by workers who have been sexually harassed by their supervisors and/or fellow employees.[52] The matter has, however, been complicated by the relatively recent decision of Mr. Justice Costello in *The Health Board v. B.C. and the Labour Court*.[53] In that case the worker in question was seriously sexually assaulted by colleagues. In a somewhat controversial decision Mr. Justice Costello held that the Health Board was not vicariously liable for the acts of its employees as their actions were not within the scope of their contractual duties. As a result of the decision in the *B.C.* case there is some academic debate as to when exactly an employer can be found to be vicariously liable. In such a context, the safest course of action for employers is to pursue vigorous anti-harassment policies. If they choose to do so they will invariably escape any potential liability and will reduce the number of incidents of harassment occurring on their premises.

The Maternity Protection Act, 1994

The Maternity Protection Act, 1994 guarantees women[54] the right to take maternity leave and the right to return to work having taken such leave.[55] It does not, however, confer on them any right to obtain pay while on maternity leave. Rather, the Department

---

[52]In such cases the employer is described as being "vicariously" liable.

[53][1994] E.L.R. 27. For comment on the case, see Harvey and Twomey (1995, pp. 55-72).

[54]The Act does not provide for parental leave for men, except where the mother of a child dies within fourteen weeks of the birth of the child in question.

[55]In order to be able to rely on the Act a woman has to be in employment which is insurable for the purposes of the Social Welfare Code.

of Social Welfare is responsible for the payment of employees who fulfil the required PRSI contribution conditions.

The Act entitles women to take fourteen consecutive weeks' maternity leave. An employee must take at least four of the fourteen weeks before the end of the week in which her baby is due, and four weeks after that week. She may also take up to four additional weeks unpaid leave immediately after her maternity leave.

The Adoptive Leave Act, 1995

The Adoptive Leave Act entitles an adopting mother (or a sole male adopter) who is in employment to:

- A minimum of ten consecutive weeks of adoptive leave from work, beginning on the day of placement of the child, and
- Up to four weeks additional adoptive leave.

The ten week period of adoptive leave attracts a social welfare benefit in most cases.

THE PAYMENT OF WAGES ACT, 1991

Three basic rights are enshrined in the 1991 Act:[56]

- The right of every employee to a readily negotiable mode of wage payment
- The right of every employee to protection against unlawful deductions from their wages, and
- The right of every employee to a written statement of wages detailing their gross pay and the nature and amount of any deductions.

Section 2(1) of the Act sets out the ways in which wages can be paid (i.e. by way of cheques, bills of exchange, drafts, money orders, postal orders or cash). Only one method of payment can be used, although section 2(2) of the Act provides that if there hap-

[56] It should be noted that no qualifying periods of service or minimum hours thresholds apply to the Payment of Wages Act.

pens to be a bank strike the employer may pay in another non-cash mode, but only if the employee consents. If the employee does not consent, he must be paid in cash. In recognition of the notion of collective bargaining the Act also provides that if there is to be any change in the form in which employees are to be paid both the employer and employees must consent.

Section 5 of the Act details deductions which an employer is allowed to make from wages, such as tax or other deductions authorised by statute or deductions made with the consent of the employee. An employer can also make deductions of a compensatory nature in lieu of acts or omissions of an employee or in respect of goods given to an employee, but any such deductions must be authorised by the employee's contract and they must be both fair and reasonable having regard to the amount of the wages of the employee. The employee must be given a copy of the Act or notice in writing of section 5 at least one week before any such deduction is made.

THE MINIMUM NOTICE AND TERMS OF EMPLOYMENT ACT, 1973

The Minimum Notice and Terms of Employment Act, 1973, lays down minimum periods of notice to be given by employers and employees when terminating a contract of employment. It originally also gave employees the right to have information about the terms of their employment set out in writing. In that respect, however, the Act has been superseded by the Terms of Employment (Information) Act, 1994.

Section 4 of the 1973 Act deals provides that if employees have been in "continuous service" with the same employer for at least thirteen weeks, they are entitled to such a minimum period of notice before the employer may dismiss them. The period of notice to which employees are entitled depends on the length of their service with the employer. The appropriate minimum periods of notice are set out in Table 19.1. below.

TABLE 19.1: MINIMUM NOTICE PERIODS UNDER THE 1973 ACT

Length of Service	Minimum Notice
13 weeks–2 years	1 week
2–5 years	2 weeks
5–10 years	4 weeks
10–15 years	6 weeks
15+ years	8 weeks

In contrast, section 6 of the Act provides that an employer is entitled to only one week's notice from an employee who has been employed by him for 13 weeks or more and who proposes to resign from his position.[57]

Any provision in a contract of employment for shorter periods of notice than the minimum periods stipulated in the Act has no effect. Despite the provisions of the Act, however, the employer is at all times entitled to dismiss an employee without notice if that employee has been guilty of gross misconduct.

THE TERMS OF EMPLOYMENT (INFORMATION) ACT, 1994

The Terms of Employment (Information) Act was enacted in order to comply with an EC Directive which required that certain information must be provided to employees concerning their contracts of employment.[58] Section 3 of the Act provides that not later than two months after the commencement of an employee's employment, the employer must provide a statement in writing to the employee setting out the following particulars of the terms of the employee's employment:

- The full names of the employer and the employee
- The address of the employer
- Either the place of work or a statement specifying that the employee is required or permitted to work at various places

[57] The contract, however, may require that the employee give the employer a greater period of notice before leaving his employment.

[58] Council Directive 91/533/EEC of 14 October, 1991.

- The title of the job or nature of the work for which the employee is employed
- The date of commencement of the employee's contract of employment
- In the case of a temporary contract of employment, the expected duration thereof, or, if the contract of employment is for a fixed term, the date on which the contract expires
- The rate or method of calculation of the employee's remuneration
- The length of the intervals between the times at which remuneration is paid
- Any terms or conditions relating to hours of work
- Any terms or conditions relating to incapacity for work due to sickness or injury and paid leave, as well as any terms or conditions relating to pensions and pension schemes
- The period of notice which the employee is required to give and entitled to receive, or the method for determining the length of such notice periods
- A reference to any collective agreements which directly affect the terms and conditions of the employee's employment.

The employee must be notified in writing of any change occurring in any of the particulars furnished within one month of such change occurring.

Section 6 provides that, in the case of contracts of employment entered into before the commencement of the Act, an employer must, on request by the employee, furnish the employee with a statement containing the required particulars.

THE WORKER PROTECTION (REGULAR PART-TIME EMPLOYEES) ACT, 1991

The Worker Protection (Regular Part-time Employees) Act, 1991, extends the benefits of a range of protective legislation to regular part-time employees. Section 1 of the Act defines "regular part-time employee[s]" as being those who are in the continuous employment of the employer for not less than 13 weeks, are normally expected to work not less than eight hours per week and who, but for the Act, would be excluded from benefits under the legislation which the Act amended. The Act extended (to regular part-time employees) the benefits of, *inter alia*, the:

- Unfair Dismissals Act, 1977
- Minimum Notice and Terms of Employment Acts, 1973 and 1984
- Worker Participation (State Enterprises) Acts, 1977 and 1988;
- Redundancy Payments Acts, 1967 to 1990, and
- Protection of Employees (Employers' Insolvency) Acts, 1984 and 1990.

THE PROTECTION OF YOUNG PERSONS (EMPLOYMENT) ACT, 1996

The Protection of Young Persons (Employment) Act, 1996 has the effect of regulating the employment of persons who have not attained the age of majority. Whereas the common law has traditionally classed all persons under the age of eighteen as "minors" or "infants" and dealt with their legal capacity and affairs in a consistent manner regardless of age, the 1996 Act sub-divides the larger classification into two groups; "children" and "young persons". For the purposes of the Act, a child is defined as "a person who is under 16 years of age or the school leaving age, whichever is the higher".[59] A young person, on the other hand, is "a person who has reached 16 years of age or the school leaving age (whichever is higher) but is less than 18 years of age".[60]

---

[59]Section 1(1). As the 1995 *White Paper on Education* explained, "[a]t present, the compulsory school leaving age is fifteen. In future, the school-leaving age will be sixteen or the completion of three years of junior cycle education, whichever is later" (Department of Education, 1995, p. 63). The recommendation in relation to raising the school-leaving age to sixteen has yet to be acted on.

[60]Section 1(1).

Section 3(1) of the Act imposes a blanket ban on the employment of children. The ban is, however, subject to a number of exceptions which are detailed in section 3. So, for example, children over the age of fifteen may be employed to do light work[61] for up to eight hours a week during school term time.[62] Similarly, children who are over the age of fourteen may, according to section 3(4), be employed to do light work[63] as long as:

- The work is not undertaken during school term-time
- Such work is not harmful to the safety, health and development of the child[64]
- The child has a break from work of at least 21 days over the summer holidays[65] and
- The child is not required to work for more than seven hours a day or 35 hours a week.[66]

The employment of thirteen-year-olds[67] is permitted only where the Minister for Enterprise, Trade and Employment introduces regulations authorising such employment:

---

[61]The term "light work" is defined in section 1(1) of the Act as meaning "all work which is not industrial work and which, on account of the inherent nature of the tasks which it involves and the particular conditions under which they are performed, is not likely to be harmful to the safety, health or development of children, and is not such as to be harmful to their attendance at school, their participation in vocational guidance or training programmes approved by the competent authority or their capacity to benefit from the instruction received."

[62]Section 3(5). In addition, section 3(10) permits an employer to "retain in his or her employment any child of 15 years of age who was in his or her employment immediately before the commencement" of section 3. In such circumstances, however, the child is limited to working 7 hours a day or 35 hours a week.

[63]The term "light work" is defined in section 1(1). See footnote 61.

[64]Section 3(4)*(b)*.

[65]Section 3(4)*(c)*.

[66]Section 3(4)*(a)*.

[67]The employment of children under the age of thirteen is permitted only where the Minister for Enterprise, Trade and Employment grants a licence *individually* authorising such employment ". . . in cultural, artistic, sports or

> . . . in cultural, artistic, sports or advertising activities which are not harmful to the safety, health or development of children and which are not likely to interfere with their attendance at school, vocational guidance or training programmes or capacity to benefit from the instruction received.[68]

Even where the employment of a child is permitted by section 3, the hours of work of such children is subject to statutory regulation.[69]

Section 6(1) of the Act imposes a blanket ban on the employment of young persons except where:

- The employment lasts no longer than 8 hours a day or 40 hours a week.[70]
- The young person is not required to work between 10.00 p.m. and 6.00 a.m.[71] (or between 11.00 p.m. and 7.00 a.m. "where the Minister [for Enterprise, Trade and Employment] is satisfied . . . that there are exceptional circumstances" which arise in relation to the area or kind of work in question).[72]
- The young person is afforded a minimum rest period of at least 12 hours in every 24 hour-period.[73]

---

advertising activities which are not harmful to the safety, health or development of children and which are not likely to interfere with their attendance at school, vocational guidance or training programmes or capacity to benefit from the instruction received." (Section 3(2)).

[68]Section 3(3).

[69]See section 4.

[70]Section 6(1)*(a)*.

[71]Section 6(1)*(b)*(i).

[72]Section 6(1)*(b)*(ii).

[73]Section 6(1)*(c)*. Section 6(2), however, provides that such rest periods "may be interrupted by an employer in the case of a young person employed on activities that do not extend beyond 2 hours in each day or are separated, exclusive of breaks, over the day, provided that, in each period of 24 hours, the young person receives a minimum rest period of 12 hours." Expressly exempted from the application of the minimum rest periods specified in section 6(1)*(c)* are those employed in the shipping or fishing sectors (section 6(4)) and in the Defence Forces (section 6(5)).

- The young person is allowed a minimum of two days off in any seven-day period.[74] Where possible, the two days in question should be consecutive.
- The young person is not allowed to work for more than four-and-a-half consecutive hours without being given at least a thirty minute break.[75]

In exceptional circumstances, however, employers may avoid the application of section 6(1) where they obtain a licence enabling them to do so from the Minister for Enterprise, Trade and Employment.[76]

Where employers decide to employ either a child or a young person, they are obliged, by section 5(1) of the Act, to obtain a copy of the prospective employee's birth certificate or some other "satisfactory evidence" of their age before the child or young person commences employment.[77] In the case of a child, the employer must also obtain the written permission of one of the child's parents or legal guardians.[78]

Employers are also required to keep a register of children and young persons in their employment.[79] The register must detail the full names,[80] dates of birth,[81] starting times,[82] finishing times,[83]

---

[74]Section 6(1)*(d)*. Section 6(3), however, provides that such rest periods "may be interrupted by an employer in the case of a young person employed on activities that do not extend beyond 2 hours in each day or are separated, exclusive of breaks, over the day, provided that, in each period of 7 days, the cumulative rest period is 2 days." Expressly exempted from the application of the minimum rest periods specified in section 6(1)*(d)* are those employed in the shipping or fishing sectors (section 6(4)) and in the Defence Forces (section 6(5)).

[75]Section 6(1)*(e)*. The child need not be paid in respect of his break-time (section 6(6)).

[76]Section 7(1).

[77]Section 5(1)*(a)*.

[78]Section 5(1)*(b)*.

[79]Section 5(1)*(c)*.

[80]Section 5(1)*(b)*(i).

[81]Section 5(1)*(b)*(ii).

[82]Section 5(1)*(b)*(iii).

rates of pay[84] and total remuneration[85] paid to each of the children or young persons in question.

THE ORGANISATION OF WORKING TIME ACT, 1997

The Organisation of Working Time Act, 1997 was introduced in order to give effect to the EU Working Time Directive[86] but also deals with a number of matters not referred to in the Directive as well as repealing and replacing some relatively outdated protective legislation. The following categories of employees are expressly excluded from the application of the Act:

- Members of the Garda Síochána and the Defence Forces[87]
- Persons engaged in sea-fishing or other work at sea[88]
- Doctors in training[89]
- Persons employed by relatives[90]
- Persons who determine their own working time.[91]

Working Time

Section 15 of the Act provides that an employer may not permit an employee to work more than an average of 48 hours in a seven-

---

[83]Section 5(1)*(b)*(iv).

[84]Section 5(1)*(b)*(v).

[85]Section 5(1)*(b)*(vi).

[86]Council Directive 93/104/EC of 23 November 1993. As Butler (1997, p. 34) explains, "[t]he Directive . . . was adopted by the Council of Social Affairs Ministers on 23 November 1993, by qualified majority vote, with the UK abstaining. The Directive, however, applies to all member states of the European Union including the UK."

[87]Section 3(1); subject to qualifications contained in section 3(4).

[88]Section 3(2)*(a)*; subject to qualifications contained in section 3(4).

[89]Section 3(2)*(a)*; subject to qualifications contained in section 3(4).

[90]Where the employee is a member of the employer's household and the place of employment is a private dwelling house or a farm where they both reside. Section 3(2)*(b)*; subject to qualifications contained in section 3(4).

[91]Section 3(1)*(c)*.

day period.[92] The average number of weekly working hours is calculated, in most cases, over a period of four months.[93]

The legislation also requires that employees be given 11 consecutive hours rest in each period of 24 hours;[94] a 15-minute break after working for four hours and 30 minutes (or 30 minutes during a six-hour period of work);[95] and 24 hours consecutive rest in each seven-day period.[96]

Annual Leave

The 1997 Act also sets out the minimum statutory holiday entitlements of employees. Significantly, the Act increases the minimum entitlement from the previous level of 15 working days[97] to four working weeks.[98] The new four week entitlement is, however, being introduced on a phased basis with employees being entitled to:

- One extra day in 1997 (a total of 16 days)
- An additional two days in 1998 (a total of 18 days)
- A further two days in 1999 (a total of 20 days).[99]

Supervisors should, however, remember that employees in occupations covered by Labour Court Employment Regulation Orders or Registered Employment Agreements generally have a legally enforceable entitlement to more generous terms. In other words,

---

[92]The 1997 Act also regulates nightworking (section 16).

[93]Section 15(1).

[94]Section 11.

[95]Section 12.

[96]Section 13(2).

[97]As provided for in the now repealed Holidays (Employees) Acts, 1973-1991.

[98]Section 19(1).

[99]Corresponding increases in the minimum entitlements of part-time workers will result in an increase in their holiday entitlement from 6 hours for every 100 hours worked in 1997 to 8 hours for every 100 hours worked in 1999 (the corresponding figures for 1997 and 1998 are 6.4 hours and 7.2 hours respectively).

the Act merely sets a minimum or floor level of holidays below which one cannot go.

The time at which annual leave may be taken is determined by the employer provided that the employees or their trade union are consulted at least one month beforehand. Regard must also be had to the employee's opportunities for rest and relaxation.

TRANSFER OF UNDERTAKINGS: THE ACQUIRED RIGHTS DIRECTIVE

Before 1977 the courts in most EU member states regarded the sale or transfer of a business as effecting the termination of the contracts of employment of all those employed by the original owner of the business. In other words, the new owners of a business could not have its old employees foisted upon them against their wishes. Obviously, the adoption of such a stance by the courts left employees with little protection.

EEC Directive 187 of 1977 (Daly, 1993, p. 7), which is usually referred to as the "Acquired Rights Directive", was intended to ensure that employees were afforded some protection where their employers sought to terminate their contracts of employment by selling or transferring the businesses in which they worked. Article 3(1) of the Directive provides that:

> The transferor's rights and obligations arising from a contract of employment or from an employment relationship existing on the date of a transfer . . . shall, by reason of such transfer, be transferred to the transferee. . . .

In like manner, Article 4 provides that:

> The transfer of an undertaking, business or part of a business shall not in itself constitute grounds for dismissal by the transferor or the transferee. This provision shall not stand in the way of dismissals that may take place for economic, technical or organizational reasons entailing changes in the workforce.

While the effect of the Directive is relatively clear, some difficulty has been encountered by those attempting to determine precisely when it applies. Article 1(1) provides that the Directive applies "to the transfer of an undertaking, business or part of a business to another employer as a result of a legal transfer or merger."[100] Unfortunately, no real further clarification of the meaning of the term "transfer" is provided in the text of the Directive.[101] For that reason, one has to turn to a series of decisions of the Court of Justice in order to obtain guidance on the matter. Among the more instructive decisions is that in *Spijkers v. Gebroeders Benedik Abattoir C.V.*[102] In that case the Court held that:

> It is clear from the scheme of Directive No. 77/187 and from the terms of Article 1(1) thereof that the directive is intended to ensure the continuity of employment relationships existing within a business, irrespective of any change of ownership. It follows that the decisive criterion for establishing whether there is a transfer for the purposes of the directive is whether the business in question retains its identity.
>
> Consequently, a transfer of an undertaking, business or part of a business does not occur merely because its assets are disposed of. Instead it is necessary to consider . . . whether the business was disposed of as a going concern, as would be indicated, *inter alia*, by the fact that its operation was actually continued or resumed by the new employer, with the same or similar activities.
>
> In order to determine whether those conditions are met, it is necessary to consider all the facts characterizing the transaction in question, including the type of undertaking or business, whether or not the business's tangible assets, such as buildings and movable property, are transferred, the value of its intangible assets at the time of the transfer, whether or not the majority of its employees are taken over by the new employer, whether or not its customers are

---

[100]Article 1(2) qualifies the broad sweep of Article 1(1) by limiting its application to situations where "the undertaking, business or part of the business to be transferred is situated within the territorial scope of the Treaty." Article 1(3) precludes the Directive from applying to "sea-going vessels".

[101]Even though the terms "transferor", "transferee" and "representatives of the employees" are defined in Article 2.

[102][1986] E.C.R. 1119.

> transferred and the degree of similarity between the activities carried on before and after the transfer and the period, if any, for which those activities were suspended. It should be noted, however, that all those circumstances are merely single factors in the overall assessment which must be made and cannot therefore be considered in isolation.[103]

The Acquired Rights Directive was implemented in Ireland by way of the European Communities (Safeguarding of Employees' Rights on Transfer of Undertakings) Regulations, 1980.[104] In determining when those regulations apply, Blayney J. held, in *Bannon v. The E.A.T. and Drogheda Town Centre Ltd.*,[105] that the relevant test has two distinct parts.[106] The regulations will, therefore, apply if:

- The business retained its identity,[107] and
- There was a change in the legal or natural person responsible for carrying on the business regardless of whether or not ownership of the business was transferred (Daly, 1993, p. 7).

THE UNFAIR DISMISSALS ACTS, 1977-1993

As Fennell and Lynch (1993, p. 205) point out, historically, Irish workers have had little legal protection against arbitrary dismissal. Because of the lack of a means of obtaining legal redress against employers who unfairly dismissed workers a significant number of strikes disrupted Irish workplaces in the 1960s and early 1970s. In 1975, for example, 116,000 working-days were lost because of strikes resulting from dismissals and related matters.

---

[103] At 1128-1129; as cited by Tony Kerr, "Implementation of Directive 77/187 into Irish Law and Case Law of the Court of Justice", in *Transfer of Undertakings*, 1, at 7-8.

[104] S.I. No. 306 of 1980.

[105] [1993] 1 I.R. 500.

[106] Blayney J. extrapolated the two elements of his test from the decisions of the Court of Justice in *Spijkers, op. cit.*, and *Landsorganiationer i Danmark v. Ny Moelle Kro*, [1987] E.C.R. 5465; (1989) I.R.L.R. 37.

[107] In line with the test established in the *Spijkers* case discussed above.

For that reason, Michael O'Leary, TD, the then Minister for Labour, introduced the first Unfair Dismissals Act in 1977, stating at the time that the Act was designed "to give the individual greater protection against being unfairly fired from his job, and to contribute towards better industrial relations by reducing the number of disputes caused by dismissals." The Act, which is broadly similar to its English equivalent, has, by and large, fulfilled both of those functions. In 1987, for example, Tom Murphy (1987, p. 36) of UCD's Department of Industrial Relations, stated that:

> the Act and the [Employment Appeals] Tribunal have made a major impact on the practices of employers and trade unions at workplace level leading to an improved ability on their parts to resolve dismissal issues without resort to industrial action.

The main provisions of the 1977 Act and the Unfair Dismissals (Amendment) Act, 1993, which amended and up-dated it, are outlined below.

Categories Excluded from Protection by the 1977-1993 Acts

The Unfair Dismissals Acts preclude a significant number of categories of employees from claiming to have been unfairly dismissed.[108] The main categories of employees excluded are:

- Those who have less than one year of continuous service with the employer who dismissed them (except where the employee concerned was dismissed because of her involvement in trade union activities, pregnancy or matters related thereto)[109]
- Those who have reached the normal retiring age for employees of the same employer in similar employment

---

[108]Somewhat unusually, however, the 1993 Act provides that employees may bring an unfair dismissals action against their employer even if their contract of service is in breach of the tax or social welfare codes.

[109]In addition, s.3(b) of the 1993 Act prevents employers from seeking to avoid the application of the Acts by employing workers under a succession of short, fixed-term contracts.

- Civil servants
- Officers of Health Boards and VECs
- Persons employed by close relatives, who are members of their employer's household and are employed at a private dwelling-house or a farm in or on which both the employee and the employer reside
- Members of the Gardaí and Permanent Defence Forces
- FÁS trainees.

Unfair Reasons for Dismissal

The 1977-1993 Acts provide that dismissals for certain specified reasons are deemed automatically to be unfair. The reasons in question are as follows:

- Section 6(2)*(b)* of the 1977 Act deems dismissals resulting wholly or mainly from the religious or political opinions of the claimant to be automatically unfair. The section in question has not appeared to have been considered very often either by the Employment Appeals Tribunal or the courts. In *Merriman v. St. James' Hospital,*[110] however, a nurse's aide who refused, for reasons of conscience, to bring a crucifix and a candle to a dying patient was found to have been unfairly dismissed.
- Similarly, dismissals resulting wholly or mainly from the claimant's race, colour, sexual orientation, age or membership of the travelling community are deemed by section 6(2)[111] to be unfair.
- Section 6(2)*(c)* deems unfair any dismissals resulting wholly or mainly because of civil proceedings[112] against the employer to which the employee is or will be a party, or in which the employee was or is likely to be a witness. Likewise, section 6(2)*(d)* deems unfair any dismissal because of criminal proceedings against the employer, whether actual, threatened or proposed,

---

[110]Unreported, Circuit Court (Clarke J.), 24 November, 1986.

[111]As amended by the 1993 Act.

[112]Whether actual, threatened or proposed.

in relation to which the employee has made, proposed or threatened to make a complaint or statement to the prosecuting authority or to any other authority connected with or involved in the prosecution of the proceedings or in which the employee was or is likely to be a witness.

- Section 6(2)*(f)* of the 1977 Act deems unfair all dismissals resulting wholly or mainly from pregnancy "or matters connected therewith" save where the employee has proven to be unable, because of the pregnancy, to do adequately the work for which she was employed, or has proven to be unable to continue to do such work without contravention by her or her employer of a statutory provision. In order for employers to be able to sustain such a defence, however, they must prove that there was not, at the time of the dismissal, any vacancy which might suitably be filled by the employee, or that the employee refused an offer by her employer of alternative employment on equally favourable terms and conditions.
- Also automatically deemed to be unfair is any dismissal resulting from an employee's participation in a strike or other industrial action if other employees who took part in the industrial action were not also dismissed for that reason, or another employee who was dismissed for taking part in the action is subsequently offered reinstatement or re-engagement and the claimant is not. Similarly, section 4 of the 1993 Act deems unfair the refusal of an employer to allow an employee who has been "locked-out" to resume work following the end of the lockout, where other similar employees are allowed to resume their work.
- Finally, section 6(2)*(a)* deems unfair dismissals resulting wholly or mainly from the claimant's membership of or proposal to become a member of a trade union, or engaging in activities on behalf of a union. While it has been held that the mere fact that claimants are trade union members does not mean that any dismissal of them is unfair,[113] the Employment Appeals Tribunal held in 1989 that the dismissal, for poor

[113] *A La Francaise v. Monaghan*, UD 13/1977.

work performance, of trade union members is unfair where the employer is prepared to tolerate similar poor performance from non-union members.[114]

Fair Reasons for Dismissal

If employers are to avoid liability under the Unfair Dismissals Acts they must be able to prove to the Tribunal that the dismissal resulted "wholly or mainly" from reasons relating to the employee's capability, qualifications, competence, conduct, redundancy, or other substantial grounds.[115]

Section 6(4)*(a)* of the 1977 Act provides that the dismissal of an employee is deemed not to be unfair if it results wholly or mainly because of his lacking the necessary capability to perform work "of the kind which he was employed by the employer to do". Dismissals for reasons relating to capability usually arise in the context of employees having problems in relation to regular attendance at work. Thus, employees who fail to attend work regularly, who are persistently late, or who are absent for long periods may be regarded as being incapable of performing the work they were employed to do. In both *Reardon v. St. Vincent's Hospital*[116] and *Bevan v. Daydream Ltd.*,[117] therefore, employees who were out of work due to illness for periods close to the equivalent of one-third of the working year were found not to have been unfairly dismissed.

Similarly, an employee will be deemed to have been fairly dismissed if the employer can prove that the dismissal came about because the employee lacked necessary qualifications. In *Flynn v. C.I.E.*,[118] for example, a road freight driver was success-

---

[114] *McElhinney v. Sheridan*, UD 470/1989.

[115] In addition, a dismissal is not considered to have been unfair if the continuance of the employee in the job would have resulted in the breach of a provision in a statute or statutory instrument.

[116] UD 74/1979.

[117] UD 31/1978.

[118] UD 254/1980.

fully dismissed when he was disqualified from driving because he had committed a road traffic offence.

As has been pointed out above, employers may also dismiss employees for reasons relating to the employee's lack of competence. It has traditionally been the case that the issue of competence arises when poor work performance is alleged. In *Kearns v. Levi Strauss Ireland,*[119] for example, it was held that the failure of an employee to meet reasonable targets set by his employer provides grounds for dismissal. It was, however, pointed out in *McGinlay v. Disabled Aid Ltd.*[120] that an employee cannot be legally dismissed because of his alleged poor performance if no targets have been set for him.

The most common ground on which employers seek to rely when attempting to justify a dismissal is that of misconduct. The nature of the misconduct must be such that it undermines the relationship of trust necessary between an employer and his employee. Even minor acts of misconduct may suffice if they breach that relationship. In pleading misconduct on the part of the employee, an employer will usually seek to pin the dismissal on a single act of gross misconduct or a series of less significant acts followed by a series of warnings.[121]

Not surprisingly, a dismissal will also be deemed to be in compliance with the Act if it results wholly or mainly from the necessity to make an employee redundant. As the Tribunal pointed out in *Hogan v. Keadeen (Carlow) Ltd.*,[122] however, the employer must be able to prove that a genuine redundancy situation existed. For that reason, in *O'Connell v. Healy*[123] the employer's attempt to justify the claimant's dismissal on the basis of redundancy failed because his business was actually improving.

---

[119]UD 527/1981.

[120]UD 773/1983.

[121]In *Wheatley v. Ulster Bank Ltd.*, UD 18/1977, for example, the claimant had been warned on several occasions about deliberately mis-stating the times at which he clocked in and out. His subsequent dismissal was, for that reason, deemed to have been fair.

[122]UD 307/1982.

[123][1990] E.L.R. 36.

Section 6(3) of the 1977 Act, however, significantly delimits the ambit of the redundancy defence, providing that if the circumstances necessitating the redundancy applied equally to one or more other employees in similar employment, with the same employer, who have not been dismissed and either the employee's selection was partly dependant on an unfair reason, or there was a contravention of procedures agreed between the employer and the employees or their union, the dismissal is unfair. In *Dillon v. Wexford Seamless Aluminium Gutters*,[124] for example, the claimant was selected for redundancy because of his trade union activities. The dismissal was, for that reason, held to have been unfair.

Section 6(4) of the 1977 Act allows for other substantial grounds to justify dismissals. Without attempting to define tightly the ambit of section 6(4), however, one can justifiably describe it as a catch-all provision designed to deal with unusual cases where the dismissals in question are morally justifiable but cannot be excused under one of the other headings detailed above.

Unfair Dismissals Acts Remedies

An employee who is not precluded from claiming to have been unfairly dismissed under the Acts has six months from the date of the dismissal within which to initiate a claim and may choose to have the case heard either by a Rights Commissioner or by the Employment Appeals Tribunal. The Commissioner or Tribunal, if satisfied that the claimant has been unfairly dismissed, can opt to award any one of three remedies. The first of those remedies is reinstatement, in which case the employee is legally deemed never to have been dismissed. The employee simply goes back into the job and is entitled to receive back pay. The second remedy is re-engagement which involves the employee returning to the same or a similar position. Unlike reinstatement, however, re-engagement involves the employee losing seniority and accumulated rights. The third, and most commonly awarded, remedy is financial compensation. Such compensation is limited to a maxi-

---

[124]UD 539/1983.

mum of 104 weeks remuneration although the maximum sum is rarely awarded.

WRONGFUL DISMISSALS

Given the limited ambit of the Unfair Dismissals Acts, 1977-1993, employees will often find themselves having to challenge the legality of their dismissals on other bases. Such challenges usually involve an allegation that the impugned dismissal was carried out in breach of the employee's contract or in breach of what lawyers refer to as the "principles of natural justice". The nature of both of these types of legal challenges is briefly outlined below.

Dismissals in Breach of Contract

Dismissals in breach of contract are those dismissals which are inconsistent with one or more of the terms of an employee's contract. Such dismissals can be challenged in the civil courts and are usually deemed to have been "wrongful". In *Gunton v. Richmond-upon-Thames London Borough Council*,[125] for example, the plaintiff was held to have been wrongfully dismissed because the defendant employer had failed to comply with the procedure for dismissal expressly provided for in the plaintiff's contract of employment.[126]

Dismissals in Breach of the Principles of Natural Justice

Where there are no agreed procedural arrangements for dealing with dismissals the courts usually imply minimum standards of fair procedures consistent with the rules of natural justice. The two rules in question are:

- *Audi alteram partem*,[127] and

---

[125] [1981] Ch. 448.

[126] Similarly, in *Allied Irish Banks Ltd. v. Lupton*, Unreported, High Court (Murphy J.), 1983, a bank official was held to have been wrongfully dismissed because the Bank, in dismissing Mr. Lupton, failed to comply with disciplinary procedures which had been agreed by the Bank and the Irish Bank Officials Association and implied into his contract of service.

[127] Murdoch (1988, pp. 39-40) literally translates this as "[h]ear the other side" and explains that the rule requires "that no judicial or quasi-judicial decision may be taken without giving the party affected an opportunity of stating his case and being heard in his own defence".

- *Nemo iudex in causa sua.*[128]

The first of these rules is more important in an employment context. *Audi alteram partem* does not simply require that the employee be given a hearing by his employer prior to dismissal. It can also extend to giving him time to prepare for the hearing, allowing him to call witnesses and showing him any relevant documents or written accusations against him. As Lord Wilberforce has pointed out in the House of Lords, the very possibility of a dismissal occurring without reasons being given is an action which may vitally affect a man's career or his pension. For that reason it is all the more important that he be able to "state his case".[129] The Irish Supreme Court has adopted a similar stance in relation to dismissals and the rules of natural justice. In *State (Gleeson) v. The Minister for Defence*,[130] for example, Private Gleeson was dismissed from the Army in accordance with section 73 of the Defence Act, 1954. He was given no information in respect of the proceedings and was given no opportunity of being heard. For those reasons, Mr. Justice Henchy held that the dismissal was not in line with the principles of natural justice and was, therefore, invalid.

Remedies for Wrongful Dismissal

Traditionally, two standard remedies have been awarded in wrongful dismissals cases. The first of these remedies is a simple declaration by the court that the dismissal was unlawful. Such declarations are of little benefit to most employees, in that their employers are not legally obliged by virtue of the declaration to reinstate them or to pay them compensation. Public sector employers, however, are inclined to reinstate employees who obtain declarations. In the private sector, however, the principal legal remedy for an employee who has been wrongfully dismissed is damages. The normal measure of the damages awarded is that

---

[128]Murdoch (p. 335) literally translates this as "[n]o one can be a judge in his own cause" and explains that the rule requires that "[t]he person or body making a decision must be without bias. . . ."

[129]*Malloch v. Aberdeen Corporation*, [1971] 1 W.L.R. 1578.

[130][1976] I.R. 280.

which employees would have earned had they been allowed to remain working during the period for which notice should have been given. The employees may also be awarded some compensation for loss of benefits (such as company cars) or, very unusually, for loss of reputation.

THE REDUNDANCY PAYMENTS ACTS, 1967-1979[131]

When a qualified employee is made redundant[132] the employer must pay a lump-sum, the amount of which is calculated as follows:

---

[131]See generally, Department of Labour (1992).

[132]The word "redundancy" is statutorily defined in section 7(2) of the Redundancy Payments Act, 1967 as amended by the Redundancy Payments Act, 1971. Section 7(2) provides that: [A]n employee . . . shall be taken to be dismissed by reason of redundancy if the dismissal is attributable wholly or mainly to:

(a) the fact that his employer has ceased, or intends to cease, to carry on the business for the purposes of which the employee was employed by him, or has ceased or intends to cease, to carry on that business in the place where the employee was so employed, or

(b) the fact that the requirements of that business for employees to carry out work of a particular kind in the place where he was so employed have ceased or diminished or are expected to cease or diminish, or

(c) the fact that his employer has decided to carry on the business with fewer or no employees, whether by requiring the work for which the employee had been employed (or had been doing before his dismissal) to be done by other employees or otherwise, or

(d) the fact that his employer has decided that the work for which the employee has been employed (or had been doing before his dismissal) should henceforward be done in a different manner for which the employee is not sufficiently qualified or trained, or

(e) the fact that his employer has decided that the work for which the employee had been employed (or had been doing before his dismissal) should henceforward be done by a person who is also capable of doing other work for which the employee is not sufficiently qualified or trained.

An employee may also be entitled to a redundancy payment if he has been laid off or kept on short-time for a certain period. No question of redundancy payment can arise, however, until the employee has been laid off or kept on short-time or a mixture of both either for four consecutive weeks or for a broken series of six weeks where all six weeks fall within a thirteen week period.

- A half-week's pay for each year of employment continuous and reckonable between the ages of 16 and 41 years
- A week's pay for each year of employment continuous and reckonable over the age of 41 years
- In addition, the equivalent of one week's normal pay subject to the statutory ceiling.

An employer who has made a lump-sum payment to an employee may obtain a rebate of part of the lump-sum from the Social Insurance Fund at the rate of 60 per cent of the lump-sum if the minimum period of two-weeks notice of dismissal is given to the employee. If an employer fails to comply with any provision concerning redundancy notice, the Minister for Enterprise, Trade and Employment may, at his or her discretion, reduce the amount of rebate payable to that employer to 40 per cent of the lump sum.

Categories Excluded from Relying on the 1967-1979 Acts

As with the Unfair Dismissals Acts, 1977-1993, a substantial proportion of the Irish labour force is precluded from relying on the provisions of the Redundancy Payments Acts, 1967-1979. The Acts expressly exclude, *inter alia*, the following groups:

- All those who are neither employees within the meaning of the 1967 Act[133] nor apprentices
- All those who have not been in the continuous employment of their employers for at least 104 weeks[134]
- All those who have not been insured for all benefits under the Social Welfare Acts for at least four years[135]
- All those employed by close relatives in domestic situations[136]

---

[133] See section 2(1).

[134] Section 4(2), Redundancy Payments Acts, 1967-1979, as amended by the Worker Protection (Regular Part-Time Employees) Act, 1991.

[135] See sections 4(1) and 7(1)(b) of the Redundancy Payments Act, 1967, as amended by the Redundancy Payments Act, 1971. This provision causes, *inter alia*, many public servants to fall outside the scope of the Acts.

- All those who normally work less than eight hours per week for the same employer
- All those who have reached pensionable age under the Social Welfare Acts[137]
- All those ordinarily working outside the State who, at the time they are dismissed, are outside the State.[138]

REFERENCES

There is no general obligation on employers to provide character references to or on behalf of employees. As the House of Lords explained in *Spring v. Guardian Assurance plc*,[139] however:

> an employer is under a duty to a departing employee, or indeed to any person who had been working for him, to take reasonable care in the preparation of a reference, and is liable for pecuniary loss suffered by the employee as a result of an inaccurate and negligently prepared reference (Milmo, p. 1477)

Similarly, an employer who provides a negligently prepared reference may be liable to a subsequent employer.

CHAPTER SUMMARY

The legal relationship between an employer and an employee is based on a contract negotiated by the two parties concerned. Where the contract can be classed as a contract of service (following the application of the control, integration or mixed

---

[136]Section 4(3) of the Redundancy Payments Act, 1967, as amended by the 1971 Act (schedule).

[137]Section 4(1), Redundancy Payments Act, 1967, as amended by section 5 of the Redundancy Payments Act 1979.

[138]See section 25 of the Redundancy Payments Act, 1967.

[139][1994] 3 All E.R. 129; [1995] 2 A.C. 296. For comments on the decisions of the Court of Appeal and the House of Lords, see Allen, (1994, p. 111) and Milmo (1994, p. 1477), respectively. The House of Lords overturned the decision of Glidewell L.J. in the Court of Appeal, which had been criticised by Allen.

tests) it is deemed to contain a number of terms implied into it by the common law, legislation and, potentially, by collective bargaining agreements.

The body of regulatory legislation in this area has significantly increased in size and importance since the late 1960s. Among the more important pieces of statutory regulation are:

- The Safety, Health and Welfare at Work Act, 1989 which complements the existing common law rules on workplace health and safety
- The Anti-Discrimination (Pay) Act, 1974 which prohibits sex-based discrimination in relation to remuneration
- The Employment Equality Act, 1977 which prohibits direct and indirect discrimination based on sex or marital status in relation to conditions of employment other than those concerning remuneration
- The Maternity Protection Act, 1994 which guarantees women the right to take maternity leave and the right to return to work having taken such leave
- The Adoptive Leave Act, 1995 which entitles and adopting mother to take parental leave
- The Payment of Wages Act, 1991 which protects employees against unlawful deductions from their wages, entitles them to a readily negotiable mode of wage payment and entitles them to a written statement of wages
- The Minimum Notice and Terms of Employment Act, 1973 which dictates minimum periods of notice to be given by employers and employees when terminating a contract of employment
- The Terms of Employment (Information) Act, 1994 which requires that employers provide employees with written statements detailing specified terms of their employments
- The Worker Protection (Regular Part-Time Employees) Act, 1991 which extends the benefits of a range of protective legislation to regular part-time employees

- The Protection of Young Persons (Employment) Act, 1996 which regulates the employment of children and young persons
- The Organisation of Working Time Act, 1997 which regulates hours of work and guarantees full-time employees a minimum of four weeks holidays per annum[140]
- The European Communities (Safeguarding of Employees' Rights on Transfer of Undertakings) Regulations, 1980 which serves to protect employees where their employer sells on or transfers the ownership of their business
- The Unfair Dismissals Acts, 1977-1993 which, combined with the common law rules relating to wrongful dismissals, serve to protect employees who have been unlawfully dismissed, and
- The Redundancy Payments Acts, 1967-1979 which entitle employees to a lump sum payment when they are made redundant.

References and Further Reading

Allen, Thomas (1994) "Liability for References: *Spring v Guardian Assurance*", [1994] 57 *M.L.R.* 111

Butler, Brendan, "The Organisation of Working Time Bill 1996", (1997) 3 (1) *Running Your Business*

Carr, C.J. and P.J. Kay (1994) *Employment Law*, sixth edition, London: M+E.

Curtin, Deirdre (1989) *Irish Employment Equality Law*, Dublin: Round Hall Press.

Daly, Marie (1993) "Transfer of Undertakings: Where to From Here?", 11 (254) *I.R. DataBank* 7.

Department of Education (1995) *Charting our Education Future: White Paper on Education*, Dublin: Stationery Office.

Department of Enterprise & Employment (1994) *Guide to Labour Law*, Dublin: Department of Enterprise & Employment, 1994.

Department of Labour (1992) *Guide to the Redundancy Payments Scheme*, Dublin: Department of Labour.

---

[140]Subject to the transitional arrangements in 1997 and 1998. See pp. 336-37.

Drake, Charles D. (1981) *Labour Law*, third edition, London: Sweet & Maxwell.

Fennell, Caroline & Irene Lynch (1993) *Labour Law in Ireland*, Dublin: Gill & Macmillan.

Forde, Michael (1991) *Industrial Relations Law*, Dublin: Round Hall Press.

Forde, Michael (1992) *Employment Law*, Dublin: Round Hall Press.

Friel, Raymond J. (1995) *The Law of Contract*, Dublin: Round Hall Press.

Harvey, Noel & Adrian F. Twomey (1995) *Sexual Harassment in the Workplace*, Dublin: Oak Tree Press.

IBEC (1996) *A Guide to Employment Legislation*, sixth edition, Dublin: IBEC, 1996.

Lavery, Paul (1996) *Commercial Secrets: The Action for Breach of Confidence in Ireland*, Dublin: Round Hall Sweet & Maxwell.

McMahon, Bryan and William Binchy (1990) *Irish Law of Torts*, second edition, Dublin: Butterworths.

Meenan, Frances (1994) *Working Within the Law*, Dublin: Oak Tree Press.

Milmo, Patrick (1994) "Liability for references", 144 *New Law Journal* 1477

Murdoch, Henry (1988) *A Dictionary of Irish Law*, Dublin: Topaz Publications.

Murphy, Tom (1987) "The Impact of the Unfair Dismissals Act on Workplace Industrial Relations", (1987) 6 J.I.S.L.L. 36, 36.

Twomey, Adrian, "'Macho Management', Moral Outrage and the IBOA: Limited Industrial Action and the Law", (1993) 3 *I.S.L.R.* 131.

von Prondzynski, Ferdinand and Charles McCarthy (1989) *Employment Law in Ireland*, second edition, London: Sweet & Maxwell

Wayne, Naomi (1980) *Labour Law in Ireland: A Guide to Workers' Rights*, Dublin: ITGWU.

Wedderburn, Lord (1986) *The Worker and the Law*, third edi tion, London: Pelican.

Whincup, Michael (1980) *Modern Employment Law: A Guide to Job Security and Safety*, third edition, London: Heinemann.

Chapter 20

THE SUPERVISOR AND HEALTH AND SAFETY

THE OBJECTIVE OF THIS CHAPTER

Supervisors have to be more concerned about health and safety issues. This view came across very clearly in interviews with senior management; they are placing greater emphasis now on work monitoring and prevention of accidents and are requiring supervisors to uphold high safety standards among their work groups. This change is the result of a variety of factors, notably recent legislative changes and the high costs of accidents (including costs relating to litigation and compensation). Poor safety standards place employees at risk of serious injury if not death; employers suffer in terms of lost productivity and potentially higher insurance premiums; and the morale of a work group, as well as the industrial relations climate in the organisation, can be adversely affected.

A greater stress on health and safety in the workplace is the result of other factors too, including a greater awareness among Irish people in general of the need to conform to higher standards in the workplace. Finally, competition in the marketplace and the shortage of skilled labour force organisations to make sure that the most efficient use is made of resources.

At a minimum, supervisors should have a practical understanding of the law in this area. They should also ensure, if necessary by enforcement, that employees follow proper safety procedure. In addition, supervisors are expected to take preventative steps to ensure high safety standards, and possibly conduct or at least participate in accident investigations. Finally, increased safety awareness imposes other duties on supervisors, such as keeping accurate records, some of which may have to be computerised, and to work in closer contact with safety specialists. Furthermore, the Health and Safety Authority (HSA), the statutory agency charged with responsibility for health and safety, advise in a number of publications that, if in doubt about safety, employees should consult with their supervisor. In all, the responsibility for health and safety cannot be taken lightly by supervisors.

This chapter provides a broad overview of health and safety legislation in Ireland, with a particular emphasis on the framework 1989 Safety, Health and Welfare at Work Act, the most comprehensive act in this area. Because of the important influence of the European Union on health and safety, the chapter also summarises the recent European directives, as well as the important common law duty on employees to provide a safe working environment.

After reading and studying this chapter, the reader should have an understanding of:

- Health and safety legislation in Ireland
- The supervisor's responsibility for health and safety
- EU directives in this area.

At the end of the chapter, information is provided on material that is available from the HSA. Supervisors are encouraged to liaise with their safety representative and the local HSA for further information. This is particularly important as area can be quite complex with major legal implications.

ACCIDENTS AT WORK

Employers are legally required to report any major accident to the Health and Safety Authority[1]. The HSA acknowledges that under-

---

[1] The term "major accident" is defined in the 1993 regulations as one which leads to loss of life to an employee or non-employee, or results in any employee or self-employed person missing three days from work plus the day of the accident. There are special forms (Form IR1 deals with notice of accidents, and Form IR3 deals with notice of dangerous occurrence) which employers must complete and return to the HSA. Records must be kept by the employer for ten years.

reporting of accidents is very common. Hence the statistics for 1995, the last time the HSA issued an annual report, show that close to 5,000 accidents occurred in work. A more accurate assessment of the number of accidents at work is given in Table 20.1. This table is a summary of statistics from the annual labour force survey conducted by the Central Statistics Office. The table points out that close to 16,000 accidents work accidents occurred in 1995, resulting in the loss of over half a million working days.

Independent research puts the average costs of accidents in the Republic of Ireland at over twice the rate of Northern Ireland, and estimates that the hidden cost of accidents (such as lost time, redeployment and recruitment of other staff) is roughly ten times the direct costs (that is, those refundable through insurance).

TABLE 20.1: LABOUR FORCE SURVEY WORK ACCIDENTS, 1994 AND 1995 (NO. OF PERSONS > THAN 3 DAYS ABSENCE)

	1994	**1995**
Agriculture, forestry and fishing	2,100	2,200
Mining, quarrying and turf production	200	—
Manufacturing	3,400	3,800
Building and Construction	1,300	1,500
Electricity, gas and water	200	200
Commerce, insurance and finance	1,900	2,000
Transport, communications and storage	1,200	900
Public administration and defence	1,000	1,100
Other non-agricultural	2,300	2,500
SUBTOTAL ALL SECTORS	13,400	14,500
Unclassified by sector	1,100	1,500
GRAND TOTAL	14,500	15,900

Notes: Total due to rounding of figures or non-statement of specific category in some cases.

Unclassified includes persons who retired from work during the year, and persons who were unemployed when the survey was conducted.

Source: Health and Safety Authority, Annual Report, 1995. p. 61.

It is recognised that certain industries, notably construction and agriculture, remain by far the most accident-prone industries in Ireland. Similarly, certain jobs, notably where there is a high degree of manual effort, are more prone to injury than others. Finally, the profile of employees — in particular age, gender, and inexperience — can add to the likelihood of an accident happening. Young people are most likely to have accidents, being less likely to follow safety procedures; similarly, older employees may be too tired. Men, largely because they are more likely than women to occupy manual jobs, have higher accidents rates. However, it is known too that men are less likely to follow safety procedures; a macho attitude can mean that men adopt an almost cavalier approach to work safety.

Mosley et al. (1993, p. 528) group causes of accidents into three categories: human, technical and environmental. Subsumed under the heading human factors are such items as carelessness, horseplay, fighting, drunkenness, limited understanding of processes and equipment, poor attitudes and fatigue. Technical factors account for such items as unsafe mechanical, chemical and physical conditions, such as those caused by defective tools and equipment, poor mechanical construction or design, or improper personal protective equipment. Finally, environmental factors are those that surround the job, such as poor housekeeping, inadequate lighting and ventilation, or pressure from management to increase output.

In all, the reasons that cause accidents are many, hence the need for a broad and proactive response on the part of employers. Accident prevention is not an additional burden on the employer nor is it a medical issue. It is rather part of the organisation of work and working conditions and a legal and moral obligation employers have to employees.

Table 20.2 reports some of the major findings of a major EU survey. As can be seen, health and safety is a real issue for employees.

TABLE 20.2: RESEARCH ON HEALTH AND SAFETY

In 1996, the European Foundation for the Improvement of Living and Working Conditions (Pascal, 1997) conducted a representative sample of 1,000 in each EU member state (a total of 15,800 workers of which 1,006 were Irish). The overall survey found that:

- 29 per cent of employees questioned consider that their work affects their health. The most common work-related health problems are back pain (30 per cent of employees), stress (28 per cent) and muscular pains in arms or legs (17 per cent).
- Health problems are most often connected with poor working conditions.
- Absenteeism due to work-related health problems affects 23 per cent of employees each year (averaging out at 4 working days lost per worker). Absenteeism increases significantly with the arduousness of the work (multiplied by three for painful or tiring positions, multiplied by two for repetitive motions).
- 28 per cent of employees are exposed to intense noise; 45 per cent of employees to painful or tiring working positions.
- 37 per cent of employees perform short repetitive tasks and 45 per cent monotonous tasks thus increasing the likelihood of injury, especially carpal tunnel syndrome.
- The client has replaced the machine as the main factor dictating the pace of work.
- 38 per cent of employees now use computers.
- Casual and temporary work is characterised by poor working conditions.

THE RESPONSIBILITY FOR HEALTH AND SAFETY AT WORK

Gunnigle and Flood (1990, p. 261) point out that:

> the primary responsibility for the prevention of accidents, health risks and the enforcement of relevant regulations rests first and foremost with management. Particular emphasis should be placed on identifying causes of accidents and the conditions under which they are most likely to occur.

Supervisors, because of their unique role in the organisation, have to make sure that senior management's concern with safety is translated into positive action in the workplace. Not only should supervisors have the capacity to communicate important safety concerns to employees, they must also be able to respond correctly to employee's queries about health and safety. They also have an important role in educating employees in safety awareness, ensuring procedures are followed and equipment maintained, taking corrective action when necessary, and carrying out inspections and investigations after accidents happen.

Perhaps the most important duty of a supervisor is to promote a climate of "safety first" and to instil in each employee the need always to think about safety. This can be done in a variety of ways and in particular by good housekeeping. That means, among other things, that both the supervisor and the employees follow proper and full procedures, rather than taking short cuts and rushing jobs that compromise the safety of others; keep work areas and tools clean; and maintain tools and equipment. The supervisor has also to ensure that the equipment provided — safety clothing, eyeglasses, earplugs, etc. — be used in accordance with the manufacturer's specifications. Third, through the use of training and educational courses, employees can be shown the proper working practices, the right way to use equipment, how equipment should be cared for and finally how to recognise hazards. Proper standards can be reinforced by the supervisor's own behaviour and enforced where employees don't follow rules: if a job requires protective eyeglasses to be worn, then they should be worn. Failure by an employee to do so should result in some form of disciplinary action initiated by the supervisor. Accurate records should be kept, and equipment monitored at all times. Finally, when accidents do occur, a thorough investigation should be conducted, in order that the incident won't be repeated.

Gunnigle and Flood (1990, p. 263) advise making a variety of checks, including safety audits, spot checks, daily checks and regular inspections, to ensure that the necessary safety standards are being met. Inspections are particularly important in light of the constant changes in any workplace. These include wear and tear on facilities and equipment and changes in layout, such as the addition of new machinery and depletion of others. Table 20.3 provides some guidelines on what to include in a safety check. Note in particular the broadness of such checks.

TABLE 20.3: WHAT TO CHECK WHEN CONDUCTING INSPECTIONS

- Personal Protective Equipment: check that the supply of PPE is adequate and is being used properly.
- Personnel: check that all employees are following correct procedures, using PPE correctly, and are properly trained. Check that employees are aware of safety standards and emergency procedures.
- Buildings: check that floors, stairs, entry ways, etc., are clean and unobstructed.
- Electricity: check that all electrical points, wires, switches, etc., are working in accordance with manufacturers requirements.
- Lighting: check that all lighting is adequate, working and suitable for work areas.
- Fire prevention: check fire equipment (extinguishers, alarms, sprinklers) are adequate and working.
- Machinery: check that machinery is in proper working order, is serviced in accordance with manufacturers recommendations, and that all safety measures, such as guards, are present and being used.
- Heating and ventilation: check that the temperature and humidity, and supply of natural air, is adequate in all areas, and check to see if all controls are working properly.

Gunnigle and Flood however warn about potential problems in inspections:

> There is a danger that involving direct supervision in all inspections may result in their developing a "perceptual blindness" to hazards in their area. Hence a system of checklists can be helpful. It may also be useful to use members of the safety committee to conduct some of the different inspection methods. Involvement of employees in safety inspections may help increase employee awareness of safety matters.

Therefore, the supervisor should work in conjunction with the safety officer and/or safety committee, seeking advice and support, and in carrying out inspections employ some form of follow-up system to ensure that problems, when noted, are attended to. The supervisor should encourage employee involvement and acknowledge the support of employees.

Table 20.4 lists a number of guidelines for supervisors to follow in regard to health and safety. Note that health and safety issues vary from industry to industry, and from work group to work group. The supervisor is well advised to seek as much material as possible from the safety officer/committee in their organisation, and develop good safety practices that are relevant to their job.

TABLE 20.4: GUIDELINES FOR SUPERVISORS TO PROMOTE HEALTH AND SAFETY AWARENESS

- Set the right example by following the correct proper procedures yourself. Don't encourage or condone employees taking short cuts that undermine safety regulations.
- Study health and safety legislation and communicate these and an appreciation of health and safety to employees.
- Make sure employees, and especially new ones, understand and follow safety rules. Enforce regulations fairly and evenly.
- Build safety in to the job. Anticipate hazards and plan ahead. Pay particular attention to unsafe jobs.
- Review procedures and processes with a view to continuous improvement.
- Stamp out bad behaviour, such as horseplay, larking, etc. Encourage employees to follow safety rules.
- Conduct regular safety meetings with employees. Involve and consult with them and seek their input into safety programmes.
- Think prevention by conducting regular checks as well as spot checks.
- Check equipment regularly. Fix or get rid of unsafe equipment. Make sure the proper equipment is worn/used at all times. Keep equipment and work areas clean and accessible.
- Don't rush a job: Follow procedure. Don't push employees unnecessarily or risk their safety to meet deadlines.

- When accidents do occur, make a complete investigation. Try to avoid recurrence.
- Liaise as much as possible with the safety representative and/or safety committee and keep management informed. Be aware of the safety representative's rights.

Accident investigations have two main goals: determining the details and, in particular, the cause of the accident, and recommending corrective action. Table 20.5 contains a sample accident reporting form. As indicated, the supervisor aims to obtain as much information as possible (and as soon as possible) about the accident. This can be achieved by meeting with the person or persons directly involved, as well as any witnesses. Any accident, no matter how trivial, has potential legal consequences. The supervisor, therefore, should consult with, and ideally be accompanied by, a representative of the firm before undertaking an accident report.

TABLE 20.5: SAMPLE ACCIDENT REPORTING FORM

Personal Details:	
	Name of employee(s):
	Occupation:
	Any other pertinent details:
Specifics of Accident:	
	Date:
	Time:
	Place:
Nature of Accident:	
	What happened:
	How did it happen:
	Why did it happen:
Post-Accident Action:	
	Immediate action:
	Recommendation:

GETTING EMPLOYEES INTERESTED IN SAFETY

The more employees are educated and trained in safety awareness, and the more they are interested in and encouraged to participate in safety programmes, the more successful a programme of safety prevention will be. Employees have a vested interested in maintaining a safety-first environment. However, an inability of management to acknowledge and foster employee interest, along with carelessness on the part of employees, can contribute to a high accident rate.

Developing employee interest in safety can be achieved in a variety of ways including holding regular meetings, using (appropriate) visual aids and circulating periodicals such as company newsletters or HSA documentation. Meetings with employees can be used as a way of educating and informing them about safety, as well as providing the mechanism for soliciting employee's opinions on the subject. Getting employees to attend voluntarily, and thereafter to participate in such meetings is acknowledged as a difficulty. It is not necessary, of course, to meet with employees in formal meetings: in many cases, during on-the-job inspections a supervisor can reiterate the importance of health and safety to individual employees as well as soliciting their views on the matter.

Signs can be used with great effect to warn employees about hazards and safety standards, for example notices requiring safety helmets on construction sites. The HSA can also advise on safety films which can be instructional for new employees and visitors in particular, and can supply a variety of leaflets advising on health and safety. At the very least, the supervisor can provide an important communications link between the HSA and the employee.

The remainder of this chapter deals with health and safety legislation in this area: supervisors should have a working knowledge of the law.

THE LAW IN IRELAND ON HEALTH AND SAFETY

There are three aspects to the law that have a bearing on health and safety:

- The common law
- Statutory law
- European Union directives.

Common Law

The common law places an important duty on the employer to take "reasonable care" for the safety and well-being of their employees. Every employer is legally required to provide, as far as is reasonably practicable, a safe working environment, including safe premises, safe equipment and safe systems of work, as well as competent and trained fellow staff and proper supervision. Failure to provide a safe working environment may result in the employer being sued for negligence in the event of an accident. It is the duty of the courts, therefore, to decide, in the event of an accident, first, if the employer is at fault, and second, the amount of compensation, if any, to be awarded to the injured or "wronged" employee.

The common law duty applies to all employers and forms part of every employee's contract of employment. Therefore, employers, large or small, unionised or non-unionised, in the services sector or in manufacturing, are legally obliged to provide safe working conditions. Employers have been sued in the courts for failure to meet these obligations, and most employers carry some form of insurance to protect against litigation. However, as Gunnigle et al. (1992, p. 132) note:

> It should be noted that the common law only addresses liability arising out of actual illness or injury. Thus, the common law is not concerned with anticipating damages or setting standards of good behaviour in order to prevent accidents. The common law only comes into play after the event and its main function is to compensate your employees for any injuries they receive while at work.

Compensation is often very little, and most cases are settled out of court. However, the general principle enshrined in the common law of providing a reasonable duty of care is given a greater force of law in a variety of acts and regulations passed in recent years.

Statutory Law

In the early part of the industrial revolution there was a reluctance on the part of the courts to impose any duties on employers to ensure the safety of employees. Rather, the belief was prevalent that factory work was beneficial to society as a whole, and that industrial work was, by its nature, dangerous, a condition which employees readily accepted. Hence, a successful defence of any employer being sued for negligence under the common law was that the worker voluntarily accepted the risk. However, as knowledge spread of the pathetic conditions workers toiled under, and industrial accidents occurred in greater numbers, often resulting in fatalities, particularly in mining and textiles, the government was forced to take action. In 1802, the House of Commons passed the first health and safety law. This dealt with textiles and placed limits on the hours an employee could work, particularly at night, as well as requiring certain safety standards in factories, notably relating to ventilation. A number of other health and safety laws were passed but it was not until 1901 that the first piece of comprehensive legislation — the Factories and Workshops Act — was passed which provided some measure of protection for workers.

The introduction of the Factories Act 1955, followed by the Safety in Industry Act 1980 (collectively known as the Safety in Industry Acts, 1955 and 1980) extended further the provisions first introduced in 1901. These acts deal primarily, though not entirely, with manufacturing, though the 1958 Office Premises Act and the 1965 Mine and Quarries Act did provide some protection for workers in those respective fields. However, in 1989 the government passed the Safety, Health and Welfare at Work Act which extended blanket coverage to all employees. Since joining the EEC in 1973 a number of directives — notably the 1992 framework directive —have had bearing on safety standards in Ireland. These directives have been encompassed in one form or another in the Safety, Health and Welfare at Work (General Application) Regulations, 1993. In 1995 the government introduced into law the Safety, Health and Welfare at Work (Miscellaneous Welfare Provisions) Regulations, which deal with welfare issues which arose out of the repeal of the Office Premises

Act and other repealed national legislation. As the relevant minister has the power to issue directives under a variety of acts, these directives are known as statutory instruments. It is estimated that there are 214 statutory instruments, in addition to 16 acts, in the area of health and safety.

Safety in Industry Acts, 1955 and 1980

A central tenet of these Acts, and indeed enshrined in later acts, is that both employers and employees have a common concern with safety. This extends as far as legally requiring employees to co-operate with employers in maintaining safety standards, say, in informing employers of defective equipment and reporting any accidents or injuries at work. Finally, the Safety in Industry Acts makes provision for the Minister of Enterprise, Trade and Employment to make recommendations which are given the force of law.

The 1955 Act introduced as a voluntary measure, but mandated in the 1980 Act, the concept of the safety committee. Organisations employing more than 20 employees must set up a committee, made up of managerial and non-managerial employees — with a majority of worker representatives — to oversee health and safety (organisations with fewer employees may have a safety representative rather than a committee). If employees fail to nominate worker representatives, the employer is free to appoint them. The thrust of the legalisation is to make these committees consultative and encourage employees and managers to work closely together to develop a safety-first environment. Despite the emphasis on consultation, the act does provide instruction on how, why and when meetings should be held.

The 1980 provisions on safety committees have been changed by section 13 of the 1989 act and section 12 of the General Applications Regulations 1993 (both discussed later). Moving away from the proscriptive view of the 1980 Act, the 1993 Act makes allowance for an employer to implement alternative procedural arrangements as long as they conform to the 1989 Act and the general provisions. This is why one finds in organisations a variety of forms of safety committees which range from joint union/management (or joint safety) committees, to management committees. Similarly, some organisations have technical committees made up largely of engineers, while others may have an overall committee in addition to special committees for handing particular aspects of safety. Regardless of the composition of a safety committee, its role is advisory, educational and investigative; it does not therefore deal with complaints or grievances. Table 20.6 lists some of the responsibilities of safety committees.

TABLE 20.6: THE RESPONSIBILITIES OF THE SAFETY COMMITTEE

- Overseeing health and safety and making sure the organisation fulfils its legal obligations
- Promoting safety awareness in the workplace through a variety of means, including the holding of training and educational seminars
- The keeping of accurate and comprehensive records in line with legal and organisational requirements
- Ensuring that the organisation stays abreast of new developments in law
- Providing a supportive and advisory role to management and utilising specialist advice.

The Barrington Report

In 1983 a government committee issued it long-awaited report on health and safety. Termed the Barrington Report[2] (after its chair, Justice Barrington), it was highly critical of the complex and technical nature of Irish legalisation on health and safety. The Report cited over 20 pieces of legalisation dealing with health and safety, and over 200 regulations, with input from 10 different government departments. Despite the abundance of law in this area, it was estimated that only 20 per cent of the labour force was covered. The Safety in Industries Acts (1955 and 1980) covered employees primarily in the manufacturing and the construction sectors only, together with a small number of other concerns, which the Barrington Report estimated at about 200,000 employ-

[2]Its full title was the "Commission of Inquiry on Safety, Health, and Welfare at Work".

ees. It identified a second group of acts that regulate the hours of work, such as the Conditions of Employment Act, and finally a third group of acts, such as the Dangerous Substances Act which provide protection against hazards and the like. Collectively, these acts provided limited and inadequate coverage. It recommended that the law be simplified and codified into a smaller number of relevant acts which would provide blanket coverage for all employees.

The report also concluded that far too many accidents occur in Irish industry, that there was not enough attention paid to health and safety in the first place, and bemoaned the lack of attention afforded to the prevention of accidents. Thus, despite the breadth of legislation, enforcement was weak. The Barrington Report, conscious of the overtly legislative approach to this area, advocated that responsibility for health and safety belongs to management, although joint consultative methods should be established to ensure the active support of employees and to function as a mechanism to ensure greater training and safety awareness in the workplace. Finally, the report made the argument that a new national authority be established which would oversee health and safety for the country as a whole. Until then, responsibility for health and safety varied between the Department of Labour and the Local Authorities with little co-ordination between them.

The Safety, Health and Welfare at Work Act 1989

The government's first response to the Barrington Report was to establish in 1986 the Interim Board on Health and Safety to oversee the legislative changes Barrington recommended. Following on the work of that board, and as part of a commitment in the 1987-1990 Programme for National Recovery, the government introduced in 1989 the Safety, Health and Welfare at Work Act. Though a wide-ranging piece of legislation, it solidified the existing thrust of earlier laws, and introduced some new requirements to the area. With the stated aim of the prevention of accidents in the workplace and the promotion of a safe working environment through the identification of potential hazards, the Act differs in one fundamental aspect from previous legislation, in that it applies to all employers and the self-employed, regardless of the type of work performed, and to all employees regardless of their place of employment. It is also referred to as a framework act in that its provisions are much less detailed than those of previous statutes — Barrington argued that the ineffectiveness of existing legislation was in large part due its detail and its rigidity — but rather places on management the primary responsibility to promote health and safety, with corresponding duties on employees.

Duties of the Employer

Section 6 of the 1989 act reads:

> It shall be the duty of every employer to ensure, so far as is reasonably practicable, the safety, health and welfare at work of all his employees.

The act specifically mentions areas which must be considered, including the safe design and provision of a place of work, safe entry to and exit from work, the safe provision and maintenance of machinery, safe systems of work, the provision of information, instruction, training and supervision to ensure the safety of employees, the provision of protective clothing where hazards exist, the provision of procedures and plans in the event of emergencies, the prevention of risk in the use of any article or substances at work, and the use of the specialist services to assist and advise in the maintenance of a safe working environment. Employers are also required to provide compulsory medical examinations for employees who are exposed to particular type of hazards, such as carcinogenic agents or compressed air.

As with the common law, failure to undertake this obligation may result in an employer being prosecuted. Section 7 also places important duties on the employer to provide for the safety of non-employees, which would include visitors, contractors, suppliers, etc.:

> It shall be the duty of every employer to conduct his undertaking in such a way as to ensure, so far as is reasonably practicable, that persons not in his employment who may be affected thereby are not exposed to risks to their safety or health.

Safety Statement

Every employer is obliged (Section 12) to have a safety statement which must be made known to all employees:

> Every employer shall, as soon as may be, after the coming into operation of this section prepare or cause to be prepared, a statement in writing to be known and hereinafter referred to as a "safety statement".

That safety statement shall:

- Specify the manner in which the safety, health and welfare of persons employed by an employer shall be secured at work.
- Be based on an identification of the hazards and an assessment of the risks to health and safety at the place of work to which the safety statement relates.
- Specify clearly the co-operation required from employees and the names of the persons responsible for safety in the organisation.

It is the duty of every employer to make each employee aware of the safety statement and allow them access to it. The Act provides for penalties for any employers not fulfilling these requirements. The HSA document "Safe to Work" provides a model safety statement for small businesses. It is particularly applicable to low-technology organisations, such as those in the retail and finance sectors.

Consultation and the Safety Representative

It shall be the duty of every employer (section 13):

> to consult his employees for the purpose of the making and maintenance of arrangements which will enable him and his employees to co-operate effectively in promoting and developing measures to ensure their safety, health and welfare at work and in ascertaining the effectiveness of such measures.

In addition, the employer is legally required to take account of any representations made by employees. Representation can be made directly by employees, or indirectly by a safety representative elected by employees. The safety representative is entitled to information on health and safety "as is necessary to ensure the health and safety of employees at the place or work. The rights of safety representatives also include the right to investigate accidents, or potential hazards (but not obstruct the scene of the accident or interfere with the investigation of such); the right to be informed of any impending visit by a safety inspectors, to accompany them on a tour, and to talk and/or write to them.

Safety representatives are entitled to time off to perform their duties and, if necessary, to attend training and have protection against being put at a personal disadvantage. Procedures for appointing safety representatives are not specified in the Act, although it is generally accepted that there should be at least one safety representative per organisation. Moreover, in union shops the accepted practice is to integrate the safety representative's role into the union representation structure.

Despite the law, O' Kelly (1994)[3] reported that employee participation in health and safety issues represents at best an aspiration rather than a reality, and is limited to permanent employees in medium and large-sized companies. Also, he notes that the success of health and safety programmes in organisations depends much on the training and powers afforded to the safety representative, as well as the undertaking of a proactive role on the part of a trade union by making health and safety a key industrial relations issue.

The following document is available free of charge from the HSA: "Guidelines on Safety Consultation and Safety Representatives". As its name suggests, the short booklet sets out the rights and obligations of employers and employees with regard to consultation and representation.

Table 20.7 summarises employers' responsibilities for health and safety.

---

[3] For a comparative study of EU countries which was critical of Irish law on consultation rights for Irish workers, see Gill, 1993.

TABLE 20.7: SUMMARY OF EMPLOYERS' RESPONSIBILITIES

- They must provide a safety statement
- They must consult with employees with respect to health and safety
- They must obtain specialist advice on health and safety
- They must ensure:
    1. A safe working place
    2. Safe access and egress
    3. Safe systems of work
    4. Competent supervision.

Employees' Responsibilities

Section 9 of the 1989 Act requires of each employee:

> to take reasonable care for his own safety, health and welfare and that of any other person who may be affected by his acts or omissions while at work;
>
> to co-operate with his employer and any other person to such extent as will enable his employer or the other person to comply with any of the relevant statutory provisions;
>
> to use in such manner so as to provide the protection intended, any suitable appliance, protective clothing, convenience, equipment or other means or thing provided (whether for his use alone or for use by him in common with others) for securing his safety, health or welfare while at work; and
>
> to report to his employer or his immediate supervisor, without unreasonable delay, any defects in plant, equipment, place of work or system of work, which might endanger safety, health or welfare, of which he becomes aware.

The latter section is the only difference from the 1980 Act. Aside from these duties, employees are afforded a wide array of rights under the Act, including the right to be consulted in matters relating to health and safety, and the entitlement to representation (either individually or through the safety representative and/or the safety committee).

Table 20.8 summarises employees' obligations for health and safety.

TABLE 20.8: EMPLOYEES' OBLIGATIONS FOR HEALTH AND SAFETY

- Take reasonable care to ensure their own and other's safety
- Co-operate with the employer
- Use protective equipment, operate machinery properly and follow the correct procedures
- Report any hazards as soon as possible (usually to their immediate supervisor)
- Report any injuries/accidents immediately
- Recognise their obligation in the promotion of a safe working environment.

National Authority for Occupational Health and Safety

Part III of the 1989 Act established the National Authority for Occupational Health and Safety on November 1, 1989 (now more commonly referred to as the Health and Safety Authority or HSA). It is the primary statutory agency dealing with health and safety in Ireland and it takes over many of the responsibilities of the then Department of Labour. The agency's main duties include reviewing existing legislation, issuing codes of practice, overseeing health and safety regulations, advising the Minister, as well as having education, training and research responsibilities. Inspectors from the agency are empowered to make spot checks on employers, and can issue directives to enforce the law. Under Section 39, Part IV of the Act, inspectors can apply to the High Court for an *ex parte* injunction to ensure enforcement of its directives or restrict a place of work where there is a potential threat to the safety and well-being of people.

The Authority is an independent body, overseen by a governing body made up as follows:

- Chairperson
- Three members nominated by employer organisations
- Three members nominated by trade unions

- Four representatives nominated by government departments and state agencies.

EU DIRECTIVES AND THE 1993 AND 1995 REGULATIONS

Article 118A of the Single European Act allows for the Council of Ministers, under recommendation of the EU Commission, to issue health and safety directives. These directives are given force of law within the EU community of nations. Each member state, including Ireland, is required to incorporate into national law the provisions of all directives, thus ensuring uniformity in health and safety law across the EU. However, where member states fail to do so, an employee can rely directly on that directive.

On January 1, 1993, to coincide with the conclusion of the European Year of Safety, Hygiene and Health Protection at Work, member states adopted a framework directive, and since then a number of "daughter" or "individual" directives. In all, the EU have adopted over 20 daughter directives since 1993. In Ireland, EU directives are incorporated in part in the 1993 Safety, Health and Welfare at Work Regulations. The Act, as well as the directives, extend the 1989 Act and the responsibilities and obligations of these regulations are enforceable by the same procedures and penalties as the 1989 Act. The regulations apply to all employees, regardless of employment status, but there are limited exceptions in the case of members of the Defence Forces, the Garda Siochánά and Firefighters engaged in emergency work.

Although there is a large number of directives, most of which relate to specific industries — to give one example, the 1993 Directive on Fishing Vessels — the main regulations that supervisors should be aware of are:

- The Physical Environment of Work
- The Safe Use of Equipment
- Personal Protective Equipment (PPE)
- Manual Handling of Loads
- Visual Display Units (VDUs)

- The Use of Electricity
- First Aid
- Emergency Procedures.

In addition to the above areas, there are also regulations regarding the duties of employers, particularly regarding protective and preventative services. These are examined below.

In terms of the physical environment of work, employers must ensure that each work area has, *inter alia*, adequate ventilation, lighting, and heating. In addition the work area must be large enough for the required purpose, and provide safe access to and from the area for vehicles and people. Employees with special needs — such as pregnant women, nursing mothers, people with disabilities — must be provided for. The 1995 Regulations also require that workplaces be kept cleaned, that rubbish be removed, and that, in certain instances, drinking and eating facilities be provided. Finally, the law provides specific guidelines on the size of sanitation facilities per size of organisation. Toilets must be kept cleaned, well-ventilated, with an adequate provision of cold and hot (or warm) water. There are also specific regulations on the location of toilets.

It is mandatory for employers to provide the right equipment which must, of course, be in working order. All equipment should be equipped with safety devices, on/off switches and, where appropriate, guards and should be used in accordance with the manufacturer's specifications. Such equipment must carry the proper warning notices and should be properly maintained and regularly checked. Employers must also ensure that employees are adequately and properly trained to use it.

It is a requirement that personal protective equipment (PPE) be provided to and used by employees, normally one piece of equipment per individual employee. PPE may include, but is not limited to, headgear, eye glasses, earplugs, gloves, etc. As with the regulations on equipment in general, PPE must be suited to the task, used properly, and properly maintained. Employees must be trained to use PPE, and are required to report any defective equipment.

As with risks in general, it is obligatory on employers to minimise the amount and degree of manual handling that must be done by employees. Where handling is done, it is a requirement that risk-taking be minimised by having proper equipment, and by strict adherence to safety procedures. Employees should be provided with information on weight, centre of gravity, and any special handling requirements for any load, in addition to being trained to handle equipment properly.

There are regulations on the use of VDUs (such as computer screens). An employee constantly using a VDU is entitled to adequate rest periods, and to free vision tests and eyeglasses if required. It is imperative on employers to analyse each work unit by conducting a risk assessment to see if the workstation and working environment complies with the law.

Electrical equipment must be designed and used to minimise the degree of risk to the employee. Electrical sockets may not be overloaded, for example, and faulty wiring must be replaced. A proper identification system must be used with each piece of electrical equipment along with the proper marking scheme. Electrical equipment which is used outdoors, for example, electricity on farms or construction sites, must comply with stringent safety requirements. All new electrical installations have to be installed by a certified person. Employees have a duty to report faulty electrical requirement.

All commercial premises are required to have minimum first aid equipment. Depending on the size of the organisation, the activity conducted and the frequency of accidents, organisations may be required to have first aid-trained staff and properly equipped medical rooms. Arrangements regarding first aid must be recorded in the safety statement.

Employer Duties under the EU Directives for Protective and Preventative Services

Employers are legally required to have emergency plans that include provision for the safe evacuation of employees and the provision of notices relating to such. Emergency plans may be attached to the safety statement and must be in located in full view of employees. In addition, fire drills must be held.

Employers are required to nominate an employee with responsibility for emergency plans. Such a person has to be competent. Competence is not defined in the regulations but is understood to mean knowledge and training in the area of health and safety. Lacking such expertise internally, a company can utilise the services of an employment agency. However, the employer is required to provide the employment agency with information on the level of skill necessary to perform the job, and the agency must pass on this information to job applicants. The employment status of this individual, commonly referred to as the safety officer or manager, depends to a large degree on the size of the organisation. In small organisations the safety officer can be a part-time position. In large organisations not only must the position be full-time, but for very large organisations more than one safety officer may have to be employed. The employer must inform the part-time or full-time safety officer, before commencing employment, of the skills required for the job, and any risks to be faced. This information can be contained in the safety statement.

The employer is required to provide the safety officer with information on known or suspected hazards, as well as brief him or her on emergency plans. Safety officers must also be given data on accidents and dangerous occurrences which the employer is required to report to the HSA.

The regulations, as noted above, also extend the rights of employees to consultation as prescribed by section 13 of the 1989 Act. Consultation is required on any proposed measure which would affect health and safety, including any measures to be taken under the Regulations. Employees, directly or through their representatives, have a right to be informed about measures introduced in regard to protective and preventative services, including the names of employees employed to carry out emergencies duties, or external experts employed to advise on health and safety. Employees have a right to be consulted in regard to any proposed changes in the safety statement, and to information as to whether the introduction of new technology or changes in the organisation of work will affect their health and safety.

In regard to the introduction of new technology or changes in the organisation of work, there must be "balanced" participation such that a joint health and safety committee, made up of employer and employee representatives, would seek a non-adversarial solution on the basis of consensus. That consensus should influence the choice of the employer with regard to major change. Employees are also entitled to information arising from risk assessment and from the reporting of accidents to the HSA. The Regulations stipulate that safety representatives should not be disadvantaged in terms of their conditions of employment by their participation in consultation. There is also a duty on the employer to provide training to employees in the area of health and safety with no loss of pay for training time.

Under the 1993 General Application Regulations, there are nine principles of prevention. These are listed in Table 20.9. A supervisor should be aware of these preventative principles.

TABLE 20.9: PREVENTATIVE PRINCIPLES

a) Avoidance of risks
b) Evaluation of unavoidable risks
c) Combating of risks at source
d) Adaptation of work to the individual, especially through design of workplaces, the choice of work equipment and systems of work, and by alleviating monotonous work or work at a predetermined rate.
e) Adaptation to technical progress
f) Use of non-dangerous or less dangerous articles, substances or systems of work
g) Development of a prevention policy taking account of: technology, work organisation, working conditions, social factors, and the working environment
h) Priority for collective over individual measures
i) Provision of appropriate training and instruction to employees.

Source: Irish Congress of Trade Unions (1993).

CHAPTER SUMMARY

There is little doubt that there is a plethora of legislation on health and safety in this country, and most of it is very detailed and complex (and complicated further still in certain industries, such as pharmaceuticals, by the technical nature of the processes). Despite this complexity, there are certain principles which should be known, and supervisors should have, at the very least, a working knowledge of the law. They should also be aware that there is a particular responsibility on all supervisors, by virtue of their place in the organisation, to ensure that all safety rules are obeyed. Supervisors should know that aside from an enforcement role, they also play an educative, preventative and investigative role in regard to health and safety.

Despite concerns about work safety, and a clear legal duty on employers and employees, not all organisations have good safety records. Indeed in certain industries, notably construction, it has been pointed out that the accident rate is exceptionally high by European standards. In other industries such as in finance, there is very little awareness of health and safety, save for fire regulations, despite the fact that increasingly, issues like the effects of visual display units (VDUs or computer screens), stress and bullying are becoming important health and safety issues. Finally, as noted, there is a strong correlation between size of organisation and safety regulations: large firms, by and large, are more likely to follow safety guidelines. Whatever about Ireland's poor record in health and safety, and the variety and complexity of legislation, Irish and European, in this area, it is imperative that supervisors be aware of their responsibilities and duties in regard to health and safety and exercise them.

References and Further Reading

Garavan, T. (1997) *The Irish Health and Safety Handbook*, Dublin: Oak Tree Press.

Gill, C. (1993) Participation in Health and Safety within the European Community, Dublin: European Foundation for the Improvement of Living and Working Conditions, EF/93/06/EN.

Gunnigle, P. & Flood, P. (1990) *Personnel Management in Ireland: Practice, Trends, Developments*, Dublin: Gill & Macmillan.

Gunnigle, P., Garavan T.N. & G. Fitzgerald (1992) *Employee Relations and Employment Law in Ireland*, Limerick: The Open Business School, Plassey Management and Technology Centre, in association with the College of Business, University of Limerick.

Higgins, E. & Keher, N. (1994) *Your Rights At Work*, Dublin: Institute of Public Administration.

Irish Congress of Trade Unions, with the assistance of the UCD Centre for Health and Safety (1993) "The Law of Health & Safety at Work: Safety, Health and Welfare at Work (General Application) Regulations, 1993".

Jacobson, David and Ziene Mottiar (1997) *Irish Times*, Business Section, Friday, June 27, p. 2.

Meenan, F. (1995) *Working Within the Law*, Dublin: Oak Tree Press.

Mosley, D., L. Megginson, P. Pietri (1993) *Supervisory Management: The Art of Empowering and Developing People*, third edition, Cincinnati, OH: South-Western.

O'Kelly, K. (1994) Employee Participation in Health and safety: Report on the Foundation Conference, Dublin, February 1993, in *European Participation Monitor*, European Foundation for Improvement of Living and Working Conditions, Issue No. 8, pp. 3-10.

Pascal, P. (1997) "Second European Survey on Working Conditions", Dublin: European Foundation for the Improvement of Living and Working Conditions.

Appendix

TRAINING AND SELF-DEVELOPMENT

The supervisor, whether new to the job or well-established in the position, needs to be conscious of the need for self-development. Knowledge gained from training and education is crucial to those entering supervisory positions. Even where people have experience in supervisory management, training helps them to learn from experience better and more quickly. With increasing demands, the possibility is high that the job may eventually overwhelm even an experienced supervisor. Further study is, therefore, advantageous for both newly-appointed and experienced supervisors.

Finding an appropriate training course can be difficult. Unlike, say, Britain, in Ireland there is no national certification programme for supervisors and there is the tendency to undervalue the role of the supervisor. There are, however, a number of courses available leading to an certified award in supervisory management. They are:

- National College of Industrial Relations, Diploma in First Line Management (Supervision)
- Irish Management Institute, Certificate in Supervisory Management
- FÁS (Irish Training Authority), Community Supervisory Development Programme.

The NCIR's Diploma in First Line Management (Supervision) and the IMI's Certificate in Supervisory Management are both two year, part-time educational courses. In both cases, students take classes either one evening (NCIR) or two evenings (IMI) a week; two hours in the case of the NCIR, and four in the case of the IMI.

Classes are offered in a variety of subjects, including management, industrial relations, employment law, safety and health, and teamwork. Assessment for the IMI students is by examination and for the NCIR students by project. Both institutions have an excellent reputation in the business community and the award in both cases offers opportunities for students to progress further with each institution or alternatively to pursue further educational courses in any NCEA[1] (National Council for Educational Awards) accredited course. Both the NCIR and the IMI courses are offered in many centres around Ireland.

The FÁS Community Supervisory Development programme, as its name suggests, is aimed at community leaders. As such, unlike the NCIR and the IMI courses, it incorporates non-business subjects that are relevant to community work. Students take roughly 140 hours of classroom instruction, with 40 hours individual tutorial instruction. Instruction is provided in three- and five-day workshops offered in various sites throughout Ireland. Unlike entry to the NCIR or IMI course, which is typically by paying a fee, entry to the FÁS programme is restricted mainly to people on the live register.

Aside from these courses, which are geared specifically towards supervisory management, whether in the community or in business, there are many other business courses which are of interest and value to any supervisor (or budding supervisor). The Regional Technical Colleges, for example, run National Certificate in Business Studies courses. Individual subjects, such as business management or human resource management, have great application to supervisory management. Private colleges, which are also accredited by the NCEA, are receptive to individuals taking single subject certification. The NCEA publishes a yearly booklet of NCEA-accredited courses. It is available direct from the NCEA for a small fee. Finally, consultants offer many training courses, both in-house and off-site. Readers should consult with management in their organisation for details of company-sponsored courses.

---

[1] In a policy document released in 1997, the (rainbow coalition) government announced the abolition of the NCEA in favour of an organisation likely to be called INIT (Irish National Institute of Technology).

READING MATERIAL

Educational courses are not the only means of learning. There are many books on supervisory management, mainly British and American, and a still greater number of management books which may be consulted for further information. Many of the British books on supervisory management are designed for educational courses, and thus are fairly detailed. This detail, while making them sometimes more difficult to read, ensures that these books, such as Evans (1995) or Betts (1993), provide a wealth of information covering every aspect of the supervisory function. Many other British books are practical in focus, including White (1986) and the excellent trio of handbooks by Bennett (1994a, 1994b, 1994c).

American books tend to be easier to read, and are very much geared towards the practising supervisor. The best of the American books on sale in Ireland include Bittel and Newstrom (1990) and Mosley et al (1993). As noted, books on the general subject of management have wide application to the supervisor. There are some excellent Irish books on management including Tiernan et al. (1996) and Lynch and Roche (1995) and, dealing with personnel management, Gunnigle and Flood (1990). There is, finally, a great deal of information on specific topics, such as such industrial relations, labour law, safety and health, teamwork and communication. Information on these and other books can be found at the end of each chapter, or collectively in the bibliography at the end of this book. Finally, browsing through municipal libraries and reputable bookstores the reader can stumble on many interesting and valuable management books.

Reading as a means of self-development and learning should not be overlooked. However, it has its disadvantages. Compared to attendance at educational course, reading suffers from a motivational aspect. The combination of education and reading, combined with the willingness to implement ideas learned in the classroom or from reading, will make for a better supervisor. The choice of material for a budding or experienced supervisor is a matter of preference (and budget).

A SKILLS ASSESSMENT EXERCISE

Printed below is a skills assessment instrument (Table A.1). In the first column is a list of skills relevant to supervisory management positions. By filling out the assessment readers can obtain a sense of what their skills are. Gaps may be filled in by reading and/or undertaking a course of study. Readers may add skills which are pertinent to their particular job, such as technical requirements.

TABLE A.1: PERSONAL SKILLS ASSESSMENT

	Weak	Adequate	Needs Improvement	Strong
Management				
Ability to understand and apply management concepts				
Assertiveness				
Ability to handle situations openly and honestly				
Presentation Skills				
Ability to speak clearly and effectively in public				
Writing Skills				
Ability to write clearly and concisely				
Time Management				
Ability to use my own time effectively				
Problem-solving and Decision-making				
Ability to analyse, solve problems and implement decisions				
Understanding People				
Ability to understand and work with people				

	Weak	Adequate	Needs Improvement	Strong
Motivation				
Ability to create and sustain an atmosphere of high productivity				
Leadership				
Ability to influence people in a positive, non-forceful way				
Interviewing				
Ability to conduct interviews properly				
Organising Meetings				
Ability to organise meetings				
Organising Work				
Ability to design and redesign work				
Industrial Relations				
Understanding of industrial relations and trade unions				
Labour Law				
Understanding of employment law				
Health and Safety				
Understanding of health and safety regulations and procedures				

Source: Adopted with modifications from Bittel and Newstrom (1990, p. 529).

BIBLIOGRAPHY

Adair, J.(1973) *Action Centred Leadership*, London: McGraw-Hill.

Adair, J. (1986) *Effective Teambuilding*, Aldershot: Gower.

Adair, J. (1988) *The Effective Supervisor*, London: The Industrial Society.

Ainger, A., Kaura R. & R. Ennals (1995) *Executive Guide to Business Success through Human-Centred Systems*, London: Springer.

Back, Ken & Kate Back (1982) *Assertiveness at Work, A Practical Guide to Handling Awkward Situations*, London: McGraw-Hill.

Belbin, R.M. (1981) *Management Teams: Why they Succeed or Fail*, London: Heinemann.

Bennett, R. (1994) *Managing Activities and Resources*, second edition, London: Kogan Page.

Bennett, R. (1994) *Managing People*, second edition, London: Kogan Page.

Bennett, R. (1994) *Personal Effectiveness*, second edition, London: Kogan Page.

Betts, P.W. (1993) *Supervisory Management*, sixth edition, London: Pitman.

Betts, P.W. (1983) *Supervisory Studies: A Managerial Perspective*, London: Pitman.

Bittle, L.R. & J. Newstrom (1990) *What Every Supervisor Should Know*, London: McGraw-Hill.

Blake, R.E. & J. Mouton (1964) *The Management Grid*, Houston, TX: Gulf Publishing.

Blanchard, K. & S. Johnson (1981) *The One Minute Manager*, Blanchard-Johnson Publishers, California.

Bolton, W. (1986) *Supervisory Management*, London: Heinemann, 1986.

Boyd, A. (1985) *The Rise of Irish Trade Unions, 1729-1980*. second edition, Dublin: Anvil Books.

Child, J. (1972) "Organisation Structure, Environment and Performance: The Role of Strategic Choice", *Sociology* (6) (1), pp. 1-22.

Christenson, C., Johnson T. & J. Stinson (1982) *Supervising*, Reading, MA: Addison-Wesley.

Cole, G.A. (1993) *Management: Theory and Practice*, London: DP Publications.

Cole, K. (1993) *Crystal Clear Communication: Skills for Understanding and Being Understood*, Prentice Hall, Australia.

Daunt, S. (1996) *Communication Skills*, Dublin: Gill & Macmillan.

Davis, L. (1966) "The Design of the Job", *Industrial Relations*, 6, pp. 21-45.

de Bono, E. (1992) *Serious Creativity: Using the Power of Lateral Thinking to Create New Ideas*, London: Fontana.

Deverell, C.S. (1973) *Supervisory Development*, London: G. Bell & Sons Ltd.

Dickson, A. (1982) *A Woman In Your Own Right; Assertiveness and You*, London: Quartet Books.

Drucker, P. (1967) "The Effective Decision", *Harvard Business Review*, January-February, pp. 92-98.

Drucker, P. (1966) *The Effective Executive*, New York: Harper and Row.

Dunlop, J. (1958) *Industrial Relations Systems*, Carbondale, IL: Southern Illinois University Press.

European Foundation for Improvement of Living and Working Conditions (1995) "A Joint Approach to Direct Participation: Ireland", Working Paper No. WP/95/01/EN, Dublin.

Evans, D. (1995) *Supervisory Management, Principles and Practices*, fourth edition, London: Cassell.

Foley K. & P. Gunnigle (1995) "The Personnel Function: Change or Continuity", in Turner, T., & M. Morley, with J. MacMahon, K. Foley & P. Gunnigle, *Industrial Relations and the New Order: Case Studies in Conflict & Co-operation*, Dublin: Oak Tree Press, pp 155-8.

Fox, A. (1974) *Beyond Contract: Work, Power and Trust Relations*. London: Faber & Faber.

Fuller, G. (1994) *The Supervisor's Big Book of Lists*, New York: Prentice Hall.

Geary, J. (1994) "New Forms of Work Organisation: Implications for Employers, Trade Unions and Employees", Working Paper IR-HRM No. 94-9, Graduate School of Business, UCD, Dublin.

Geary, J. (1996) "Working at Teamwork: Lessons from Europe", *European Participation Monitor*, European Foundation for Improvement of Living and Working Conditions, Issue No. 12, pp. 18-24.

Geary, J. (1995) "Working Practices: The Structure of Work", in Edwards, P.K., (ed) *Industrial Relations: Theory and Practice in Britain*, Oxford: Basil Blackwell.

Gill, C. (1993) "Participation In Health and Safety within the European Community", European Foundation for the Improvement of Living and Working Conditions, EF/93/06/EN, Dublin.

Gillespie, K. (1994) *Creative Supervision*, New York: Harcourt Brace Jovanovich.

Gray, J.L. (1984) *Supervision: An Applied Behavioural Science Approach to Managing People,* Boston: Kent Publishing Company.

Gunnigle P., M. Morley, N. Clifford & T. Turner (1997) *Human Resource Management in Irish Organisations: Practice in Perspective*, Dublin: Oak Tree Press.

Gunnigle, P, P. Flood & T. Turner (1995) *Continuity and Change in Irish Employee Relations*, Dublin: Oak Tree Press.

Gunnigle, P. & P. Flood (1990) *Personnel Management in Ireland: Practice, Trends, Developments*, Dublin: Gill & Macmillan.

Gunnigle, P. (1996) "Collectivism and the Management of Industrial Relations in Greenfield Sites", *Human Resource Management Journal*, Vol. 5, No. 3, pp. 24-40.

Gunnigle, P., Garavan T.N. & G. Fitzgerald (1992) *Employee Relations and Employment Law in Ireland*, The Open Business School, Plassey Management and Technology Centre, in association with the College of Business, University of Limerick.

Gunnigle, P., McMahon, G. & G. Fitzgerald (1995) *Industrial Relations in Ireland: Theory and Practice*, Dublin: Gill & Macmillan.

Gunnigle, P., Morley, M., & C. Brewster (1993) "Changing Patterns in Industrial Relations: Differentiation and Convergence", in *European Participation Monitor*, European Foundation for Improvement of Living and Working Conditions, Issue No. 7, pp. 27-32.

Hackman, J. & G. Oldman (1980) *Work Redesign*, Reading, MA: Addison-Wesley.

Haimann, T. (1994) *Supervisory Management for Healthcare Organizations*, Iowa City< IA: Wm. C. Brown.

Handy, C. (1993) *Understanding Organizations*, fourth edition, London: Penguin.

Harris, T. (1973) *I'm OK, You're OK,* London: Pan Books.

Harvey, N. & A. Twomey (1995) *Sexual Harassment in the Workplace: A Practical Guide for Employers and Employees in Ireland*, Dublin: Oak Tree Press.

Harvey, N. & M. von Behr (1994) "Group Work in the American and German Non-Automotive Metal Manufacturing Industry", *International Journal of Human Factors in Manufacturing*, Vol. 4, No. 1, pp. 1-16.

Harvey, N. (ed) (1996) Proceedings of the Workplace Partnership for Competitiveness, EU Irish Presidency/European Foundation Conference, Dublin.

Harvey, N. (1993) "Automation and Restructuring: How Industrial Relations Affects Change in the Wisconsin Metal Working Industry", *IFAC Symposium on Automated Systems Based on Human Skill (and Intelligence)*. Madison, Wisconsin. September 22-25, 1992, London: Pergammon Press.

Harvey, N. (1994) "How Unions Should Respond to Cells", *Labor Studies Journal*, Vol. 18, No. 4, pp. 21-38.

Harvey, N. (1994) "Socio-Technical Organization of Cell Manufacturing and Production Islands in the Metal Manufacturing Industry in Germany and the U.S.", *International Journal of Production Research*, Vol. 32, No. 11, pp. 2669-2681.

Harvey, N. (1994) "The Changing Face of Manufacturing: New Compensation Practices in the German and American Metal Working Industries", *Control Engineering Practice*, Vol. 2, No. 4, pp. 697-705.

Herzberg, F., Mausner, B. & Synderman, B. (1967) *The Motivation to Work*, New York: Wiley.

Herzberg, F. (1987) "One More Time: How Do You Motivate Employees?", *Harvard Business Review*, September/October.

Higgins, E. & N. Keher (1994) *Your Rights At Work*, Dublin: Institute of Public Administration.

Holland, S. & C. Ward (1990) *Assertiveness: A Practical Approach*, Bicester, Oxon: Winslow Press.

Hyman, R. (1975) *Industrial Relations: A Marxist Introduction*, London: Macmillan.

Irish Business and Employers Confederation, "Directory of Services to Members", Dublin, undated.

Irish Business and Employers Confederation (1993) "Teams in Action: A Report on Teamworking in Leading Irish Companies", Dublin.

Irish Business and Employers Confederation, "Who We Are, What We Do", Dublin, undated.

Irish Congress of Trade Unions (1993) "New Forms of Work Organisation: Options for Unions", Dublin.

Keegan, R. & J. Lynch (1995) *World Class Manufacturing ... in an Irish Context*, Dublin: Oak Tree Press.

Kelly, G. & R. Armstrong (1991) *20 Training Workshops for Developing Managerial Effectiveness*, Volumes 1 and 2, Aldershot: Gower.

Keys, B. & J. Henshall (1990) *Supervision: Concepts, Skills and Assessment*, New York: Wiley.

Koontz, H., O'Donnell, C. & H. Weirich (1980) *Management*, seventh edition, New York: McGraw-Hill.

Lewin, K. (1936) *Principles of Topological Psychology*, New York: McGraw-Hill.

Likert, R. (1967) *New Patterns of Management*, New York: McGraw-Hill.

Lynch, J. & Roche, F. (1995) *Business Management in Ireland: Competitive Strategy for the 21st Century*, Dublin: Oak Tree Press.

Malone, S. (1996) *Learning to Learn*, London: CIMA.

Malone, S. (1997) *Mind Skills for Managers*, Aldershot: Gower.

Manz. C. & H. Sims (1989) *Superleadership: Leading Others to Lead Themselves*, New York: Prentice-Hall.

Maslow, A. (1943) "A Theory of Human Motivation", *Psychological Review*, Vol. 50, pp. 370-396.

Mayo, E. (1949) *The Social Problems of an Industrial Civilisation*, London: Routledge & Kegan Paul.

McClave, H. (1986) *Communication for Business in Ireland*, Dublin: Gill & Macmillan.

McDuffie, J.P. & T. Kochan (1988) "Human Resources, Technology, and Economic Performance: Evidence from the Automobile Industry". Industrial Relations Research Association, Allied Science Social Sciences Meeting, New York.

McGregor, D. (1960) *The Human Side of Enterprise*, New York: McGraw-Hill.

McNamara, G., Williams, K. & D. West (1994) *Understanding Trade Unions: Yesterday and Day*, Dublin: ELO Publications in association with the Irish Congress of Trade Unions.

Meenan, F. (1994) *Working Within the Law: A Practical Guide for Employers and Employees*, Dublin: Oak Tree Press.

Monden, Y. (1983) *Toyota Production System*. Atlanta, GA: Industrial Engineering and Management Press.

Mooney, P. (1993) "Changing Patterns in Irish Industrial Relations", *Irish Industrial Relations Review*, May, pp. 20-34.

Mooney, P. (1996) *Developing the High Performance Organisation: Best Practice for Managers*, Dublin: Oak Tree Press.

Mosley, D., L. Megginson & P. Pietri (1993) *Supervisory Management: The Art of Empowering and Developing People,* third edition, Cincinnati, OH: South-Western.

Mulvey, K., "The Labour Relations Commission — One Year On", Unpublished Paper, The Labour Relations Commission, Dublin, undated.

Murphy, T. & W.K. Roche (ed) (1997) *Irish Industrial Relations In Practice*, second edition, Dublin: Oak Tree Press.

Murphy, T. (1989) "The Impact of the Unfair Dismissals Act, 1977, on Workplace Industrial Relations", in *Industrial Relations in Ireland, Contemporary Issues and Developments*, Department of Industrial Relations, Faculty of Commerce, University College Dublin, pp. 247-52.

Naughton, M. (1994) A Case Study for the Joint International Project on New Forms of Work Organisation, International Metalworkers Federation and the European Metalworkers Federation, June, Dublin.

Naughton, M. (1993) Report of a Survey of SIPTU Members on their Experience of World Class Manufacturing and Total Quality Management, SIPTU Education and Training Department, Dublin.

Naughton, M. (1995) "The Implications of Teamwork on Industrial Relations", A Presentation to the ICM Conference on Creating, Leading and Motivating High Performance Teams, 24-25th. January, Dublin.

Naughton, M. (1992) "The People Dimension: Employee Flexibility in the Changing Environment, Its Impact on Industrial Relations", A Presentation to the National Human Resources Conference, Burlington Hotel, September 22-24th, 1992.

Neumann, J., Holti, R. & H. Standing (1995) *Change Everything At Once!: The Tavistock Institute's Guide to Developing Teamwork in Manufacturing*, Oxford: Management Books 2000.

Nevin, D. (ed) (1994) *Trade Union Century*, Dublin: Mercier Press in association with the Irish Congress of Trade Unions and Radio Telefís Éireann.

O'Brien, S. (1994) "Autonomous Working at Galtee Food Dairygold", *European Participation Monitor*, European Foundation for Improvement of Living and Working Conditions, Issue No. 9, p. 38.

O'Kelly, K. (1994) "Employee Participation in Safety and Health: Report on the Foundation Conference", Dublin, February 1993, in *European Participation Monitor*, European Foundation for Improvement of Living and Working Conditions, Issue No. 8, pp. 3-10.

Ouchi, W. (1981) *Theory Z*, Reading, MA: Addison-Wesley.

Pascal, P. (1997) "Second European Survey on Working Conditions", European Foundation for the Improvement of Living and Working Conditions, Dublin.

Peppard, J. & P. Rowland (1995) *The Essence of Business Process Re-engineering*, London: Prentice Hall.

Pettinger, R. (1994) *Introduction to Management*, London: Macmillan.

Piore, M. & C. Sabel (1984) *The Second Divide: Possibilities for Posterity*, New York: Basic Books.

Roche, W.K. & J. Larragy (1989) "The Trend of Unionisation in the Irish Republic", in *Industrial Relations in Ireland: Contemporary Issues and Developments*, University College Dublin, 1989, pp. 21-37.

Roche, W.K. (1995) "The New Competitive Order and Employee Relations in Ireland: Challenges and Prospects", Summary of Address to IBEC Annual Employee Conference, Human Resources in the Global Market, November 16th.

Roche, W.K. (1996) "Trade Unions and Industrial Relations", Working Paper IR-HRM No. 2, Centre for Employment Relations and Organisational Performance, University College Dublin.

Roethlisberger, F.J. & W.J. Dickson (1939) *Management and the Worker*, Cambridge, MA: Harvard University Press.

Schonberger, R. (1986) *World Class Manufacturing: The Lesson of Simplicity Applied*, New York: The Free Press.

Scott, M. (1993) *Time Management*, London: Century Business.

Simmel, G. (1902) "The Number of Members as Determining the Sociological Form of the Group", *American Journal of Sociology*, 8, 1-46, pp. 158-96.

Simon, H. (1979) *Models of Thought*, New Haven, CT: Yale University Press,.

Simon, H. (1971) "The New Science of Management Decisions", in Welch, L., & R. Cyert, (eds), *Management and Decision-Making,* London: Penguin.

SIPTU (1994) "Guide for Union Representatives", National Executive Council of SIPTU, Dublin.

Sisson, K. (1996) "The Nature and Extent of Direct Participation in Europe: Preliminary Results from the EPOC Workplace Survey", in N. Harvey (ed) Proceedings of the Workplace Partnership for Competitiveness, EU Irish Presidency/European Foundation Conference, Dublin, pp. 26-34.

Stanton, Nicky (1996) *Mastering Communication*, third edition, London: Macmillan.

Stone, Brian W. (1988) *Supervisory Skills*, London: Pitman.

Stott, K. & A. Walker (1995) *Teams, Teamwork and Teambuilding: The Manager's Complete Guide to Teams in Organisations*, New York: Prentice Hall.

Tannenbaum, R. & W. Schmidt (1973) "How to Choose a Leadership Pattern", *Harvard Business Review*, 51, May-June, pp. 162-80.

Taylor, F. (1911) *The Principles of Scientific Management*, New York: Harper & Bros.

Tiernan, S., Morley, M. & Foley, E. (1996) *Modern Management: Theory and Practice for Irish Students*, Dublin: Gill & Macmillan.

Tuckman, B.W. (1965) "Development Sequences in Small Groups", *Psychological Bulletin*, 63, pp. 384-389.

Turner, T. & M. Morley (1995) *Industrial Relations and the New Order, Case Studies in Conflict and Co-operation*, Dublin: Oak Tree Press.

von Prondzynski, F. (1992) "Ireland: Between Centralism and the Market", in A. Ferner & R. Hyman (eds.), *Industrial Relations in the New Europe*, Oxford: Basil Blackwell, pp. 69-87.

Vroom, V. (1964) *Work and Motivation*, New York: Wiley.

Wall, T. (1994) "Union Involvement in Teamworking in Ireland", *European Participation Monitor*, European Foundation for Improvement of Living and Working Conditions, Issue No. 9, pp. 35-37.

Weber, M. (1968) *Economy and Society*, New York: Bedminster Press.

Weber, M. (1930) *The Protestant Ethic and the Spirit of Capitalism*, London: Allen & Unwin.

White, J. (1968) *Successful Supervision*, second edition, London: McGraw-Hill.

Wobbe, W. (1992) Commission of the European Communities, "What are Anthropocentric Production Systems? Are They A Strategic Issue for Europe?", FAST Report EUR 13968 EN.

Womack, J.P., Jones, D.T. & D. Roos (1990) *The Machine that Changed the World*, New York: Macmillan.

INDEX